T0125029

AN ESSAY ON THE NATURE AND CONDUCT OF THE PASSIONS AND AFFECTIONS, WITH ILLUSTRATIONS ON THE MORAL SENSE

NATURAL LAW AND
ENLIGHTENMENT CLASSICS

Knud Haakonssen
General Editor

Francis Hutcheson

NATURAL LAW AND
ENLIGHTENMENT CLASSICS

An Essay on the Nature and Conduct of the Passions and Affections, with Illustrations on the Moral Sense

Francis Hutcheson

Edited and with an Introduction
by Aaron Garrett

The Collected Works of Francis Hutcheson

LIBERTY FUND

Indianapolis

This book is published by Liberty Fund, Inc., a foundation established to encourage study of the ideal of a society of free and responsible individuals.

The cuneiform inscription that serves as our logo and as the design motif for our endpapers is the earliest-known written appearance of the word "freedom" (*amagi*), or "liberty." It is taken from a clay document written about 2300 B.C. in the Sumerian city-state of Lagash.

© 2002 Liberty Fund, Inc.

All rights reserved

Frontispiece: Detail of portrait of Francis Hutcheson by Allan Ramsay (c. 1740–45), oil on canvas, reproduced courtesy of the Hunterian Art Gallery, University of Glasgow.

Printed in the United States of America

| 11 | 15 | 16 | 17 | 18 | C | 6 | 5 | 4 | 3 | 2 |
| 15 | 16 | 17 | 18 | 19 | P | 6 | 5 | 4 | 3 | 2 |

Library of Congress Cataloging-in-Publication Data
Hutcheson, Francis, 1694–1746
An essay on the nature and conduct of the passions and affections: with illustrations on the moral sense / Francis Hutcheson; introduction by Aaron Garrett.
p.   cm.
(The collected works of Francis Hutcheson)
Includes bibliographical references and index.
ISBN 978-0--86597-386-2 (hbk.)—ISBN 978-0-86597-387-9 (pbk.)
1. Emotions—Early works to 1850.   2. Ethics.   I. Title.
B1501.E6 2003
171'.2—dc21   2002029652

LIBERTY FUND, INC.
8335 Allison Pointe Trail, Suite 300
Indianapolis, Indiana 46250-1684

CONTENTS

INTRODUCTION

An Essay on the Nature and Conduct of the Passions and Affections, with Illustrations on the Moral Sense (1728), jointly with Francis Hutcheson's earlier work *Inquiry into the Original of Our Ideas of Beauty and Virtue* (1725),[1] presents one of the most original and wide-ranging moral philosophies of the eighteenth century. These two works, each comprising two semiautonomous treatises,[2] were widely translated and vastly influential throughout the eighteenth century in England, continental Europe, and America.

The two works had their greatest impact in Scotland and influenced many well-known Scottish philosophers, particularly those writing after the last Jacobite upheaval, in 1745. This can be seen in the concern of the post-1745 generation with analyzing human nature as the foundation of moral theory, with the "moral sense" and moral epistemology more generally, with the impartial spectator and the calm passions, and with the independence of benevolence from self-interest. In addition to the influence of his writings, Hutcheson was also a famed teacher whose Glasgow students, notably Adam Smith, held sway over generations of Scottish moral philosophers.

Despite their impact on Scottish letters, the four treatises were in fact written in Dublin, and the philosophers to whom Hutcheson re-

---

1. I refer to these as, respectively, *Essay with Illustrations* and the *Inquiry*.

2. Hutcheson seems to have thought of the works as four independent but interconnected treatises, and he generally cites by treatise and section number (i.e., *Inquiry on Beauty* as Treatise 1, *Inquiry on Virtue* as Treatise 2, *Essay on the Passions* as Treatise 3, and the *Illustrations* as Treatise 4) as opposed to by book and page number. This is further reflected in the titles of the two works.

sponded and with whom he debated were in the main not Scottish but English, Irish, French, Roman, and Greek. Consequently, part of Hutcheson's legacy was a cosmopolitan outlook among enlightened Scots, who learned to turn their eyes far from home.

Early Life

Hutcheson was born in 1694[3] in County Down, near Saintfield. His father and grandfather were respected Presbyterian ministers in the Scots emigrant community of Ulster. Unlike their brethren in Scotland, where the Presbyterian Kirk was the established church, the Irish Presbyterians were Dissenters. Like the English Dissenters, they were discriminated against by the Anglican state church, which considered them marginally less unsavory than Catholics.[4] They were excluded from Trinity College, Dublin, as well as from Oxford and Cambridge, and, after 1704, they could not take public office.[5] The major difference between Irish Presbyterians and English Dissenters was that the former had strong ties to Scotland, including the Scottish universities, especially Glasgow.

Irish Presbyterians were divided between traditionalists and more rationally inclined "New Light" ministers. John Hutcheson, Francis's father, was a traditionalist who wrote the church's response to the claims of "liberal" nonsubscribers. Francis associated with the nonsub-

---

3. My chronology of Hutcheson's early life is based on William Robert Scott, *Francis Hutcheson: His Life, Teaching and Position in the History of Philosophy* (Cambridge: Cambridge University Press, 1990); M. A. Stewart, "Abating Bigotry and Hot Zeal," in Damian Smyth (ed.), *Francis Hutcheson: A Supplement to* Fortnight, 308 (1992), 4–6; M. A. Stewart, "Rational Dissent in Early Eighteenth-Century Ireland," in Knud Haakonssen (ed.), *Enlightenment and Religion* (Cambridge: Cambridge University Press, 1996), 42–63; James Moore, "The Two Systems of Francis Hutcheson: On the Origins of the Scottish Enlightenment," in M. A. Stewart, *Studies in the Philosophy of the Scottish Enlightenment* (Oxford: Clarendon, 1990), 37–59.

4. See Robert Eccleshall, "Anglican Political Thought in the Century After the Revolution of 1688," in D. George Boyce, Robert Eccleshall, and Vincent Geoghegan (eds.), *Political Thought in Ireland Since the Seventeenth Century* (London: Routledge, 1993), 41.

5. Ian McBride, "The School of Virtue: Francis Hutcheson, Irish Presbyterians and the Scottish Enlightenment," in *Political Thought in Ireland*, 80.

scribing clergymen in Belfast and leaned toward the tolerationist theology of love that was associated with the New Light.[6]

Hutcheson was schooled in classics in Ireland and moved to Glasgow in 1711 when the university was just recovering from a period of decline, thanks to the influence of some charismatic and theologically moderate teachers and of politically active Irish students who challenged the arbitrariness of university authority.[7] Upon graduating, Hutcheson returned to Ireland to head a Dissenting Academy in Dublin, a major undertaking of the Ulster Kirk in which he appears to have prospered. Hutcheson associated with Robert Molesworth, a close friend of Shaftesbury and of radical intellectuals such as John Toland and Anthony Collins. In Ireland, Molesworth cultivated a circle of talented intellectuals who wrote in the *Dublin Journal,* notably Hutcheson's friend James Arbuckle. Hutcheson was also in contact with open-minded Anglican intellectuals such as William King, the archbishop of Dublin. At the same time, Hutcheson no doubt felt the impact of the more bigoted world about him.

In intellectual circles, clubs, and, particularly, publications such as the *Dublin Journal* and the *London Journal,* provincial intellectuals flourished, fought, and exchanged ideas. Like Bayle's Rotterdam, with its Huguenot diaspora, Hutcheson's Dublin felt the weight of sectarian controversy and the tug of another country. In this context Hutcheson wrote his early masterpieces.

The Inquiry

Treatise 1, the *Inquiry on Beauty,* is relatively independent of the *Essay with Illustrations* except that it presents the sense of the "beautiful" as a model for Hutcheson's subsequent considerations of the "internal" senses. Treatise 2, however, is presupposed in the *Essay with Illustrations* (see the Preface). The first section of Treatise 2 considers the moral

---

6. See Wolfgang Leidhold, *Ethik und Politik bei Francis Hutchison* (Freiburg: Alber, 1985), chaps. III and IV.

7. See M. A. Stewart, "John Smith and the Molesworth Circle," *Eighteenth-Century Ireland* 2 (1987): 89–102.

sense, and the validity and the importance of the arguments for it in Treatise 2 are assumed in Treatises 3 and 4.

Hutcheson's basic premise—in both the *Inquiry* and the *Essay*—is that our immediate perceptions of the moral qualities of an action or a character are derived from a "sense," like the external senses, that perceives external, adventitious qualities. To this end, Hutcheson argued that the *content* of a moral perception, the quality perceived, cannot be forced upon us. Moral perceptions are, like the perceptions of other senses, independent of the will.

As we cannot will the perception of something, for example, stimulated by a reward or punishment, our volitions either result from or are independent of our experience of moral qualities; they do not prompt them. This is the basis for Hutcheson's argument against the view that morality arises from sanctions associated with Locke's *Essay* and Pufendorf's *Law of Nature and Nations* (although Hutcheson is at pains not to deny all influence of sanctions). On the same basis, Hutcheson argued that benevolence toward mankind is "disinterested"; we are capable of having benevolent sentiments toward those in whom we have no interest and whose "lovely disposition" our moral sense tells us to approve (T2 148).

Hutcheson's best explanation of this moral sense was that nature determines us to apprehend moral qualities and that our apprehension is issued with a moral sense that approves of good moral qualities (T2 180). Our judgments are sometimes incorrect, but there is nevertheless a perceived quality of which we judge. When we perceive as benevolent someone who is in fact malicious, what we approve of is still the *perceived* benevolence. Thus, Hutcheson attempted to rest the approval of benevolence on our perceptions and, ultimately, on our natures.

Gilbert Burnet and John Clarke of Hull

The *Essay with Illustrations* followed the *Inquiry* by almost three years, during which time a number of acute thinkers criticized the *Inquiry*, and Hutcheson became widely known. The *Essay with Illustrations* is distinctive, therefore, both for its content and for the altered intellectual context. In 1725, Hutcheson entered into a debate in the *London Jour-*

nal with Gilbert Burnet concerning the newly published *Inquiry*—and this bore fruit in Treatise 4, the *Illustrations*. In the same year, John Clarke published an attack on the then-anonymous author of the *Inquiry* (along with criticisms of Samuel Clarke) and then communicated further comments to Hutcheson directly. The first section of Treatise 3, the *Essay,* is a response to John Clarke that sets the agenda for much that follows.

Gilbert Burnet (1690–1726) was the son of Bishop Gilbert Burnet of Salisbury (1643–1715), one of the best-known latitudinarian divines of the era, admired by Shaftesbury[8] and many others. His son, Hutcheson's correspondent, was chaplain to George I and a promising young churchman. John Clarke was master of the Hull grammar school when he entered into argument with Hutcheson. He was referred to as John Clarke of Hull to distinguish him from Samuel Clarke's better-known nephew. Clarke of Hull was known in the eighteenth and early nineteenth centuries primarily for his popular Latin manuals, but he was also an able philosopher who produced two undervalued but significant works: *An Examination of the Notion of Moral Good and Evil* (1725) and *The Foundation of Morality in Theory and Practice Considered* (1726)

In an enterprising piece of self-advertisement, Hutcheson published an anonymous letter, "To Britannicus," in the *London Journal,* praising the *Inquiry*. Shortly afterward, Burnet responded skeptically: How do we know the moral sense is not erroneous or deceitful? Pleasure does not make it true; rather, reason does, and that is the proper internal or moral sense by which we judge. Once we know that a given act or quality *is* really good, then we take pleasure in its intrinsic moral qualities.

Hutcheson thus confronted moral rationalism of the sort presented by Samuel Clarke, who had argued that morality was found in the "fitnesses" of things. Obligations and duties flowed from eternal relations, ends, and offices forming a system as certain as mathematics and, like mathematics, discerned through reason.[9]

---

8. Isabel Rivers, *Reason, Grace, and Sentiment: A Study of the Language of Religion and Ethics in England: 1600–1780* (Cambridge: Cambridge University Press, 2000), 24, 89.

9. See particularly *A Discourse Concerning the Unchangeable Obligations of Nat-*

Hutcheson provided a bevy of arguments against Burnet and criticized the clarity and coherence of his terminology. One argument is particularly notable. Hutcheson took over Grotius's distinction between exciting and justifying reasons, arguing that "*Desires, Affections, Instincts,* must be previous to all *Exciting Reasons;* and a *Moral Sense* antecedent to all *Justifying Reasons.*"[10] Neither justifying reason nor exciting reason is adequate to the purposes to which Samuel Clarke and Burnet would put reason. For moral reasoning, "reasonableness," is practical and has numerous ends. Some ends may be more "fit" and "rational" than others, but we recognize ends through our practical interests, and we distinguish among competing ends.

John Clarke's *The Foundation of Morality in Theory and Practice* was a criticism of Samuel Clarke and Hutcheson. Clarke of Hull was a hedonistic theist in the mold of the elder Locke and Pierre Bayle, who viewed sanction as the basic support of morality, in contrast with both Hutcheson and the moral rationalists. His central challenge to Hutcheson concerned self-love. Clarke claimed that Hutcheson's arguments for the independence of benevolence from self-love were inadequate because they failed to recognize that "the Love of Benevolence is . . . a Desire or Inclination to do Good to others," and "the Object and Cause of Desire is Pleasure alone, or the supposed Means of procuring it."[11] Although there is a profound natural connection between the happiness of a parent and the happiness of a child, and this connection is as "disinterested" as smelling a rose or tasting a peach, it is still pleasure that reinforces and spurs action in both cases. We may have different sorts of pleasures, some brutish and bad, such as the desire for esteem, and

---

ural Religion and the Truth and Certainty of the Christian Religion (London, 1706), 5–11, 45–67. In 1717, the young Hutcheson wrote a letter (now lost) to Clarke criticizing his proof of God in *A Demonstration of the Being and Attributes of God* (1705) (Scott, *Francis Hutcheson,* 15–16).

10. Gilbert Burnet (ed.), *Letters Between the Late* Mr. *Gilbert Burnet, and* Mr. *Hutcheson, Concerning the True Foundation of Virtue or Moral Goodness. Formerly Published in the London Journal* (London: W. Wilkins, 1735), 49.

11. John Clarke, *The Foundation of Morality in Theory and Practice,* in L. A. Selby-Bigge, *British Moralists* (Oxford: Clarendon Press, 1897), v. 2, 224.

some delightful, such as eating a peach or seeking the good of a child, but this does not make them less pleasing. Their virtue must instead be related to the pain and pleasure of divine sanction.

The Essay

In the *Essay*, Hutcheson attempted to untangle these difficulties while furnishing a consistent and convincing theory of the passions. The latter was formulated with reference to two of his predecessors, Bernard Mandeville and Shaftesbury.[12] Mandeville had been publishing for twenty years, but only with the publication in 1723 of a much expanded edition of the *Fable of the Bees* did he become famous and controversial. It was on Hutcheson's generation, therefore, that he had his greatest impact. Mandeville presented an infamous Epicurean theory of the passions based on a skeptical analysis of human nature: "I believe Man (besides Skin, Flesh, Bones, &c. that are obvious to the Eye) to be a compound of various Passions, that all of them, as they are provoked, and come uppermost, govern him by turns, whether he will or no."[13] The theory was directed against Shaftesbury, as a naively optimistic aristocrat with little understanding of the realities of human nature.

Shaftesbury also championed the diversity of human nature but diminished the importance of self interest by promoting the social affections "and a thousand other springs, which are counter to self-interest, [and] have as considerable a part."[14] Following Cicero and Marcus Aurelius, Shaftesbury saw virtue, not as a Mandevillian artifice, but as a stoic harmony with man's intrinsically passionate nature.

Mandeville emphasized the complexity of self-interest, the interconnectedness of vice and virtue, and the diversity and ubiquity of plea-

---

12. The subtitle of the first edition of *Inquiry* reads "IN WHICH The Principles of the late Earl of SHAFTESBURY are Explain'd and Defended, against the Author of the *Fable of the Bees*." Hutcheson also wrote three letters to the *Dublin Weekly Journal* in 1726, in which he criticized Mandeville.

13. Bernard Mandeville, *The Fable of the Bees: Or Private Vices, Publick Benefits*, F. B. Kaye (ed.) (Indianapolis: Liberty Fund, 1988), vol. 1, 39.

14. Shaftesbury, "Sensus Communis" (1709), III.3.

sure. Hutcheson's reply to this, as to John Clarke's hedonism, was a reprise of the argument that we cannot force a sentiment, even if the result is pleasing. If feeling a certain passion makes us happy, we might wish to feel it in order to be happy, but we cannot force ourselves to feel something in order to get a reward. Instead, we sense and desire, and then we may feel pleasure as a consequence of the desire. The idea that action implies pleasure is false moral psychology.

For Hutcheson, as for many early modern philosophers, the passions were central to ethics. The most unsavory passions and sentiments—bigotry, anger, and the desire to harm—are consequences of limited and "partial Views," and they arise from emphasis on selfish interest and mistaken understandings of the public good (pp. 72, 75). Consequently, they are less present in the broader view and disappear in the universal view of the moral system. Limited views of human interest derive such validity as they have from their approximation to the most general view, the providential design of creation, and the prospect of the future state (p. 123). The general view reinforces the calm passions.

The progress of the sentiments accordingly leads us to reflection not only on the human system but also on its place in the universal system. Such reflection shows how many apparently negative features of human nature have their place—in moderation. By reflection on the universal "oeconomy," we learn to regulate passions so as to be happy and to make others happy.

Illustrations

Hutcheson's theory of the passions responded to John Clarke's claim that his moral philosophy was based on poor psychology. Clarke forced Hutcheson to draw his account of desire and sentiment more precisely than he had in the *Inquiry*, and to show how it was linked with the moral sense. But, as noted previously, other issues were afoot. Burnet's criticisms of Treatise 2 had brought out Hutcheson's conflict with moral rationalism and the view that moral judgments are like other judgments insofar as they are only valid if true.

As noted, Hutcheson emphasized in Treatise 4.1 that this was a skirmish among those who accepted the moral sense, even if some parties were not aware of it! But Burnet was not the only writer of that stripe. In the opening chapters of the *Illustrations,* Hutcheson successively criticized Samuel Clarke and William Wollaston (1659–1724), employing two related strategies. First, he used Grotius's distinction between exciting and justifying reasons to show the confusion in many rationalists' invocation of reason. Hutcheson argued that there is "no *exciting Reason* previous to *Affection*" (pp. 139–40); what we take as exciting reasons to action and to active attitudes, such as desire and affection, either presupposes affections and desires or serves as mere justifying reasons.

Furthermore, moral reasoning is practical and particular and varies from agent to agent. Consequently, supposedly fixed and eternal reasons differ drastically according to how they are viewed by individuals, and judging what is reasonable in a given situation is difficult. Rather, moral ends and actions are fixed through a moral sense; they may be justified by reason but cannot be called forth by it.

Similar arguments were deployed against Samuel Clarke's eternal moral relations and Wollaston's "significancy of truth in actions." Hutcheson attacked Samuel Clarke's "fitnesses"—real, normative predispositions among beings—and argued that the theory was incoherent and failed to support the eternal moral relations that Clarke required. Clarke's heart was in the right place, but that was because the "eternal relations" were perceived by his own moral sense.

William Wollaston argued in the *Religion of Nature Delineated* (1724; first printed privately in 1722) that actions have "significancy"; that is, they could be true or false. Any act that interferes with truth is morally wrong, and, conversely, any act in accordance with the truth is morally right. Therefore, there is a correspondence of the truth signified by actions and the morally right, and conversely the denial of truth and the morally wrong.

Hutcheson distinguished between logical and moral truths. Many logical truths and falsehoods are not moral truths and falsehoods. Notably, actions that unintentionally hinder truth are rarely considered evil; they may be logically but not morally false.[15] False ideas often may result in moral evil, but they are evil not because of falsity but because we recognize them as evil through our moral sense.

The moral sense in parallel with the senses of beauty, honor, and imagination does not mean that Hutcheson saw morals as nothing but spontaneous reactions. Although we do not divine eternal moral relations in the fitnesses of things, we are capable of exact knowledge of natural law and civil laws, which constitute "the most useful Subject of *Reasoning* . . . as certain, invariable, or eternal Truths, as in any Geometry" (pp. 174/10, 216). But these "relations" arise from the nature of people in social interaction, not from eternal logical relations in abstraction from human nature. The absolute principles of the universal moral system are inaccessible to humanity, but we can gain more extensive views by exploring our nature and its place in a wider world.

In the final chapter of *Illustrations,* Hutcheson is concerned with balancing the importance of toleration with the need for belief in and love of God. Our love of God amplifies the social affections and reinforces benevolence. Consequently, the best signs of piety are social affections and public virtue, and we should not attempt further divination of the beliefs of others. Instead, we should broaden our views through reflection on the general moral system and thereby cultivate the calm passions. The *Illustrations* thus concludes with a "moderate" vision of humanity that connects the theory of the passions with Hutcheson's later discussions in the System.[16]

Remarks Concerning the Editions

Three editions of the *Essay with Illustrations* were printed during Hutcheson's lifetime, with two variants of the first edition:

15. This argument is perhaps derived from John Clarke, *An Examination of the Notion of Moral Good and Evil,* 12.

16. On Hutcheson as model for Moderatism, see Richard Sher, *Church and University in the Scottish Enlightenment* (Princeton: Princeton University Press, 1985), 69.

1A An Essay on the Nature and Conduct of the Passions and Affections. With Illustrations On the Moral Sense. By the Author of the Inquiry into the Original of our Ideas of Beauty and Virtue. London: Printed by J. Darby and T. Browne, for John Smith and William Bruce, Booksellers in Dublin; and sold by J. Osborn and T. Longman in Pater-Noster-Row, and S. Chandler in the Poultrey. M.DCC.XXVIII.

1B An Essay on the Nature and Conduct of the Passions and Affections. With Illustrations On the Moral Sense. London: Printed and Dublin re-printed by S. Powell for P. Crampton, at Addison's Head, Opposite the Horse Guard in Dame's-Street, and T. Benson, at Shakespear's Head in Castle-Street, MDCCXXVIII.

2 An Essay on the Nature and Conduct of the Passions and Affections. With Illustrations on the Moral Sense. By Francis Hutcheson, Professor of Moral Philosophy in the University of Glasgow; and Author of the Inquiry into the Original of our Ideas of Beauty and Virtue. London. Printed for James and John Knapton, and John Crownfield in St. Paul's Church-Yard; John Darby in Bartholomew-Close; Thomas Osborne Jun. At Greys Inn; and Lauton Gilliver in Fleetstreet. M.DCC.XXX.

3 An Essay on the Nature and Conduct of the Passions and Affections. With Illustrations On the Moral Sense. The third edition, with Additions. London: Printed for A. Ward, J. and P. Knapton, T. Longman, S. Birt, C. Hitch, L. Gilliver, T. Astley, S. Austen, and J. Rivington. MDCCXLII.

There is some question about the order of appearance of 1A and 1B. Scott notes that 1B was advertised as having "the errors of the London Edition emended."[17] But 1A has fewer errors than 1B, which might seem according to Scott's comment to make it the "emended" edition. Fur-

---

17. Scott is quoting an advertisement in the March 23, 1728 edition of the *Dublin Intelligencer*. See Scott, *Francis Hutcheson*, 53.

thermore, IA and not IB was repackaged as the "second edition." But IB clearly reads, "London: printed and Dublin re-printed," and according to Mautner, IA is advertised in the *London Journal* as having been printed on January 13, 1728.[18] Thus, unless IB was printed in the first two weeks of January, which seems unlikely, IB was an inferior edition that appeared after IA.

IA and IB appeared anonymously as penned by "the Author of the Inquiry into the Original of our Ideas of Beauty and Virtue" (which did carry Hutcheson's name). The second edition of 1730, which introduced Hutcheson's name on the title page, is not an independent edition but rather IA reprinted with Francis Hutcheson's name on the title page. This was, it seems, the only revision. The authorship read in full, "Francis Hutcheson, Professor of Moral Philosophy in the University of *Glasgow;* and Author of the *Inquiry into the Original of our Ideas of* Beauty *and* Virtue." The point of this reissue was probably to boost sales of both of Hutcheson's works by means of his newly acquired academic distinction. He became a professor in Glasgow in 1730, and the third edition of the *Inquiry* (1729) had been published too early to make note of Hutcheson's new standing.

The third edition of 1742 is a distinct and revised edition with many additions and emendations, mainly to the *Illustrations.* There were a number of posthumous editions of *Essay with Illustrations.* Jessop mentions a 1751 Dublin edition, a 1756 London fourth edition, and a 1772 Glasgow "3rd edition."

18. See Thomas Mautner, *Francis Hutcheson: On Human Nature* (Cambridge: Cambridge University Press, 1993), 173–4. Mautner provides the most extended and up-to-date discussion of the lifetime editions of Hutcheson's texts. Other bibliographical discussions are to be found in Bernard Peach (ed.), *Francis Hutcheson: Illustrations on the Moral Sense* (Cambridge, Mass.: Belknap, 1971), 97–100; T. E. Jessop, *A Bibliography of David Hume and of Scottish Philosophy from Francis Hutcheson to Lord Balfour* (New York: Russell and Russell, 1966), 143–7; and the "Bibliographical Note" that introduces each volume of Bernard Fabian (ed.), *Collected Works of Francis Hutcheson* (Hildesheim: Olms, 1969/1971), 7 v.

Editorial Principles

Of the two extant variorum editions,[19] Peach used a posthumous 1769 reprint of 3 as the copy text for his edition of the *Illustrations*.[20] This is the best approach to the *Illustrations* when presented independently of the *Essays*. I have adopted 1A as the copy text for this edition of the entire *Essay with Illustrations* for a simple reason. It allows the reader to view the actual chronological alteration of the text: that is, how Hutcheson himself initially presented it and then altered it fourteen years later.

Turco's excellent Italian edition uses internal citation to make the body of the text neutral to the specific edition.[21] Unfortunately, that approach becomes far too unwieldy when noting punctuation changes. As Turco's edition is a translation into Italian with textual apparatus, minute changes of punctuation go for the most part unremarked.

Why 1A and not 1B? Because 1A has fewer mistakes than 1B, is more common, and is the basis for 2 (more accurately, it is identical to 2, aside from a new title page). I have not noted any variations among 1A, 1B, and the "second edition," as they have only bibliographic interest (and limited bibliographic interest at that), since Hutcheson appears to have had little or no hand in them. For the same reason, I have not noted variations found in posthumous editions.

Hutcheson made numerous alterations in the third edition, although the differences between the two editions are not as dramatic

19. There are a number of reprints without variorum. Volume II of Fabian (op. cit.) reprints 1A, as does the Garland (New York: 1971). Andrew Ward (ed.), *Essay with Illustrations* (Manchester: Clinamen, 1999) is a modernized version of 1A; and 3 has been reprinted in Paul McReynolds (ed.), *Four Early Works on Motivation* (Gainesville, Fla.: Scholars' Facsimiles and Reprints, 1969).

20. Peach (ed.), op. cit., 97.

21. Luigi Turco (ed.), Giovanni Grandi and Monica Saccani (trans.), *Francis Hutcheson: Saggio sulla natura e condotta delle passioni* (Bologna: Cooperativa Libraria Universitaria Editrice Bologna, 1997).

as one might expect, given the fourteen years between them. The significant varia are at the end of this text and are indicated by page and line number of the present volume. Hutcheson's notes and my editorial notes are attached to the main body of the text, as is the pagination for IA and 3 (IA appears in italic typeface; 3 appears in regular typeface).

The lengthiest emendations are found in the preface to the work and in the *Illustrations;* generally, these are subtractions from the preface and additions to the *Illustrations.* Many of the specific references to his contemporaries Joseph Butler, Jean Le Clerc, and John Clarke are trimmed from the preface in 3.

There are numerous other changes to the text, additions and subtractions of words, lines, and paragraphs, as well as countless modifications and alterations to punctuation, capitalization procedures, italics, and typeface. A number of footnotes were added to the later edition as well, including a diatribe against Hutcheson's critic John Balguy. A sole reference to the New Testament is also added. There are even alterations in the marginal titles.

I have restricted my variorum to changes that could alter the sense of the text, although what could affect sense is a point of debate. I have noted all changes of wording and all changes of relevant punctuation. These are clearly the two most important types of textual varia. There are many varia, though, that have not been noted.

I have not noted most changes in capitalization, as there is little or no rhyme or reason to Hutcheson's use of them. Although capitals are often used for emphasis in twentieth-century prose, they are not used with great consistency in earlier eighteenth-century English-language philosophical texts. Furthermore, capitalization was often a printer's decision. The same holds for italics. I have noted very few changes in capitals and italics—only those that could possibly be construed as providing a change in emphasis. Readers are strongly cautioned, however, against reading too much into even those changes.

Among other variorum that have not been noted are the following:

1. Differences in spelling, broadly conceived, among the editions.

A. The first edition prefers the idiomatic contraction of -ed: "join'd"/ "joined," "gratify'd"/"gratified," "alter'd"/"altered." There are other variations in contraction, such as "though"/"tho'"/"tho," "it is"/"'tis."

B. There are numerous differences in spelling more narrowly construed. A few representative examples are: "alledge"/"alledg," "threatned"/ "threatened," "inadvertencies"/"inadvertences," "suspence"/"suspense," "shews"/"shows."

C. There are also differences in the hyphenation and separation of words. A few representative examples are "nobody"/"no body," "pre-suppose"/"pre suppose," "fellow-creatures"/"fellow creatures," "our-selves"/ "our selves."

2. The placement of Hutcheson's footnote markers—inside or outside punctuation marks. I have noted variations in the marks used, and of course the absence of notes.

3. Changes in the use of roman and arabic numerals in the footnotes, as well as changes in the footnote markers themselves

Finally, I have corrected obvious printer's errors (e.g., "deipise" for "despise") and missing punctuation (e.g., a period missing at the end of a sentence), without remark. I have also substituted regular capitalization for the small caps used in the first word of every paragraph.

Aaron Garrett

ACKNOWLEDGMENTS

A number of people and institutions have helped in producing this edition of Hutcheson's *Essay with Illustrations*. As to institutions, special thanks are due Boston University, the Humanities Research Centre of the Australian National University, the Houghton Library at Harvard University, Liberty Fund and its unfailingly helpful staff, and the Australian National Cricket Team, which kept me awake through long nights of collation. As to people, James Moore has shown great generosity in helping me with my many queries about Hutcheson. He suggested Gershom Carmichael as the possible identity of the man of "real merit" in Glasgow (cf. p. 10, note x) and has aided in numerous other notes. Stephen Scully and Morgan Meis have suggested and corrected translations. I am also grateful to Bob Brown, Alfredo Ferrarin, Ian Hunter, Thomas Mautner, and Åsa Söderman.

Three people deserve very special thanks. First, Shelly Kroll labored with me over the proofs and caught many errors with her eagle eye. Second, I have benefited beyond measure from Luigi Turco's masterly Italian edition of the *Essay with Illustrations*. Through his scholarship I have avoided many pitfalls, and most of the notes in my edition are indebted in one way or another to his far more copious and erudite discussions. In particular, he has identified all of Hutcheson's classical sources. I refer to Turco in a few of my notes, when I am deriving a particular point from him, but his mark is on virtually everything in this volume. All readers who can read Italian and want to know more about the *Essay with Illustrations* are referred to his work. Finally, thanks to Knud Haakonssen, the editor of this series, who has helped with many notes, edited my prose, and been a constant support and resource. Without him this edition would not exist.

AN ESSAY ON THE NATURE AND CONDUCT
OF THE PASSIONS AND AFFECTIONS, WITH
ILLUSTRATIONS ON THE MORAL SENSE

AN

ESSAY

ON THE

Nature *and* CONDUCT

OF THE

Passions and *Affections.*

WITH

ILLUSTRATIONS

On the MORAL SENSE.

By the Author of the Inquiry into the Original
of our Ideas of *Beauty* and *Virtue,*

---

*Hoc opus, hoc studium, parvi properemus, & ampli,
Si Patriae volumus, si Nobis vivere chari.* Hor.[1]

LONDON:

Printed by *J. Darby* and *T. Browne,* for *John Smith* and *William Bruce,*
Booksellers in *Dublin;* and sold by *J. Osborn* and *T. Longman* in
Pater-Noster-Row, and *S. Chandler* in the *Poultrey.*
M.DCC.XXVIII.

1. Horace, *Sermones,* I.3.28–29. "This work, this study, let us hasten it far and wide, if we would wish to live in our country and to live happily with ourselves." Horace is the most quoted of the classical authors in the *Essay with Illustrations,* although Cicero, Marcus Aurelius, Plato, and Aristotle are also frequently cited.

THE PREFACE

[*iii*] Altho the main *practical Principles,* which are inculcated in this Treatise, have this Prejudice in their Favour, that they have been taught and propagated by the best of Men in all Ages, yet there is reason to fear that renewed Treatises upon Subjects so often well manag'd, may be look'd upon as *superfluous;* especially since little is offer'd upon them which has not often been well said before. But [*iv*] beside that general Consideration, that old Arguments may sometimes be set in such a Light by one, as will convince those who were not [iv] moved by them, even when better express'd by another; since, for every Class of *Writers* there are Classes of *Readers* adapted, who cannot relish any thing higher: Besides this, I say, the very *Novelty* of a Book may procure a little Attention, from those who over-look the Writings which the World has long enjoy'd. And if by *Curiosity,* or any other means, some few can be engag'd to turn their Thoughts to these important Subjects, about which a little *Reflection* will discover the Truth, and a thorow *Consideration* of it may occasion a great Increase of real Happiness; no Person need be asham'd of his Labours as useless, which do such Service to any of his Fellow-Creatures.

[*v*] If any should look upon some Things in this *Inquiry into the Passions,* as too subtile for common Apprehension, and consequently not [v] necessary for the Instruction of Men in *Morals,* which are the common business of Mankind: Let them consider, that the Difficulty on these Subjects arises chiefly from some *previous Notions,* equally difficult at least, which have been already receiv'd, to the great Detriment of many a *Natural Temper;* since many have been discourag'd from all Attempts of cultivating *kind generous Affections* in themselves, by a pre-

3

vious Notion that there are no such Affections in Nature, and that all Pretence to them was only *Dissimulation, Affectation,* or at best some *unnatural Enthusiasm.* And farther, that to discover Truth on these Subjects, nothing more is necessary than a little *Attention to what passes in our own Hearts,* [*vi*] and consequently every Man may come to Certainty in these Points, without much Art or Knowledge of other Matters.

[vi] Whatever Confusion the *Schoolmen* introduced into Philosophy, some of their keenest *Adversaries*[2] seem to threaten it with a worse kind of Confusion, by attempting to take away some of the most *immediate simple Perceptions,* and to explain all *Approbation, Condemnation, Pleasure* and *Pain,* by some intricate Relations to the Perceptions of the *External Senses.* In like manner they have treated our *Desires* or *Affections,* making the most generous, kind and disinterested of them, to proceed from *Self-Love,* by some subtle Trains of Reasoning, to which honest Hearts are often wholly Strangers.

[*vii*] Let this also still be remembred that the *natural Dispositions* of Mankind will operate regularly in those who never reflected upon them, nor form'd just Notions about them. [vii] Many are really *virtuous* who cannot explain what *Virtue* is. Some act a most generous disinterested Part in Life, who have been taught to account for all their Actions by *Self-Love,* as their sole Spring. There have been very different and opposite Opinions in *Opticks,* contrary Accounts have been given of *Hearing, voluntary Motion, Digestion,* and other *natural Actions.* But the Powers themselves in reality perform their several Operations with sufficient Constancy and Uniformity, in Persons of good Health, whatever their Opinions be about them. In the same manner our *moral Actions* and *Affections* may be in good order, when our Opinions [*viii*] are quite wrong about them. *True Opinions* however, about both, may enable us to *improve* our natural Powers, and to *rectify* accidental Disorders incident unto them. And true Speculations on these Subjects must certainly [viii] be attended with as much *Pleasure* as any other Parts of Human Knowledge.

2. Hutcheson likely had in mind modern Epicureans: Mandeville, Hobbes, La Rochefoucault, and others.

It may perhaps seem strange, that when in this *Treatise* Virtue is suppos'd *disinterested;* yet so much Pains is taken, by a *Comparison* of our several *Pleasures,* to prove the *Pleasures* of *Virtue* to be the greatest we are capable of, and that consequently it is our truest *Interest* to be *virtuous.* But let it be remember'd here, that tho there can be no *Motives* or *Arguments* suggested which can directly raise any *ultimate Desire,* such as that of our *own Happiness,* or *publick Affections* (as we attempt to prove in *Treatise* IV;) [*ix*] yet if both are *natural Dispositions* of our Minds, and nothing can stop the Operation of *publick Affections* but some *selfish Interest,* the only way to give publick Affections their full Force, and to make them prevalent [ix] in our Lives, must be to remove these *Opinions of opposite Interests,* and to shew a superior Interest on their side. If these Considerations be just and sufficiently attended to, a *natural Disposition* can scarce fail to exert it self to the full.

In this *Essay on the Passions,* the Proofs and Illustrations of a *moral Sense,* and *Sense of Honour* are not mention'd; because they are so, in the *Inquiry into Moral Good and Evil,* in the first and fifth *Sections.* Would Men reflect upon what they feel in themselves, all *Proofs* in such Matters would be needless.

[*x*] Some strange Love of *Simplicity* in the Structure of human Nature, [x] or Attachment to some favourite *Hypothesis,* has engag'd many *Writers* to pass over a great many *Simple Perceptions,* which we may find in our selves. We have got the Number *Five* fixed for our *external Senses,* tho *Seven* or *Ten* might as easily be defended. We have Multitudes of Perceptions which have no relation to any *external Sensation;* if by it we mean *Perceptions, occasion'd by Motions or Impressions made on our Bodies,* such as the Ideas of *Number, Duration, Proportion, Virtue, Vice, Pleasures of Honour, of Congratulation; the Pains of Remorse, Shame, Sympathy,* and many others. It were to be wish'd, that those who are at such Pains to prove a beloved Maxim, that "all Ideas arise from *Sensation* and *Reflection,*" had so explain'd [*xi*] themselves, that none should take their Meaning to be, that all our Ideas are either *external Sensations,* [xi] or *reflex Acts* upon *external Sensations:* Or if by *Reflection* they mean an *inward Power of Perception,* as I fancy they do, they had as carefully examin'd into the several kinds of *internal Perceptions,* as they

have done into the *external Sensations:* that we might have seen whether
the former be not as *natural* and *necessary* as the latter. Had they in like
manner consider'd our *Affections* without a previous Notion, that they
were all from *Self-Love,* they might have felt an *ultimate Desire* of the
Happiness of others as easily conceivable, and as certainly implanted in   5
the human Breast, tho perhaps not so strong as *Self-Love.*

The Author hopes this imperfect *Essay* will be favourably re[*xii*]
ceiv'd, till some Person of greater Abilities [xii] and Leisure apply himself to a more strict Philosophical Inquiry into the various *natural Principles* or *natural Dispositions* of Mankind; from which perhaps a more   10
exact Theory of Morals may be formed, than any which has yet appear'd: and hopes that this Attempt, to shew the fair side of the human
Temper, may be of some little use towards this great End.

The principal Objections offer'd by Mr. *Clarke* of *Hull,* against the
second Section of the second *Treatise,* occurr'd to the Author in Con-   15
versation, and had appriz'd him of the necessity of a farther illustration
of *disinterested Affections,* in answer to his Scheme of deducing them
from *Self-Love,* which seem'd more ingenious than any which the Author of the *Inquiry* ever yet saw in print. He takes better from Mr.
Clarke, all [*xiii*] other Parts of his Treatment, than the raising such an   20
Outcry against him as *injurious to Christianity,*[3] for Principles which
some of the most *zealous Christians* have publickly maintain'd: He
hopes Mr. *Clarke* will be satisfy'd upon this Point, as well as about the
Scheme of *disinterested Affections,* by what is offer'd in the Treatise on
the *Passions,* Sect. I. and designedly placed here, rather than in any dis-   25
tinct *Reply,* both to avoid the disagreeable Work of *Answering* or *Re-*

3. John Clarke repeatedly criticized Hutcheson for impiety. *The Foundation of
Morality* closes: "I have naturally a peculiar Benevolence and Veneration for Persons
of Good Parts and Learning, untainted with Pride, Pedantry, or ill Nature, such as
our Author from his manner of Writing appears to me to be, and therefore I am   30
heartily grieved upon his account, to find his Doctrine bear so hard upon the
Christian Religion. Had it not clash'd so visibly with that, notwithstanding it being
false, his Character would have appeared much fairer in the Eye of the World than
it now does, or at least will do, when his Notion comes to be more generally and
thoroughly scanned." (p. 112).   35

marking upon Books, wherein it is hard to keep off too keen and offensive Expressions; and also, that those who have had any of the former Editions of the Inquiry, might not be at a loss about any *Illustrations* or additional *Proofs* necessary to complete the Scheme.

The last Treatise had never seen the Light, had not some worthy [*xiv*] *Gentlemen* mistaken some things about the moral Sense alledg'd to be in Mankind:[4] Their Objections gave Opportunity of farther Inquiry into the several *Schemes* of accounting for our *moral Ideas,* which some apprehend to be wholly different from, and independent on, that *Sense* which the Author attempts to establish. The following Papers attempt to shew, that all these *Schemes* must necessarily presuppose this *moral Sense,* and be resolv'd into it: Nor does the Author endeavour to over-turn them, or represent them as unnecessary Superstructures upon the Foundation of a moral Sense; tho what he has suggested will probably shew a considerable Confusion in some of the Terms [xiv] much used on these Subjects. One may easily see from the great *variety of Terms,* and diversity of *Schemes* invented, that all Men *feel* something in their own Hearts recommending Virtue, which [*xv*] yet it is difficult to explain. This Difficulty probably arises from our previous Notions of a small Number of *Senses,* so that we are unwilling to have recourse in our Theories to any more; and rather strain out some Explication of moral Ideas, with relation to some other natural Powers of Perception universally acknowledg'd. The like difficulty attends several other *Perceptions,* to the Reception of which Philosophers have not generally assigned their *distinct Senses*; such as *natural Beauty, Harmony,* the Perfection of *Poetry, Architecture, Designing,* and such like Affairs of Genius, Taste, or Fancy: The Explications or Theories on these Subjects [xv] are in like manner full of Confusion and Metaphor.

To define *Virtue* by *agreeableness to this moral Sense,* or describing it to be *kind Affection,* may [*xvi*] appear perhaps too uncertain; considering that the Sense of particular Persons is often depraved by *Custom, Habits,* false Opinions, Company: and that some *particular kind Pas-*

---

4. This is a reference to Hutcheson's correspondence with Burnet (who equated the moral sense with Reason). See the Introduction.

sions toward some Persons are really pernicious, and attended with very unkind Affections toward others, or at least with a Neglect of their Interests. We must therefore only assert in general, that "every one calls that Temper, or those Actions *virtuous,* which are approv'd by his *own Sense;*" and withal, that "abstracting from particular Habits or Prejudices, every one is so constituted as to approve every *particular kind Affection* toward any one, which argues no *want of Affection* toward others. And constantly to approve that Temper which desires, and those Actions which tend to procure the greatest Moment of Good in the Power of the Agent toward [*xvii*] the [xvi] most extensive System to which it can reach;" and consequently, that the Perfection of Virtue consists in "having the *universal calm Benevolence,* the prevalent Affection of the Mind, so as to limit and counteract not only the *selfish Passions,* but even the *particular kind Affections.*"

Our *moral Sense* shews this to be the highest Perfection of our Nature; what we may see to be the *End* or *Design* of such a Structure, and consequently what is requir'd of us by the Author of our Nature: and therefore if any one like these Descriptions better, he [xvii] may call Virtue, with many of the Antients, "*Vita secundum naturam;*"[5] or "acting according to what we may see from the Constitution of our Nature, we were intended for by our Creator."

[*xviii*] If this *Moral Sense* were once set in a convincing Light, those vain Shadows of Objections against a virtuous Life, in which some are wonderfully delighted, would soon vanish: alledging, that whatever we admire or honour in a *moral Species,* is the effect of *Art, Education, Custom, Policy,* or subtle Views of Interest; we should then acknowledge

Quid sumus, & quidnam victuri gignimur.[6]—Pers.

---

5. "Vita secundum naturam"—"a life according to nature"—is a central Stoical ethical doctrine as well as the name of a lost treatise by Zeno of Citium (see Diogenes Laertius, *Vitae Philosophorum,* VII.4), with whom Cicero identifies the phrase in *De Finibus Bonorum et Malorum,* IV.vi [14].

6. Persius, *Satire,* III.66. "[Learn] what we are, and for what we have come to be." It is quoted by Shaftesbury and discussed in the "Miscellaneous Reflections," III.1 (Shaftesbury, *Characteristicks,* III:97–8).

'Tis true, a *Power of Reasoning* is natural to us; and we must own, that all Arts and Sciences which are well founded, and tend to direct our [xviii] Actions, are, if not to be called *Natural,* an *Improvement upon our Nature:* yet if Virtue be look'd upon as wholly Artificial, there are I know not what Suspicions against it; as if indeed [xix] it might tend to the greater Interest of *large Bodies* or *Societies* of Men, or to that of their *Governors;* whereas a private Person may better find his *Interest,* or enjoy greater Pleasures in the Practices counted *vicious,* especially if he has any Probability of *Secrecy* in them. These Suspicions must be entirely remov'd, if we have a *moral Sense* and *publick Affections,* whose Gratifications are constituted by Nature, our most intense and durable *Pleasures.*

I hope it is a good Omen of something still better on this Subject to be expected in the learned World, that Mr. *Butler,* in his Sermons at the *Rolls Chapel,* has done so much Justice to the wise and good Order of our Nature; that the Gentlemen, who have oppos'd some other Sentiments of the Author of the *Inquiry,* seem convinc'd of a *moral* [xx] *Sense.*[7] Some of them have by a Mistake made a Compliment to the Author, which does not [xix] belong to him; as if the World were any way indebted to him for this Discovery. He has too often met with the *Sensus Decori & Honesti,*[8] and with the Δύναμις αγαθοειδὴς, to assume any such thing to himself.

7. This refers to John Clarke's remark, "The Doctrine of a Moral Sense, and a Natural Benevolence founded thereon, is a very pretty ingenious Speculation, which the World is obliged to our Author for; and has, in my Opinion, a good deal of Truth in it, tho' perhaps it may not be of that Universal Extent he pleads for," (*Foundation of Morality,* 97).

8. Hutcheson likely has *De Officiis* I [94] in mind, but the identification of what is appropriate and what is honorable is a common Ciceronian sentiment. Shaftesbury clearly had this passage in mind when he further identified it with the *venusta* (the lovely or beautiful)—"The *Venustum,* the *Honestum,* the *Decorum* of Things, will force its Way. They who refuse to give it scope in the nobler Subjects of a rational and moral kind, will find its Prevalency elsewhere, in an inferior Order of Things," Shaftesbury, "Sensus Communis," IV.2 (*Characteristicks,* I.92) further elucidated in "Miscellaneous Reflections" III.2 (*Characteristicks,* III.109–114). The phrase recurs in Hutcheson's *Reflection on Laughter* in the *Dublin Journal* (Saturday, June, 5, 1725), no. 10, 38) collected in *A Collection of Letters and Essays on Several Subjects Lately Publish'd in the Dublin Journal* (London: J. Darby and T. Longman, 1729), 2 v.

Some Letters in the *London* Journals, subscribed *Philaretus,*⁹ gave the
first Occasion to the *Fourth Treatise;* the Answers given to them bore
too visible Marks of the Hurry in which they were wrote, and therefore
the *Author* declined to continue the Debate that way; chusing to send
a private Letter to *Philaretus,* to desire a more private Correspondence   5
on the Subject of our Debate. I have been since informed, that his
Death disappointed my great Expectations from [*xxi*] so ingenious a
Correspondent. The *Objections* proposed in the first *Section* of *Treatise*
[xx] IV, are not always those of *Philaretus,* tho I have endeavour'd to
leave no Objections of his unanswer'd; but I also interspersed whatever   10
Objections occurr'd to me in Conversation on these Subjects. I hope I
have not used any Expressions inconsistent with the high Regard I have
for the Memory of so ingenious a Gentleman, and of such Distinction
in the World.

The last *Section* of the *Fourth Treatise,* was occasion'd by a private   15
Letter from a Person of the most real Merit, in *Glasgow;* representing to
me some Sentiments not uncommon among good Men, which might
prejudice them against any Scheme of *Morals,* not wholly founded
upon *Piety.*¹⁰ This Point is, I hope, so treated, as to remove the Difficulty.   20

[*xxii*] The Deference due to a Person, who has appear'd so much in
the learned World, as M. *Le Clerc,* would seem to require, that I should
make some Defense against, or Submission to, the Remarks he makes
in his *Bibliotheque Ancienne & Moderne.* But I cannot but conclude
from his Abstract, especially from that of the *last Section* of the *Inquiry,*   25

The Greek phrase, meaning the sense of the good or right, is replaced in the third
edition with "loving mankind and having the form of the good."

9. This refers to the exchange with Gilbert Burnet in 1725, and Hutcheson has
either confused the date of the exchange with the publication date of the first edition
of the *Essay with Illustrations,* or with four letters in the *London Journal* (nos. 447,   30
450, 463, 468) written in response to and in defense of the *Essay with Illustrations.*
See Bernard Fabian, "Bibliographical Note," in Bernard Fabian (ed.), *Collected
Works of Francis Hutcheson* (Hildesheim: Georg Olms Verlag, 1990), v. II vii–viii.

10. It is not clear to whom this remark refers, but a possible candidate is Gershom
Carmichael, whom Hutcheson replaced as Professor of Moral Philosophy at Glas-   35
gow University and who did not approve of Hutcheson's "new light" philosophy.

either that I don't understand his *French,* or he my *English,* or that he has never read more than the Titles of some of the *Sections:* and if any one of the three be the Case, we are not fit for a Controversy.[11]

In the References, at bottom of Pages, the Inquiry into *Beauty* is called *Treatise* I. That into the Ideas of moral Good and Evil, is *Treatise* II. The Essay on the Passions, *Treatise* III. And the Illustrations on the moral Sense, *Treatise* IV.

11. Hutcheson received two unpleasant reviews of the *Inquiry* in Francophone journals, first an anonymous notice in the *Bibliothètheque angloise* accusing him of having plagiarized Crousaz's *Traité du beau,* and then a review by Jean Le Clerc in the *Bibliothèque ancienne et moderne* that repeated the charge. The *Traité du beau* bears only a surface similarity (at best) to Treatise 1, so these reviews quite justly irked Hutcheson, who wrote a letter to the editor responding to the comments in the *Bibliothètheque angloise.*

THE CONTENTS

An Essay on the Nature and Conduct of the Passions

SECTION I

A general Account of our several Senses and Desires, Selfish or Publick

[*1*/1] The Nature of human Actions cannot be sufficiently understood without considering the *Affections* and *Passions;* or those *Modifications, or Actions of the Mind consequent upon the Apprehension of certain Objects or Events, in which the Mind generally conceives Good or Evil.* [2] In this

5 Inquiry we need little *Reasoning,* or *Argument,* since Certainty is only
[2] attainable by distinct *Attention* to what we are *conscious* happens in our Minds.

Art. I. "Objects, Actions, or Events obtain the Name of *Good,* or *Evil,* according as they are the Causes, or Occasions, mediately, or im-

10 mediately, of a grateful, or ungrateful *Perception* to some sensitive Nature." To understand therefore the several Kinds of *Good,* or *Evil,* we must apprehend the several *Senses* natural to us.

There seems to be some *Sense* or other suited to every sort of Objects which occurs to us, by which we receive either *Pleasure,* or *Pain* from a

15 great part of them, as well as some *Image,* or *Apprehension* of them: Nay, sometimes our only *Idea* is a *Perception of Pleasure, or Pain.* The Pleasures or Pains perceived, are sometimes *simple,* without any other previous Idea, or any Image, or other concomitant Ideas, save those of *Ex-*

tension, or of *Duration;* one of which accompanies every Perception, whether of *Sense,* or *inward Consciousness.* Other Pleasures arise only upon some *previous Idea,* or *Assemblage,* or *Comparison of Ideas.* These Pleasures, presupposing previous Ideas, were called *Perceptions* of an *internal* [3] *Sense,* in a former [3] Treatise.* Thus *Regularity* and *Uniformity* in Figures, are no less grateful than *Tastes,* or *Smells;* the *Harmony* of Notes, is more grateful than simple Sounds.† In [4] like manner, *Affections, Tempers,* [4] *Sentiments,* or *Actions,* reflected upon in our selves, or observed in others, are the constant *Occasions* of agreeable or disagreeable Perceptions, which we call *Approbation,* or *Dislike.* These *Moral*

---

*Inquiry into Beauty.

† It is not easy to divide definitely our several *Sensations* into Classes. The Division of our *External Senses* into the five common Classes, is ridiculously imperfect. Some *Sensations,* received without any previous Idea, can either be reduced to none of them, such as the Sensations of *Hunger, Thirst, Weariness, Sickness;* or if we reduce them to the Sense of *Feeling,* they are Perceptions as different from the other *Ideas* of Touch, such as *Cold, Heat, Hardness, Softness,* as the *Ideas* of *Taste* or *Smell.* Others have hinted at an External Sense different from all of these. The following general Account may possibly be useful. (1.) That certain Motions raised in our Bodies are by a *general Law* constituted the Occasion of *Perceptions* in the Mind. (2.) These Perceptions never come entirely alone, but have some other *Perception* joined with them. Thus every Sensation is accompanied with the *Idea* of *Duration,* and yet *Duration* is not a sensible *Idea,* since it also accompanies *Ideas* of *Internal Consciousness* or Reflection: So the *Idea* of *Number* may accompany any sensible Ideas, and yet may also accompany any other Ideas, as well as external Sensations. (3.) Some *Ideas* are found accompanying the most different Sensations, which yet are not to be perceived separately from some *sensible Quality;* such are *Extension, Figure, Motion,* and *Rest,* which accompany the *Ideas* of Sight, or Colours, and yet may be perceived without them, as in the *Ideas* of *Touch,* at least if we move our Organs along the Parts of the Body touched. *Extension, Figure, Motion,* or *Rest* seem therefore to be more properly called *Ideas accompanying* the Sensations of *Sight* and *Touch,* than the Sensations of either of these Senses. The *Perceptions* which are purely sensible, received each by its proper Sense, are *Tastes, Smells, colours, Sound, Cold, Heat,* &c. The universal Concomitant *Ideas* which may attend any *Idea* whatsoever, are *Duration,* and *Number.* The *Ideas* which accompany the most different Sensations, are *Extension, Figure, Motion, Rest.* These all arise without any previous *Ideas* assembled, or compared: the Concomitant *Ideas* are reputed Images of something External.

From all these we may justly distinguish "the Pleasures perceived upon the previous Reception and Comparison of various sensible Perceptions, with their concomitant Ideas, or intellectual Ideas, when we find Uniformity, or Resemblance among them." These are meant by *the Perceptions of the internal Sense.*

Perceptions arise in us as necessarily as any other Sensations; nor can we alter, or stop them, while our *previous Opinion* or *Apprehension* of the *Affection, Temper,* or *Intention* of the Agent continues the same; any more than we can make the Taste of Wormwood sweet, or that of Honey bitter.

If we may call *every Determination of our Minds to receive Ideas independently on our Will, and to have Perceptions of Pleasure and Pain,* A SENSE, we shall find many other *Senses* beside those commonly explained. Tho it is not easy to assign accurate Divisions on such Subjects, yet we may reduce them to the following Classes, leaving it to others to arrange them as they think convenient. A little Reflection will [5] shew that there are such *Natural* [5] *Powers* in the human Mind, in whatever Order we place them. In the 1st Class are the *External Senses,* universally known. In the 2d, the *Pleasant Perceptions* arising from *regular, harmonious, uniform* Objects; as also from *Grandeur* and *Novelty.* These we may call, after Mr. ADDISON, the Pleasures of the *Imagination;*[12] or we may call the Power of receiving them, an *Internal Sense.* Whoever dislikes this Name may substitute another. 3. The next Class of Perceptions we may call a *Publick Sense, viz.* "our Determination to be pleased with the *Happiness* of others, and to be uneasy at their *Misery."* This is found in some degree in all Men, and was sometimes called Κοινονοημοσύνη or *Sensus Communis*[13] by some of the Antients. 4. The fourth Class we may call the *Moral* [6] *Sense,* by which "we perceive *Virtue,* or *Vice* in our selves, or others." This is plainly distinct from the former Class of Perceptions, since many are strongly affected with the Fortunes of others, who seldom reflect upon *Virtue,* or *Vice* in themselves, or others, as an Object: as we may find in *Natural Affection, Compassion, Friendship,* or even *general Benevolence* to Mankind, which connect our

12. See Joseph Addison's (1672–1719) "Essay *on the Pleasures of the Imagination*" in *Spectator* 411–21. Addison's "Essay" is a discussion of aesthetics that includes extended comparisons between the external senses and the imagination. A "Table of the principal Contents" is given in *Spectator* 421.

13. Hutcheson is deriving this from Shaftesbury's extended discussion of the classical origins of *sensus communis* at "Sensus Communis," III.1 n (*Characteristicks,* I.65–6 n).

Happiness or Pleasure with that of others, even when we are not reflecting upon our own Temper, nor delighted with the Perception of our own Virtue. 5. The fifth [6] Class is a *Sense of Honour,* "which makes the *Approbation,* or *Gratitude* of others, for any good Actions we have done, the necessary occasion of Pleasure; and their *Dislike, Condemnation,* or *Resentment* of Injuries done by us, the occasion of that uneasy Sensation called *Shame,* even when we fear no further evil from them."

There are perhaps other *Perceptions* distinct from all these Classes, such as some Ideas "of *Decency, Dignity, Suitableness to human Nature* in certain Actions and Circumstances; and of an *Indecency, Meanness,* and *Unworthiness,* in the contrary Actions or Circumstances, even without any conception of *Moral* Good, or Evil." Thus the Pleasures of *Sight,* and *Hearing,* are more esteemed than those of Taste or [7] Touch: The Pursuits of the Pleasures of the *Imagination,* are more approved than those of simple external Sensations. *Plato** accounts for this difference from a constant Opinion of *Innocence* in this sort of Pleasures, which would reduce this Perception to the Moral Sense. Others may imagine that the difference is not owing to any such Reflection upon their *Innocence,* but that there is a different sort of Perceptions in these cases, to be reckoned another *Class of Sensations.*

A like Division of our Desires. [7] II. Desires arise in our Mind, from the Frame of our Nature, upon Apprehension of Good or Evil in Objects, Actions, or Events, to obtain for our *selves* or *others* the *agreeable Sensation,* when the Object or Event is good; or to prevent the *uneasy Sensation,* when it is evil. Our original Desires and Aversions may therefore be divided into five Classes, answering to the Classes of our Senses. 1. The Desire of *sensual Pleasure,* (by which we mean that of the external Senses); and Aversion to the opposite Pains. 2. The Desires of the *Pleasures of Imagination* or Internal Sense,† and Aversion to what is disagreeable to it. 3. Desires of the

---

* Hippias Major. See also *Treat.* II. *Sect.* 5. *Art.* 7.

[[See Plato, *Hippias Major,* 300a1–b5. In this passage and those surrounding it, Socrates discusses what is common to, and presupposed in, various pleasures.]]

† See *Treat.* I.

[[Notably, Hutcheson rarely identifies internal sense with imagination in Treatise I, but rather with the sense of beauty and harmony (see T1 1.10). He normally uses

Pleasures arising from *Publick Happiness*, and Aversion to the Pains arising [8] from the *Misery of others*. 4. Desires of *Virtue*, and Aversion to
Vice, according to the Notions we have of the Tendency of Actions to
the Publick Advantage or Detriment. 5. Desires of *Honour*, and Aversion to Shame.*

The third Class of *Publick Desires* contains many very different sorts
of Affections, all those which tend toward the *Happiness of others*, or the
removal of Misery; such as those of *Gratitude, Compassion*, [8] *Natural
Affection, Friendship*, or the more extensive calm *Desire of the universal
Good* of all sensitive Natures, which our moral Sense approves as the
Perfection of Virtue, even when it limits, and counteracts the narrower
Attachments of Love.

Now since we are capable of *Reflection, Memory, Observation*, and *Reasoning* about the distant Tendencies of Objects and Actions, and not
confined to things present, there must arise, in consequence of our
original Desires, "*secondary Desires* of every thing imagined useful to
gratify any of the primary Desires, with strength proportioned to the
several original Desires, and the imagined Usefulness, or Necessity, of
the advantageous Object." Hence it is that as soon as we come to apprehend the Use of *Wealth* or *Power* to gratify any of our original Desires, we must also desire them. Hence arises the *Universality* of these
Desires of Wealth and Power, since they are the Means of gratifying all
other Desires. "How foolish then is the Inference, some would make,
from the universal Prevalence of these Desires, that human Nature is
wholly selfish, or that each one is only studious of his *own Advantage;*
since Wealth or Power are as naturally fit to [9] gratify our *Publick Desires*, or to serve *virtuous Purposes*, as the *selfish* ones?"

[*9*] "How weak also are the Reasonings of some recluse Moralists,

Secondary De-
sires of Wealth
and Power.

"imagination" pejoratively (T1 VIII.1) The identification of internal sense with
imagination is primarily associated with Addison, and with the articles published
in his *Spectator* (411–21), one article of which (*Spectator* 412) Hutcheson cites with
approbation at T1 VI.13. The identification of internal sense with beauty and harmony can be found in Addison but is particularly associated with Shaftesbury. See,
for example, "The Inquiry Concerning Virtue or Merit," II.3.]]
  *See *Treat*. II. *Sect*. 5. *Art*. 3–8.

who condemn in general all Pursuits of Wealth or Power, as below a perfectly virtuous Character: since Wealth and Power are the most effectual *Means,* and the most powerful *Instruments,* even of the greatest Virtues, and most generous Actions?" The Pursuit of them is laudable, when the *Intention* is virtuous; and the neglect of them, when honourable Opportunities offer, is really a Weakness. This justifies the Poet's Sentiments:

> ——————— *Hic onus horret,*
> *Ut parvis Animis & parvo Corpore majus:*
> *Hic subit & perfert: aut virtus nomen inane est,*
> *Aut Decus & Pretium recte petit experiens Vir.*—HOR. *Epist.* 17.[14]

"Further, the *Laws* or *Customs* of a Country, the *Humour* of our Company may have made strange *Associations* of *Ideas,* so that some Objects, which of themselves are indifferent to any Sense, by reason of some *additional* grateful *Idea,* may become very desirable; or by like *Addition* of an ungrateful *Idea* may raise the strongest Aversion." Thus many a Trifle, when once it is made a *Badge* of *Honour,* an Evidence of some *generous Disposition,* a Monument of [9] some *great Action,* may be impatiently pursued, [*10*] from our Desire of Honour. When any *Circumstance, Dress, State, Posture* is constituted as a Mark of *Infamy,* it may become in like manner the Object of Aversion, tho in itself most inoffensive to our Senses. If a certain way of *Living,* of *receiving Company,* of *shewing Courtesy,* is once received among those who are honoured; they who cannot bear the Expence of this may be made uneasy at their Condition, tho much freer from Trouble than that of higher Stations. Thus *Dress, Retinue, Equipage, Furniture, Behaviour,* and *Diversions* are made Matters of considerable Importance by additional *Ideas.** Nor is it in vain that the wisest and greatest Men regard these

---

14. Horace, *Epistles,* I.17.39. "This man dreads his burden as too much for a small soul and a small body: that man submits and bears it to the end: either virtue is a word without meaning, or the venturesome deservedly gain honor and reward."

*See *Treat.* I. *Sect.* I. *Art.* 7. and *Treat.* II. *Sect.* 6. *Art.* 6.

[[Hutcheson changes the reference from T2 VI.2 in the first edition to T2 VI.6 in the third. T2 VI.2 is an appropriate reference, since Hutcheson argues in this

things; for however it may concern them to break such Associations in their own Minds, yet, since the bulk of Mankind will retain them, they must comply with their Sentiments and Humours in things innocent, as they expect the *publick Esteem,* which is generally necessary to enable Men to serve the Publick.

Should any one be surprized at this *Disposition* in our Nature to asso-ciate any *Ideas* together for the future, which once presented themselves jointly, considering what [11] great *Evils,* and how much *Corruption* [11] of Affections is owing to it, it may help to account for this Part of our Constitution, to consider "that all our *Language* and much of our *Mem-ory* depends upon it:" So that were there no such *Associations* made, we must lose the use of *Words,* and a great part of our Power of *recollecting past Events;* beside many other valuable *Powers* and *Arts* which depend upon them. Let it also be considered that it is much in our power by a vigorous *Attention* either to prevent *these Associations,* or by *Abstraction* to separate Ideas when it may be useful for us to do so.

Concerning our Pursuit of *Honour,* 'tis to be observ'd, that "since our Minds are incapable of retaining a great Diversity of Objects, the *Nov-elty,* or *Singularity* of any Object is enough to raise a particular Atten-tion to it among many of equal Merit:" And therefore were Virtue *uni-versal* among Men, yet, 'tis probable, the *Attention* of Observers would be turned chiefly toward those who distinguished themselves by some *singular Ability,* or by some Circumstance, which, however trifling in its own Nature, yet had some honourable Ideas commonly joined to it, such as *Magnificence, Generosity,* or the like. We should perhaps, when we considered sedately the [12] common Virtues of others, [12] equally love and esteem them:* And yet probably our *Attention* would be generally fixed to those who thus were *distinguished* from the Mul-titude. Hence our natural Love of Honour, raises in us a Desire of

The Uses of these Associa-tions.

---

passage that "WEALTH and EXTERNAL PLEASURES bear no small bulk in our Imaginations." T2 VI.6 concerns the power of rhetoric and has at best a tangential relation to Hutcheson's discussion in T3 to which it is referenced.]]
　*See *Treat.* II. *Sect.* 3. last Parag.

Distinction, either by higher Degrees of Virtue; or, if we cannot easily or probably obtain it this way, we attempt it in an easier manner, by any Circumstance, which, thro' a *Confusion of Ideas,* is reputed honourable.

This Desire of *Distinction* has great Influence on the Pleasures and Pains of Mankind, and makes them chuse things for their very *Rarity,* *Difficulty,* or *Expence;* by a confused Imagination that they evidence *Generosity, Ability,* or a *finer Taste* than ordinary; nay, often the merest Trifles are by these means ardently pursued. A *Form of Dress,* a *foreign Dish,* a *Title,* a *Place,* a *Jewel;* an *useless Problem,* a *Criticism on an obsolete Word,* the *Origin of a Poetic Fable,* the *Situation of a razed Town,* may employ many an Hour in tedious Labour:

> *Sic leve, sic parvum est, animum quod laudis avarum*
> *Subruit aut reficit.*—HOR.[15]

Desires, selfish and publick.

[13/13] *Art.* III. There is another Division of our Desires taken from the Persons for whose Advantage we pursue or shun any Object. "The Desires in which one intends or pursues what he apprehends advantageous to himself, we may call SELFISH; and those in which we pursue what we apprehend advantageous to others, and do not apprehend advantageous to *our selves,* or do not pursue with this view, we may call *Publick* or BENEVOLENT Desires." If there be a just Foundation for this Division, it is more extensive than the former Division, since each of the former Classes may come under either Member of this Division, according as we are desiring any of the five sorts of Pleasures *for our selves,* or desiring them *for others.* The former Division may therefore be conceived as a Subdivision of the latter.

This Division has been disputed since *Epicurus;* who with his old Followers, and some of late, who detest other parts of his Scheme,[16] maintain, "that all our Desires are *selfish:* or, that what every one intends

15. Horace, *Epistles,* II.1. 179–80, "So light, so little is what is needed to tear down or build up a soul hungry for praise."

16. This seems to be a reference to Locke's hedonistic theory of motivation, as developed in the later editions of the *Essay Concerning Human Understanding.* See particularly *Essay,* II.xxi §§41–43.

or designs ultimately, in each Action, is the obtaining Pleasure to *himself,* or the avoiding his own *private Pain.*"*

[*14*/14] It requires a good deal of Subtilty to defend this Scheme, so seemingly opposite to *Natural Affection, Friendship, Love of a Country, or Community,* which many find very strong in their Breasts. The Defences and Schemes commonly offered, can scarce free the Sustainers of this Cause from manifest Absurdity and *Affectation.* But some do† acknowledge a *publick Sense* in many Instances; especially in *natural Affection,* and *Compassion;* by which "the Observation of the Happiness of others is made the necessary Occasion of Pleasure, and their Misery the Occasion of Pain to the Observer." That this *Sympathy* with others is the Effect of the Constitution of our Nature, and not brought upon our selves by any Choice, with view to any *selfish Advantage,* they must own: whatever Advantage there may be in Sympathy with the *Fortunate,* none can be alledged in Sympathy with the *Distressed:* And every one feels that this *publick Sense* will not leave his Heart, upon a change of the Fortunes of his Child or Friend; nor does it depend upon a Man's *Choice,* whether he will be affected with their Fortunes or not. But supposing this publick Sense, they insist, "That by means [15] of it there is a *Conjunction of Interest:* the [*15*] Happiness of others becomes the Means of private Pleasure to the Observer; and for this Reason, or with a View to this private Pleasure, he desires the Happiness of another." Others deduce our Desire of the Happiness of others from Self-love, in a less specious manner.

If a *publick Sense* be acknowledged in Men, by which the Happiness of one is made to depend upon that of others, independently of his Choice, this is indeed a strong Evidence of the Goodness of the Author of our Nature. But whether this Scheme does truly account for our *Love of others,* or for *generous Offices,* may be determined from the following

---

* See *Cicero de finib. lib.* i.

[[This is discussed throughout Book I of Cicero's *De Finibus Bonorum et Malorum* and succinctly stated at I.vii [23].]]

† See Mr. *Clark* of *Hull,* his *Remarks* on *Treat.* II.

[[On John Clarke of Hull, see the Introduction to this volume.]]

Considerations; which being matters of *internal Consciousness,* every one can best satisfy himself by Attention, concerning their Truth and Certainty.

Let it be premised, that *Desire is generally uneasy, or attended with an uneasy Sensation,* which is something distinct from that uneasy Sensation arising from some *Event* or *Object,* the Prevention or Removal of which Sensation we are intending when the Object is apprehended as Evil; as this *uneasy Sensation of Desire* is obviously different from the *pleasant Sensation,* expected from the Object or Event [*16*] which we apprehend as Good. Then it is plain,

1. "That no Desire of any Event is excited by any view of removing the *uneasy Sensation attending this Desire itself.*" Sensations which are *previous* to a *Desire,* or not connected with it, may excite Desire of any Event, apprehended necessary to procure or continue the Sensation if it be pleasant, or to remove it if it be uneasy: But the *uneasy Sensation, accompanying and connected with the Desire itself,* cannot be a Motive to that *Desire* which it presupposes. The *Sensation* accompanying Desire is generally *uneasy,* and consequently our Desire is never raised with a view to obtain or continue it; nor is the Desire raised with a view to *remove* this uneasy *Sensation,* for the Desire is raised previously to it. This holds concerning all *Desire* publick or private.

There is also a *pleasant Sensation of Joy,* attending the *Gratification* of any Desire, beside the *Sensation* received from the *Object itself,* which we directly intended. "But Desire does never arise from a View of obtaining that *Sensation of Joy,* connected with the Success or Gratification of Desire; [17] otherwise the strongest Desires might arise toward any Trifle, or an Event in all respects indifferent: [*17*] Since, if Desire arose from *this View,* the stronger the Desire were, the higher would be the *Pleasure of Gratification;* and therefore we might desire the turning of a Straw as violently as we do *Wealth* or *Power.*" This Expectation of the *Pleasure of gratified* Desire, would equally excite us to desire the *Misery* of others as their Happiness; since the *Pleasure* of *Gratification* might be obtained from both Events alike.

2. It is certain that, "*that Desire* of the Happiness of others which we account virtuous, is not *directly* excited by prospects of any *secular Ad-*

vantage, Wealth, Power, Pleasure of the external Senses, Reward from the Deity, or future Pleasures of Self-Approbation." To prove this let us consider, "That no Desire of any Event can arise immediately or directly from an *Opinion* in the Agent, that his *having such a Desire* will be the Means of private Good." This *Opinion* would make us *wish* or *desire* to have that *advantageous Desire* or *Affection;* and would incline us *to use any means* in our power to raise that Affection: but no Affection or Desire is raised in us, directly by our *volition* or *desiring* it. That alone which raises in us from *Self-Love* [18] the Desire of any Event, is an *Opinion* that *that Event* is the *Means [18]* of private Good. As soon as we form this Opinion, a Desire of the Event immediately arises: But if *having the Desire or Affection* be imagined the *Means* of private Good, and not the *Existence of the Event desired,* then from *Self-Love* we should only desire or wish to have the *Desire* of that Event, and should not desire the *Event* itself, since the *Event* is not conceived as the *Means* of Good.

For instance, suppose GOD revealed to us that he would confer Happiness on us, if our *Country were happy;* then from Self-Love we should have immediately *the subordinate Desire* of our Country's Happiness, as the Means of our own. But were we assured that, whether our Country were happy or not, it should not affect our future Happiness; but that we should be rewarded, provided we *desired the Happiness of our Country;* our Self-Love could never make us now desire the *Happiness of our Country,* since it is not now conceived as the *Means* of our Happiness, but is perfectly indifferent to it. The Means of our Happiness is *the having a Desire of our Country's Happiness;* we should therefore from Self-Love only *wish* to have *this Desire.*

[19] 'Tis true indeed in fact, that, because *Benevolence* is natural to us, a little Attention [*19*] to other Natures will raise in us good-will towards them, whenever by any *Opinions* we are persuaded that there is no real *Opposition of Interest.* But had we no Affection distinct from *Self-Love,* nothing could raise our *Desire of the Happiness of others,* but conceiving their Happiness as the Means of ours. An Opinion that our having *kind Affections* would be the Means of our private Happiness, would only make us desire to have those Affections. Now that Affec-

tions do not arise upon our *wishing* to have them, or our volition of raising them; as conceiving the *Affections themselves* to be the *Means* of private Good; is plain from this, that if they did thus arise, then a *Bribe* might raise any Desire toward any Event, or any *Affection* toward the most improper Object. We might be hired to *love* or *hate* any sort of   5
Persons, to be *angry, jealous,* or *compassionate,* as we can be engaged into external Actions; which we all see to be absurd. Now those who alledg, that our Benevolence may arise from prospect of *secular Advantage, Honour, Self-Approbation, or future Rewards,* must own, that these are either *Motives only to external Actions,* or *Considerations,* shewing, that   10
having the Desire of the Happiness of others, would be the *Means* of private Good; [20] while the *Event* supposed to be desired, *viz.* the Happiness of others, is not [20] supposed the *Means* of any private Good. But the best Defenders of this part of the Scheme of *Epicurus,* acknowledge that "Desires are not raised by *Volition.*"   15

This Distinc-
tion Defended 3. "There are in Men *Desires of the Happiness of others,* when they do not conceive this *Happiness* as the *Means* of obtaining any sort of Happiness to themselves." *Self-Approbation,* or *Rewards* from the Deity, might be the *Ends,* for obtaining which we might possibly *desire* or *will* from   20
Self-Love, to raise in our selves *kind Affections;* but we could not from *Self-Love* desire the *Happiness of others,* but as conceiving it the Means of our own. Now 'tis certain that sometimes we may have this *subordinate Desire* of the Happiness of others, conceived as the *Means* of our own; as suppose one had laid a *Wager* upon the Happiness of a Person   25
of such Veracity, that he would own sincerely whether he were happy or not; when Men are *Partners in Stock,* and share in Profit or Loss; when one hopes to *succeed to,* or some way to *share in* the Prosperity of another; or if the DEITY had given such Threatnings, as they tell us *Telamon* gave his Sons when they went to War,[17] that he would reward   30
or punish one according as others were [21] happy or miserable: In such cases one might have this *subordinate Desire* [21] of another's Happiness

---

17. Telamon was the father of Ajax, the Iliadic hero.

from Self-Love. But as we are sure the DEITY has not given such Com-
minations, so we often are conscious of the *Desire of the Happiness of
others,* without any such Conception of it as the *Means* of our own; and
are sensible that this *subordinate Desire* is not that virtuous Affection
which we approve. The virtuous Benevolence must be an *ultimate Desire,* which would subsist without view to private Good. Such *ultimate
publick Desires* we often feel, without any *subordinate Desire* of the same
Event, as the *Means* of private Good. The *subordinate* may sometimes,
nay often does concur with the *ultimate;* and then indeed the *whole Moment* of these conspiring Desires may be greater than that of either
alone: But the *subordinate alone* is not that Affection which we approve
as virtuous.

Art. IV. This will clear our way to answer the chief Difficulty: "May not
our Benevolence be at least a *Desire of the Happiness of others, as the
Means of obtaining the Pleasures of the publick Sense, from the Contemplation of their Happiness?*" If it were so, it is very unaccountable that
we should approve this *subordinate Desire* as virtuous, and yet not approve the like Desire upon a *Wager,* or other Considerations of Interest.
[22] Both Desires proceed from *Self-Love* in the same [22] manner: In
the latter case the Desires might be extended to multitudes, if any one
would wager so capriciously; and, by increasing the Sum wagered, the
Motive of Interest might, with many Tempers, be made stronger than
that from the Pleasures of the publick Sense.

Don't we find that we often desire the Happiness of others without
any such selfish Intention? How few have thought upon this part of our
Constitution which we call a *Publick Sense?* Were it our only View, in
Compassion to free our selves from the *Pain of the publick Sense;* should
the Deity propose it to our Choice, either to obliterate all Ideas of the
Person in Distress, but to continue him in Misery, or on the other hand
to relieve him from it; should we not upon this Scheme be perfectly
indifferent, and chuse the former as soon as the latter? Should the DE-
ITY assure us that we should be immediately annihilated, so that we
should be incapable of either Pleasure or Pain, but that it should depend upon our Choice at our very Exit, whether our Children, our

Benevolence is
not the Desire
of the Plea-
sures of the
publick Sense,

Friends, or our Country should be happy or miserable; should we not upon this Scheme be intirely indifferent? Or, if we should even desire the [23] *pleasant Thought* of their Happiness, in our last Moment, would not this Desire be the faintest imaginable?

[*23*] 'Tis true, our *Publick Sense* might be as acute at our Exit as ever; as a Man's Taste of Meat or Drink might be as lively the instant before his Dissolution as in any part of his Life. But would any Man have as strong *Desires* of the Means of obtaining these Pleasures, only with a View to himself, when he was to perish the next Moment? Is it supposable that any *Desire* of the *Means of private Pleasure* can be as strong when we only expect to enjoy it a Minute, as when we expect the Continuance of it for many Years? And yet, 'tis certain, any good Man would as strongly desire at his Exit the *Happiness of others,* as in any part of his Life. We do not therefore desire it as the *Means of private Pleasure.*

Should any alledge, that this Desire of the Happiness of others, after our Exit, is from some *confused Association of Ideas;* as a Miser, who loves no body, might desire an Increase of Wealth at his Death; or as any one may have an Aversion to have his Body dissected, or made a Prey to Dogs after Death: [24] let any honest Heart try if the deepest Reflection will break this *Association* (if there be any) which is supposed to raise the Desire. The closest Reflection would be found rather to strengthen it. [*24*] How would any *Spectator* like the Temper of one thus rendered indifferent to all others at his own Exit, so that he would not even open his Mouth to procure Happiness to Posterity? Would we esteem it *refined Wisdom,* or a *Perfection* of Mind, and not rather the vilest Perverseness? 'Tis plain then we feel this *ultimate Desire* of the Happiness of others to be a most *natural Instinct,* which we also expect in others, and not the Effect of any confused Ideas.

The Occasion of the imagined Difficulty in conceiving *distinterested Desires,* has probably been attempting to define this simple Idea, *Desire.* It is called *an uneasy Sensation in the absence of* Good.* Whereas *Desire*

* *See* Mr. Lock's *Essay on Human Understanding in the Chap. on the Passions.*
[[This footnote was added in the third edition. See Locke, *An Essay Concerning Human Understanding,* II.20.]]

is as distinct from any *Sensation,* as the *Will* is from the *Understanding* or Senses. This every one must acknowledge, who speaks of *desiring to remove Uneasiness or Pain.*

We may perhaps find, that our Desires are so far from tending always toward *private Good,* that they are oftner employ'd about *the State of others.* Nay further, we may have a Propensity toward an Event, which we neither apprehend as the *Means of private Good, or publick.* Thus an *Epicurean* who denies a future State; or, one to [25] whom God revealed that he should be annihilated, might at his very Exit desire a *future Fame,* from which he expected no Pleasure to himself, nor intended any to others. Such Desires indeed no *selfish Being,* who had the modelling of his own Nature, would chuse to implant in itself. But since we have not this power, we must be content to be thus "befooled into a publick Interest against our Will;" as an ingenious Author expresses it.[18]

The Prospect of any *Interest* may be a Motive to us, to desire whatever we apprehend as the *Means* of obtaining it. Particularly, "if *Rewards* of any kind are proposed to those who have virtuous Affections, this would raise in us the Desire of having these *Affections,* and would incline us to use all means to raise them in our selves; particularly to *turn our Attention* to all those Qualities in the DEITY, or our Fellows, which are naturally apt to raise the virtuous Affections." Thus it is, that Interest of any kind may influence us indirectly to Virtue, and Rewards particularly may over-ballance all Motives to Vice.

[26] This may let us see, that "the Sanctions of *Rewards* and *Punishments,* as proposed in the *Gospel,* are not rendered [26] useless or unnecessary, by supposing the virtuous Affection to be *disinterested;*" since such *Motives of Interest,* proposed and attended to, must incline every Person to *desire* to have virtuous Affections, and to *turn his Attention* to every thing which is naturally apt to raise them; and must *overballance* every other *Motive of Interest,* opposite to these Affections, which could incline Men to suppress or counteract them.

---

18. This is one of the Mandeville's main contentions throughout the *Fable of the Bees* and the central theme of his attack on Shaftesbury, "An Enquiry into the Origin of Moral Virtue" (*Fable of the Bees,* I:43–50).

SECTION II

Of the Affections and Passions: The natural Laws of pure Affection: The confused Sensations of the Passions, with their final Causes

Proper Affections are Desire and Aversion.

[27/27] I. After the general account of *Sensations,* we may consider other *Modifications* of our Minds, consequent upon these Perceptions, whether grateful, or uneasy. The first which occur to any one are *Desire* of the grateful Perceptions, and *Aversion* to the uneasy, either for our selves or others. If we would confine the word *Affection* to these two, which are entirely distinct from all *Sensation,* and directly incline the Mind to *Action* or *Volition of Motion,* we should have no Debate about the Number or Division of *Affections.* But since, by universal Custom, this Name is applied to other Modifications of the Mind, such as *Joy, Sorrow, Despair,* we may consider what universal *Distinction* can be assigned between these *Modifications,* and the several *Sensations* above-mentioned; and we shall scarce find any other than this, that we call

Other Affections, wherein different from Sensation.

"the *direct immediate Perception* of Pleasure or Pain from [28] the present [28] Object or Event, the *Sensation.*" But we denote by the *Affection* or *Passion* some other "*Perceptions* of Pleasure or Pain, not directly raised by the *Presence* or *Operation* of the Event or Object, but by our *Reflection* upon, or *Apprehension* of their present or certainly future Existence; so that we are sure that the Object or Event will raise the *direct Sensations* in us." In beholding a regular Building we have the *Sensation* of Beauty; but upon our *apprehending* our selves possessed of it, or that we can procure this pleasant Sensation when we please, we feel the *Affection* of *Joy.* When a Man has a Fit of the Gout, he has the *painful Sensation;* when he is not at present pained, yet apprehends a sudden return of it, he has the *Affection of Sorrow,* which might in some sense also be called a Sensation.

Affection distinct from Passion.

When the word *Passion* is imagined to denote any thing different from the *Affections,* it includes, beside the *Desire* or *Aversion,* beside the *calm Joy* upon apprehended Possession of Good, or *Sorrow* from the Loss of it, or from impending Evil, "a* *confused Sensation* either of Pleasure [*29/29*] or Pain, occasioned or attended by some violent bodily Motions, which keeps the Mind much employed upon the present Affair, to the exclusion of every thing else, and prolongs or strengthens the Affection sometimes to such a degree, as to prevent all *deliberate Reasoning* about our Conduct."

II. We have little reason to imagine, that all other Agents have such *confused Sensations* accompanying their Desires as we often have. Let us abstract from them, and consider in what manner we should act upon the several Occasions which now excite our Passions, if we had none of these *Sensations* whence our Desires become *passionate*.

<aside>General Desires, and particular Affections or Passions.</aside>

There is a Distinction to be observed on this Subject, between "the *calm Desire* of Good, and Aversion to Evil, either selfish or publick, as it appears to our *Reason* or *Reflection;* and the *particular Passions* towards Objects immediately presented to some Sense." Thus nothing can be more distinct than the *general calm Desire* of private Good of any kind, which alone would incline us to pursue whatever Objects were apprehended as the Means of Good, and the particular *selfish Passions*, such as *Ambition, Covetousness, Hunger, Lust, Revenge, Anger,* [*30*] as they arise upon particular Occasions. [30] In like manner, our publick Desires may be distinguished into the *general calm Desire of the Happiness*

* Whoever would see subtile Divisions of those Sensations, let him read *Malebranche's Recherche de la Verite, B.* v. *c.* 3. Together with these Sensations there are also some strong *Propensities* distinct from any rational Desire: About which see *Sect.* 3. *Art.* 2. of this Treatise.

[[*Recherche de la Vérité* III.5 presents a variety of distinctions in Malebranche's neo-Augustinean theory of the passions that—roughly—correspond to the position Hutcheson ascribes to him. Hutcheson seems to be drawing more on *Elucidation* 14 (a clarification of III.5), in using Malebranche to explain the distinction between passions and affections. In the *Elucidation*, Malebranche distinguishes between two kinds of pleasures: pleasures of the body and pleasures of the soul. Examples of the latter would be "the joy excited in us as a consequence of the clear knowledge or the confused sensation we have that some good has happened or will happen to us." Malebranche particularly emphasizes that they are perceptions. All such perceptions are distinguished from love.]]

of others, or *Aversion to their Misery* upon Reflection; and the *particular Affections* or *Passions* of *Love, Congratulation, Compassion, natural Affection.* These *particular Affections* are found in many Tempers, where, thro' want of Reflection, the *general calm* Desires are not found: Nay, the former may be opposite to the latter, where they are found in the   5 same Temper. We obtain *Command* over the *particular Passions,* principally by strengthning the *general Desires* thro frequent Reflection, and making them *habitual,* so as to obtain Strength superior to the *particular Passions.**

[31] Again, the *calm public Desires* may be considered as "they either   10 regard the Good of *particular Persons* or *Societies* presented to our Senses; or that of some more abstracted or general Community, such as a *Species* or System." This latter sort we may call *universal calm Benevolence.* Now 'tis plain, that not only *particular kind Passions,* but even *calm particular Benevolence* do not always arise from, or necessarily pre-   15 suppose, the *universal Benevolence;* both the former may be found in Persons of little Reflection, where the latter is wanting: And the former two may [*31*] be opposite to the other, where they meet together in one

---

*The Schoolmen express this Distinction by the *Appetitus rationalis* and the *Appetitus Sensitivus.* All Animals have in common the *External Senses* suggesting   20 notions of things as pleasant or painful; and have also the *Appetitus Sensitivus,* or some instinctive Desires and Aversions. *Rational Agents* have, superadded to these, two higher analogous Powers; *viz.* the *Understanding,* or *Reason,* presenting farther notion, and attended with an higher sort of Sensations; and the *Appetitus rationalis.* This latter is a "constant natural Disposition of Soul to desire what the Understand-   25 ing, or these sublimer Sensations, represent as Good, and to shun what they represent as Evil, and this either when it respects ourselves or others." This many call the *Will* as distinct from the *Passions.* Some later Writers seem to have forgot it, by ascribing to the *Understanding* not only *Ideas, Notions, Knowledge;* but *Action, Inclinations, Desires, Prosecution,* and their Contraries.   30

[[By the "Schoolmen" Hutcheson likely means the seventeenth-century Scholastic textbooks taught at Glasgow—Eustachius de Sancto Paulo, *Ethica, sive Summa Moralis Disciplinae,* Adrian Heereboord, *Collegium Ethicum,* and Franciscus Burgersdijk, *Idea Philosophiae tum Moralis tum Naturalis.* The texts differ widely—Eustachius was a Catholic, Heereboord and Burgersdijk Protestants—and were very   35 eclectic and synoptic. The distinction Hutcheson draws on, though, is not particular to these authors but stems from Aristotle.]]

Temper. So the *universal Benevolence* might be where there was neither of the former; as in any superior Nature or Angel, who had no particular Intercourse with any part of Mankind.

[32] Our *moral Sense,* tho it approves all particular *kind Affection* or *Passion,* as well as *calm particular Benevolence* abstractedly considered; yet it also approves the *Restraint* or *Limitation* of all particular Affections or Passions, by the *calm universal Benevolence.* To make this Desire prevalent above all *particular Affections,* is the only sure way to obtain constant *Self-Approbation.*

The *calm selfish Desires* would determine any Agent to pursue every Object or Event, known either by Reason or prior Experience to be good to itself. We need not imagine any innate Idea of *Good in general,* of *infinite Good,* or of the *greatest Aggregate:* Much less need we suppose any *actual Inclination* toward any of these, as the *Cause* or *Spring* of all particular Desires. 'Tis enough to allow, "that we are capable by *enlarging,* or by *Abstraction,* of coming to these Ideas: That we must, by the Constitution of our Nature, desire any apprehended Good which occurs a-part from any Evil: [32] That of two Objects inconsistent with each other, we shall desire that which seems to contain the greatest *Moment of Good.*" So that it cannot be pronounced concerning any *finite Good,* that it shall necessarily engage our Pursuit; since the Agent may possibly [33] have the Idea of a *Greater,* or see this to be inconsistent with some *more valuable Object,* or that it may bring upon him some *prepollent Evil.* The certain Knowledge of any of these Things, or probable *Presumption* of them, may stop the Pursuit of any finite Good. If this be any sort of *Liberty,* it must be allowed to be in Men, even by those who maintain "the *Desire* or *Will* to be necessarily determined by the *prepollent Motive;*" since this very *Presumption* may be a prepollent Motive, especially to those, who by frequent *Attention* make the Idea of the *greatest Good* always present to themselves on all important Occasions.

The same may easily be applied to our Aversion to finite Evils.

There seems to be this Degree of Liberty about the Understanding, that tho the *highest Certainty* or *Demonstration* does necessarily engage our Assent, yet we can suspend any *absolute Conclusion* from *probable* Arguments, until we examine whether this [*33*] apparent *Probability* be not opposite to *Demonstration,* or *superior Probability* on the other side.

This may let us see, that tho it were acknowledged that "Men are *necessarily* determined to pursue their own Happiness, and to be influenced by whatever Motive [34] appears to be *prepollent;*" yet they might be proper *Subjects of a Law;* since the very *Sanctions* of the Law, if they attend to them, may suggest a Motive *prepollent* to all others. In like manner, "Errors may be criminal,* where there are sufficient *Data* or *Objective Evidence* for the Truth;" since no Demonstration can lead to Error, and we can suspend our Assent to probable Arguments, till we have examined both Sides. Yet *human Penalties* concerning Opinions must be of little consequence, since no Penalty can supply the place of *Argument,* or *Probability* to engage our *Assent,* however they may as *Motives* determine our *Election.*

In the *calm publick Desires,* in like manner, where there are no opposite Desires, the greater Good of another is always preferred to the less: And in the calm [*34*] universal Benevolence, the Choice is determined by the *Moment* of the Good, and the *Number* of those who shall enjoy it.

When the *publick Desires* are opposite to the *private,* or seem to be so, that kind prevails which is *stronger* or more intense.

Definitions. [35] III. The following *Definitions* of certain Words used on this Subject, may shorten our Expressions; and the *Axioms* subjoined may shew the manner of acting from *calm Desire,* with Analogy to the *Laws of Motion.*

Natural Good
and Evil. 1. NATURAL *Good* is Pleasure: *Natural Evil* is Pain.

2. NATURAL *good Objects* are those which are apt, either mediately or immediately to give Pleasure; the former are called *Advantageous.* Natural *Evil Objects* are such as, in like manner, give Pain.

---

*See *Treat. 4 Sect 6. Art.* 6, last Paragraph.

3. ABSOLUTE *Good* is that which, considered with all its Concomi-   Absolute.
tants and Consequences, contains more Good than what compensates
all its Evils.

4. ABSOLUTE *Evil,* on the contrary, contains Evil which outweighs
all its Good.

[35] 5. RELATIVE *Good or Evil,* is any particular Good or Evil, which   Relative.
does not thus compensate its contrary Concomitants or Consequences.
This Distinction would have been more exactly expressed by the
Bonum simpliciter, and *secundum quid* of the Schoolmen.

Cor. RELATIVE *Good* may be *Absolute Evil;* thus often sensual Pleasures are in the whole pernicious: And *Absolute Good* may be *Relative
Evil;* thus an *unpleasant Potion* may recover Health.

GOOD and *Evil,* according to the *Persons* whom they affect, may be
divided into *Universal, Particular* and *Private.*

6. UNIVERSAL *Good,* is what tends to the Happiness of the whole   Universal.
System of sensitive Beings; and *Universal Evil* is the contrary.

7. PARTICULAR *Good* is what tends to the Happiness of a Part of   Particular.
this System: *Particular Evil* is the contrary.

8. PRIVATE *Good or Evil* is that of the Person acting. Each of these   Private.
three Members may be either *Absolute* or *Relative.*

[36] *Cor.* I. PARTICULAR *or private Good* may possibly be *universal
Evil:* And *universal Good* may be *particular* or *private Evil.* The Punishment of a Criminal is an Instance of the latter. Of the former, perhaps,
there are no real Instances in the whole Administration of Nature: but
there [37] are some apparent Instances; such as the *Success of an unjust
War;* or the *Escape of an unrelenting Criminal.*

Cor. 2. WHEN *particular* or *private Goods* are entirely innocent toward others, they are *universal Good.*

Compound.   9. COMPOUND *good Objects* or *Events,* are such as contain the Powers of several Goods at once. Thus, Meat may be both pleasant and
healthful; an Action may give its Author at once the Pleasures of the
Moral Sense and of *Honour.* The same is easily applicable to *compound
Evil.*   5

Mixed.   10. A MIXED *Object* is what contains at once the Powers of Good
and Evil: Thus a virtuous Action may give the Agent the *Pleasures* of
the *Moral Sense,* and *Pains of the external Senses.* Execution of Justice
may give the Pleasures of the *publick Sense,* and the Pains of *Compassion*   10
toward the Sufferer.

Greatest   [37] 11. THE *greatest* or *most perfect Good* is that whole Series, or Scheme
Good.   of Events, which contains a greater Aggregate of Happiness in the
whole, or more absolute universal Good, than any other possible   15
Scheme, after subtracting all the Evils connected with each of them.

Moral Good.   [38] 12. AN Action is *good, in a moral Sense,* when it flows from benevolent Affection, or Intention of absolute Good to others. Men of much
Reflection may actually intend *universal absolute Good;* but with the   20
common rate of Men their Virtue consists in intending and pursuing
particular absolute Good, not inconsistent with universal Good.

Moral Evil.   13. AN Action is *morally evil,* either from Intention of *absolute Evil,*
universal, or particular, (*which is seldom the case with Men, except in   25
sudden Passions;) or from pursuit of *private* or *particular relative Good,*
which they might have known did tend to *universal absolute Evil.* For
even the *want* of a† just Degree of Benevolence renders an Action evil.

---

* See Treatise II. *Sect.* 2. *Art.* 4. *p.* 143.
   [[The page reference is not to the first edition of the *Inquiry* but to the second   30
through the fourth editions.]]
   † Treatise IV. *Sect.* 6. *Art.* 4.

[*38*] 14. COMPOUND *moral Goodness* is that to which different *moral*   Compound.
Species concur: Thus the same Action may evidence Love to our Fellows, and Gratitude to God. We may in like manner understand *compound moral Evil.* We cannot suppose *mixed moral Actions.**

[*39*] 15. AGENTS are denominated *morally good or evil,* from their Affections and Actions, or Attempts of Action.

IV. AXIOMS, or natural Laws of *calm Desire.*   Axioms, or

1. SELFISH *Desires* pursue ultimately only the private Good of the   general Laws.
Agent.

2. BENEVOLENT or *publick Desires* pursue the Good of others, according to the several *Systems* to which we extend our Attention, but
with different Degrees of Strength.

3. THE *Strength* either of the *private* or *publick* Desire of any Event,
is proportioned to the imagined *Quantity of Good,* which will arise from
it to the Agent, or the Person beloved.

[*39*] 4. MIXED *Objects* are pursued or shunned with Desire or Aversion, proportioned to the apprehended *Excess* of Good or Evil.

5. EQUAL *Mixtures* of Good and Evil stop all Desire or Aversion.

6. A COMPOUND *good or evil Object,* is prosecuted or shunned with
a *Degree* of [40] Desire or Aversion, proportioned to the *Sum* of Good,
or of Evil.

7. IN computing the *Quantities* of Good or Evil, which we pursue or
shun, either for our selves or others, when the *Durations* are equal, the
Moment is as the *Intenseness:* and when the *Intenseness* of Pleasure is the
same, or equal, the Moment is as the *Duration.*

8. HENCE the *Moment* of Good in any Object, is in a compound
Proportion of the *Duration* and *Intenseness.*

9. THE *Trouble, Pain,* or *Danger,* incurred by the Agent, in acquiring

* See Treatise II. *Sect.* 7. *Art.* 9, last Parag.
[[As T2 VII.9 seems to have little relevance to the passage, Hutcheson is likely
citing the far more relevant discussion at II.7.7 Cor. 15 added in the second through
the fourth editions. See the similar mistake in n. 23.]]

or retaining any Good, is to be subtracted from the *Sum* of the Good. So the *Pleasures* which attend or flow from the means of *prepollent Evil,* are to be subtracted, to find the *absolute Quantity.*

[*40*] 10. THE Ratio of the *Hazard* of acquiring or retaining any Good must be multiplied into the Moment of the Good; so also the   5 *Hazard* of avoiding any Evil is to be multiplied into the Moment of it, to find its comparative value.

Cor. HENCE it is, that the smallest certain Good may raise stronger Desire than the [41] greatest Good, if the *Uncertainty* of the latter surpass *that* of the former, in a greater Ratio than that of the greater to the   10 less. Thus Men content themselves in all Affairs with *smaller,* but more *probably successful* Pursuits, quitting those of greater Moment but *less Probability.*

11. To an *immortal* Nature it is indifferent in what part of its Duration it enjoys a Good limited in Duration, if its Sense be equally *acute*   15 in all parts of its Existence; and the Enjoyment of this Good excludes not the Enjoyment of other Goods, at one time more than another. The same may be applied to the Suffering of Evil, limited in Duration.

12. BUT if the Duration of the Good be *infinite,* the Earliness of Commencement increases the Moment, as *finite* added to *infinite,* sur-   20 passes *infinite* alone.

[*41*] 13. To Beings of *limited certain Duration,* Axiom 12. may be applied, when the *Duration* of the Good would not surpass the Existence of the Possessor, after the Time of its Commencement.

14. To Beings of *limited uncertain Duration,* the Earliness of Com-   25 mencement increases the Moment of any Good, according [42] to the Hazard of the *Possessor's Duration.* This may, perhaps, account for what some alledg to be a *natural Disposition* of our Minds, even previous to any Reflection on the Uncertainty of Life, *viz.* that we are so constituted, as to desire more ardently the *nearer* Enjoyments than the more   30 distant, tho of equal Moment in themselves, and as certainly to be obtained by us.

15. THE *Removal of Pain* has always the Notion of Good, and sollicits us more importunately: Its Moment is the same way computed by

Intenseness and *Duration,* and affected by the *Hazard* and by the *Uncertainty* of our Existence.

These are the general Ways of computing the Quantities of Good in any Object or Event, whether we are pursuing our own private Good from selfish Desires, or [42] the Good of others from publick Affections. Concerning these latter we may observe,

16. THAT our Desires toward *publick Good* are, when other Circumstances are equal, proportioned to the Moment of the Goods themselves.

17. OUR publick Desires of any Events, are proportioned to the *Number* of Persons to whom the good Event shall extend, when [43] the *Moments* and other Circumstances are equal.

18. WHEN the *Moments* themselves, and *Numbers* of Enjoyers are equal, our Desire is proportioned to the *Strength* or *Nearness* of the *Ties* or *Attachments* to the Persons.

19. WHEN all other Circumstances are equal, our Desires are proportional to the apprehended *Moral Excellence* of the Persons.

20. IN general, the Strength of publick Desire is in a Compound Ratio of the *Quantity of the Good itself, and the Number, Attachment, and Dignity* of the Persons.

These seem to be the general Laws, according to which our Desires arise. Our [43] *Senses* constitute Objects, Events or Actions *good;* and "we have Power to *reason,* reflect and compare the several Goods, and to find out the proper and effectual Means of obtaining the greatest for our selves or others, so as not to be led aside by every Appearance of *relative* or *particular* Good."

V. If it be granted, that we have implanted in our Nature the several *Desires* above-mentioned, let us next inquire "into [44] what *State* we would incline to bring our selves, upon the several Accidents which now raise our *Passions;* supposing that we had the Choice of our own State entirely, and were not, by the Frame of our Nature, subjected to certain *Sensations,* independently of our Volition."

If it seems too rash to assert a Distinction between *Affections* and *Pas-*

Action from pure Desire or Affection.

sions, or that *Desire* may subsist without any *uneasiness,* since perhaps
we are never conscious of any Desire absolutely free from all uneasiness;
"let it be considered, that the simple Idea of *Desire* is different from that
of Pain of any kind, or from any *Sensation* whatsoever: Nor is there any
other Argument for their Identity than this, that they occur to us at   5
once: But this Argument is inconclusive, otherwise [*44*] it would prove
Colour and *Figure* to be the same, or *Incision* and *Pain.*"

There is a *middle State* of our Minds, when we are not in the pursuit
of any *important Good,* nor know of any great *Indigence* of those we
love. In this State, when any smaller positive Good to our selves or our   10
Friend is apprehended to be in our power, we may resolutely *desire* and
pursue it, without any considerable *Sensation of Pain* or Uneasiness.
Some Tempers seem [45] to have as strong *Desires* as any, by the Constancy and Vigor of their Pursuits, either of publick or private Good;
and yet give small Evidence of any *uneasy Sensation.* This is observable   15
in some sedate Men, who seem no way inferior in Strength of Desire to
others: Nay, if we consult our selves, and not the common Systems, we
shall perhaps find, that "the noblest Desire in our Nature, that of *universal Happiness,* is generally calm, and wholly free from any confused
uneasy Sensation:" except in some warm Tempers, who, by a lively   20
Imagination, and frequent Attention to general Ideas, raise something
of Passion even toward *universal Nature.** Yea, further, Desire may be
as strong as possible toward a certainly future [*45*] Event, the fixed Time
of its Existence being also known, and yet we are not conscious of any
Pain attending such Desires. But tho this should not be granted to be   25
Fact with Men, yet the Difference of the Ideas of Desire and Pain, may
give sufficient ground for abstracting them; and for our making the
Supposition of their being separated.

Upon this Supposition then, when any Object was desired, if we
found it *difficult* or *uncertain* to be obtained, but worthy of all the La-   30

* See *Marcus Aurelius,* in many places.
[[Marcus Aurelius was Hutcheson's preferred ancient Stoic philosopher. He
translated Aurelius with James Moor as *The Meditations of the Emperor Marcus
Aurelius Antoninus* (Glasgow: Robert Foulis, 1742).]]

bour it would cost; we would set [46] about it with Diligence, but
would never chuse to bring upon our selves any *painful Sensation* accompanying our Desire, nor to increase our Toil by *Anxiety.* Whatever
Satisfaction we had in our State before the Prospect of this additional
Good, we should continue to enjoy it while this Good was in suspense;
and if we found it unattainable, we should be just as we were before:
And we should never [*46*] chuse to bring upon our selves those *Frettings*
which now commonly arise from Disappointments. Upon Opinion of
any impending Evil, we should *desire* and *use all means* to prevent it,
but should never voluntarily bring upon our selves the uneasy Sensation of *Fear,* which now naturally anticipates our Misery, and gives us a
Foretaste of it, more ungrateful sometimes than the Suffering itself. If
the Evil did befal us, we should never chuse to increase it, by the Sensations of *Sorrow* or *Despair;* we should consider what was the Sum of
Good remaining in our State, after subtracting this Evil; and should enjoy our selves as well as a Being, who had never known greater Good,
nor enjoyed greater Pleasure, than the *absolute Good* yet remaining with
us; or perhaps we should pursue some other attainable Good. In the like
manner, did our *State* and the *Modifications* of our Mind depend upon
our Choice, should we be affected upon the apprehended Approach of
Good or [47] Evil, to those whom we love; we should have *desires* of
obtaining the one for them, and of defending them from the other, accompanied with no *uneasy Sensations.* We do indeed find in fact, that
our stronger Desires, whether private or publick, are accompanied with
uneasy Sensations; but these Sensations do not seem the necessary *Result*
of the Desire itself: They depend upon the present *Constitution of our
Nature,* which might possibly have been otherwise ordered. And in fact
we find a considerable Diversity of Tempers in this matter; some *sedate
Tempers* equally desiring either publick or private Good with the more
passionate Tempers; but without that Degree of *Ferment, Confusion,*
and *Pain,* which attend the same Desires in the *Passionate.*

[47] According to the present Constitution of our Nature, we find
that the *Modifications* or *Passions* of our Mind, are very different from
those which we would chuse to bring upon our selves, upon their several Occasions. The Prospect of any considerable Good for our selves,

or those we love, raises Desire; and this Desire is accompanied with *uneasy confused Sensations,* which often occasion *Fretfulness, Anxiety,* and *Impatience.* We find violent *Motions* in our Bodies; and are often made unfit for serious Deliberation about the Means of obtaining [48] the Good desired. When it is first obtained, we find violent confused *Sensations of Joy,* beyond the Proportion of the Good itself, or its Moment to our Happiness. If we are disappointed, we feel a Sensation of *Sorrow* and *Dejection,* which is often entirely useless to our present State. Foreseen Evils are antedated by painful Sensations of *Fear;* and Reflection, attended with Sensations of *Sorrow,* gives a tedious Existence to transitory Misfortunes. Our *publick Desires* are in the same manner accompanied with painful Sensations. The Presence or Suspence of Good or Evil *to others,* is made the Occasion of the like confused Sensations. A little Reflection will shew, that none of these Sensations depend upon our Choice, but arise from the very *Frame [48] of our Nature,* however we may regulate or moderate them.

The Necessity for these Sensations.

VI. Let us then examine "for what Purpose our Nature was so constituted, that Sensations do thus necessarily arise in us." Would not those *first sorts of Sensations,* by which we apprehend Good and Evil in the Objects themselves, have been sufficient, along with our *Reason* and *pure Desires,* without those Sensations attending the very Desires themselves, for which they are called *Passions,* or those *Sensations* which [49] attend our Reflection upon the Presence, Absence, or Approach of Good or Evil?

The common Answer, that "they are given to us as useful *Incitements* or *Spurs* to Action, by which we are roused more effectually to promote our private Good, or that of the Publick," is too general and undetermined. What need is there for rousing us to Action, more than a *calm pure Desire* of Good, and Aversion to Evil would do, without these confused Sensations? Say they, "we are averse to *Labour;* we are apt to be hurried away by Avocations of *Curiosity* or *Mirth;* we are often so *indolent* and averse to the vigorous Use of our Powers, that we should neglect our true Interest without these solliciting [49] Sensations." But may it not be answered, that if Labour and vigorous Use of our Powers be attended with *Uneasiness* or *Pain,* why should not this be brought into the Account? The Pursuit of a small Good by great Toil is really foolish; violent *Labour* may be as pernicious as any thing else: Why should we be excited to any *uneasy Labour,* except for prepollent Good? And, when the Good is *prepollent,* what need of any further *Incitement* than the calm Desire of it? The same may be said of the Avocations of *Curiosity* or *Mirth;* if their *absolute Pleasures* be greater than [50] that of the good from which they divert us, why should we not be diverted from it? If not, then the *real Moment* of the Good proposed is sufficient to engage our Pursuit of it, in Opposition to our Curiosity or Mirth.

If indeed our Aversion to Labour, or our Propensity to Mirth be accompanied with these Sensations, then it was necessary that other *Desires* should be attended with like Sensations, that so a Ballance might be preserved. So if we have confused Sensation strengthning and fixing our *private Desires,* the like Sensation joined to *publick Affections* is necessary, lest the former Desires should wholly engross our Minds: If weight be cast into one Scale, as much must be put into the other to preserve [50] an *Equilibrium.* But the first Question is, "whence arose the Necessity of such additional Incitements on either side?"

It must be very difficult for Beings of such imperfect Knowledge as we are, to answer such Questions: we know very little of the Constitution of *Nature,* or what may be necessary for the Perfection of the *whole.* The Author of Nature has probably formed many active Beings, whose Desires are not attended with confused Sensations, raising them into Passions like to ours. There is probably an infinite *Variety* of Beings, of all possible Degrees, in which the Sum of Happiness exceeds that of Misery. We know that our State is *absolutely Good,* notwithstanding a considerable Mixture of Evil. The Goodness of the great Author of Nature appears even in producing the *inferior Natures,* provided their State in the whole be absolutely Good: Since we may probably conclude,* that there are in the Universe as many Species of *superior*

---

* See *Simplicius* on *Epictetus,* Cap. 34. And the Archbishop of *Dublin, De Origine Mali,* above all others on this Subject.

[[Simplicius was one of the major Hellenistic commentators on Aristotle and

Natures, as was consistent with the most perfect State of the whole. This is the Thought so much insisted upon by *Simplicius,* that the universal [*51*] Cause must produce τα μέσα, as well as τα πρῶτα, και τα ἔσχατα. We know not if this Globe be a fit Place for the Habitation of Natures superior to ours: If not, it must certainly be in the *whole* better   5 that it should have its *imperfect* [52] *Inhabitants,* whose State is absolutely Good, than that it should be desolate.

All then which we can expect to do in this Matter, is only to shew, that "these confused Sensations are necessary to such Natures as we are in other *respects:* Particularly that Beings of such Degrees of *Understand-*   10 *ing,* and such *Avenues* to Knowledge as we have, must need these *additional Forces,* which we call Passions, beside the first *Sensations* by which Objects are constituted Good or Evil, and the *pure Desire* or *Aversion* arising from Opinion or Apprehension of Good or Evil."

---

also produced a number of commentaries on other philosophical works, including   15
a major exposition of the Stoic Epictetus's *Enchiridion,* or *Manual.* Chapter 34
considers Epictetus's maxim "As no Man sets up a Mark, with a Design to shoot
beside it, so neither hath the Maker of the World formed any such real Being, as
Evil, in it" (George Stanhope [trans.], Epictetus *his Morals With* Simplicius *His
Comment* [London Richard Sare, 1704], third ed., 207). Simplicius emphasized that   20
evil is not anything real, but a deviation from the order of nature by imperfect
beings imparted with the power of choice but confused as to what course would
be best for them. The specific passage Hutcheson alludes to reads: "God, who is
the Source and Original Cause of all Goodness, did not only produce the highest
and most Excellent Things, such as are good in themselves; nor only those that are   25
of a Rank something inferior to those, and of a middle Nature; but the Extremes
too, such as are capable of falling and apt to be perverted from that which is
agreeable to Nature, to that which we call Evil" (221).

William King's (1650–1729) theodicy, *De Origine Mali* (1702), was, like Leibniz's
Theodicy, a response to the fideist challenge posed by Pierre Bayle. King attempted   30
to reconcile the existence of evil and God's goodness through the freedom of the
divine and human will, and the fact that God made an imperfect world in order
to preserve human freedom of choice with the consequence of natural and moral
evil. *De Origine Mali* was translated from Latin by Edmund Law (1703–87) in 1731
and edited with copious notes and commentary. Hutcheson sent a copy of the   35
Inquiry to King.

Now our *Reason,* or *Knowledge of the Relations* of external Things to our Bodies, is so inconsiderable, that it is generally some *pleasant Sensation* which teaches us what tends to their Preservation; and some *painful Sensation* which shews what is pernicious. Nor is this Instruction sufficient; we need also to be directed *when* our Bodies want supplies of Nourishment; to this our Reason could not extend: Here then [52] appears the first Necessity of *uneasy Sensation,* preceding Desire, and continuing to accompany it when it is raised.

[53] Again, our Bodies could not be preserved without a Sense of Pain, connected with *Incisions, Bruises,* or violent *Labour,* or whatever else tends to destroy any part of their Mechanism; since our Knowledge does not extend so far, as to judge in time what would be pernicious to it: And yet, without a great deal of human Labour, and many Dangers, this Earth could not support the tenth Part of its Inhabitants. Our Nature therefore required a Sensation, accompanying its Desires of the *Means of Preservation,* capable to surmount the Uneasiness of *Labour:* this we have in the Pains or Uneasiness accompanying the Desires of Food.

In like manner, the *Propagation of Animals* is a Mystery to their *Reason,* but easy to their *Instinct.* An Offspring of such Creatures as Men are, could not be preserved without perpetual Labour and Care; which we find could not be expected from the more general Ties of *Benevolence.* Here then again appears the Necessity of strengthning the Στοργὴ, or *natural Affection,* with strong Sensations, or Pains of Desire, sufficient to counter-ballance the Pains of *Labour,* and the Sensations of the [53] *selfish Appetites;* since Parents must often check and [54] disappoint their own Appetites, to gratify those of their Children.

"When a Necessity of joining strong Sensations to one Class of Desires appears, there must appear a like Necessity of strengthning the rest by like Sensations, to keep a just Ballance." We know, for instance, that the Pleasures of the *Imagination* tend much to the Happiness of Mankind: the Desires of them therefore must have the like *Sensations* assisting them, to prevent our indulging a nasty solitary Luxury. The Happiness of human Life cannot be promoted without *Society* and *mutual Aid,* even beyond a Family; our *publick Affections* must therefore be

From the Imperfection of our Understanding, which required Sensations of Appetite.

strengthned as well as the private, to keep a Ballance; so must also our Desires of *Virtue* and *Honour. Anger,* which some have thought an useless Passion, is really as necessary as the rest; since Men's Interests often seem to interfere with each other; and they are thereby led from Self-Love to do the worst *Injuries* to their Fellows. There could not therefore be a wiser Contrivance to restrain *Injuries,* than to make every mortal some way *formidable* to an unjust Invader, by such a violent Passion. We need not have recourse to a *Prometheus* in this matter, with the old Poets: [54] they might have ascribed it to their *Optimus Maximus.*[19]

[52]—Insani Leonis,
Vim Stomacho apposuisse nostro.[20]

A Ballance may be still preserved.

VII. With this *Ballance* of publick Passions against the private, with our *Passions* toward Honour and Virtue, we find that human Nature may be as really amiable in its low Sphere, as superior Natures endowed with higher Reason, and influenced only by *pure Desires;* provided we vigorously exercise the Powers we have in keeping this Ballance of Affections, and checking any Passion which grows so violent, as to be inconsistent with the publick Good. If we have selfish Passions for our own Preservation, we have also *publick Passions,* which may engage us into vigorous and laborious Services to *Offspring, Friends, Communities, Countries. Compassion* will engage us to succour the distressed, even with our private Loss or Danger. An Abhorrence of the injurious, and Love toward the injured, with a Sense of Virtue, and Honour, can make us despise Labour, Expence, Wounds and Death.

The Sensations of *Joy* or *Sorrow,* upon the Success or Disappointment of any Pursuit, either publick or private, have directly the Effect of *Rewards* or *Punishments,* [55] to excite us to act with the utmost Vigor, either for our own Advantage, or that of [56] others, for the fu-

---

19. *Optimus Maximus* was a Roman name for Jupiter or the ruling Deity.

20. Horace *Odes,* 1.16, 15–16. The passage quoted by Hutcheson is preceded by, "They say Prometheus had to add to the primeval slime/a particle cut from each of the animals"; Hutcheson quotes, "and grafted the violence of rabid lions/on to our stomachs." Trans. David West, *Horace: The Complete Odes and Epodes* (Oxford: Oxford University Press, 1997).

ture, and to punish past Negligence. The Moment of every Event is thereby increased: as much as the Sensations of *Sorrow* add to our *Misery*, so much those of *Joy* add to our *Happiness*. Nay, since we have some considerable *Power* over our Desires, as shall be explained hereafter, we may probably, by good Conduct, obtain more frequent *Pleasures of Joy* upon our Success, than *Pains of Sorrow* upon Disappointment.

'Tis true indeed, that there are few Tempers to be found, wherein these Sensations of the several Passions are in such a *Ballance,* as in all cases to leave the Mind in a proper State, for considering the Importance of every Action or Event. The Sensations of *Anger* in some Tempers are violent above their proportion; those of *Ambition, Avarice, desire of sensual Pleasure,* and even of *natural Affection,* in several Dispositions, possess the Mind too much, and make it incapable of attending to any thing else. Scarce any one Temper is always constant and uniform in its Passions. The best State of human Nature possible might require a Diversity of Passions and Inclinations, for the different Occupations necessary for the whole: But the Disorder seems to be much greater than is [56] requisite for this End. *Custom, Education, Habits,* and *Company,* may [57] often contribute much to this Disorder, however its Original may be ascribed to some more universal Cause. But it is not so great, but that human Life is still a desireable State, having a superiority of Goodness and Happiness. Nor, if we apply our selves to it, does it hinder us from discerning that just *Ballance* and *Oeconomy,* which would constitute the most happy State of each Person, and promote the greatest Good in the whole.

A just Ballance very rare.

Let Physicians or Anatomists explain the several Motions in the *Fluids* or *Solids* of the Body, which accompany any Passion; or the *Temperaments* of Body which either make Men prone to any Passion, or are brought upon us by the long Continuance, or frequent Returns of it. 'Tis only to our Purpose in general to observe, "that probably certain *Motions* in the Body do accompany every Passion by a fixed Law of Nature; and alternately, *that Temperament* which is apt to receive or prolong these Motions in the Body, does influence our *Passions* to heighten

Dispositions to some particular Passions.

or prolong them." Thus a certain *Temperament* may be brought upon the Body, by its being frequently put into Motion by the Passions of *Anger, Joy, Love,* or *Sorrow;* and the Continuance of this Temperament shall make Men prone to the several [57] Passions for the future. We find [58] our selves after a long Fit of *Anger* or *Sorrow,* in an uneasy State, even when we are not reflecting on the particular *Occasion* of our Passion. During this State, every trifle shall be apt to provoke or deject us. On the contrary, after *good Success,* after strong *friendly Passions,* or a State of *Mirth,* some considerable *Injuries* or *Losses,* which at other times would have affected us very much, shall be overlooked, or meekly received, or at most but slightly resented; perhaps because our Bodies are not fit easily to receive these *Motions* which are constituted the Occasion of the uneasy Sensations of Anger. This *Diversity* of Temper every one has felt, who reflects on himself at different Times. In some Tempers it will appear like *Madness.* Whether the only *Seat* of these Habits, or the Occasion rather of these *Dispositions,* be in the Body; or whether the *Soul* itself does not, by frequent Returns of any Passion acquire some greater Disposition to receive and retain it again, let those determine, who sufficiently understand the Nature of either the one or the other.

SECTION III

Particular Divisions of the Affections and Passions.

[58/59] I. The Nature of any *Language* has considerable Influence upon Men's Reasonings on all Subjects, making them often take all those Ideas which are denoted by the same Word to be the same; and on the other hand, to look upon different Words as denoting different Ideas. We shall find that this Identity of Names has occasioned much confusion in Treatises of the Passions; while some have made larger, and some smaller Collections of Names, and have given the Explications of them as an Account of the Passions.

Cicero, in the Fourth Book of *Tusculan Questions*,[21] gives from the
Stoicks, this general Division of the *Passions:* First, into *Love* and *Ha-*
tred, according as the Object is good or evil; and then subdivides each,
according as the Object is *present* or *expected.* About Good we have
these two, *Libido & Latitia, Desire* and *Joy:* About Evil we have likewise
two, *Metus & Ægritudo, Fear* and *Sorrow.* To this general Division he
[60] subjoins many [59] *Subdivisions* of each of these four Passions; according as in the *Latin* Tongue they had different Names for the several
Degrees of these Passions, or for the same Passion employed upon different Objects. A Writer of *Lexicons* would probably get the most precise Meanings of the *Latin* Names in that Book; nor would it be useless
in considering the Nature of them.

The *Schoolmen,* as their Fund of Language was much smaller, have
not so full Enumerations of them, going no further than their admired
Aristotle.

II. 'Tis strange that the thoughtful MALEBRANCHE did not consider, that "*Desire* and *Aversion* are obviously different from the other
Modifications called *Passions;* that these two directly lead to Action, or
the Volition of Motion, and are wholly distinct from all sort of Sensation." Whereas Joy and Sorrow are only a sort of Sensations; and other
Affections differ from Sensations only, by including Desire or Aversion,
or their correspondent Propensities: So that *Desire* and *Aversion* are the
only pure Affections in the strictest Sense.

If, indeed, we confine the Word *Sensation* to the "immediate Perceptions of [61] Pleasure and Pain, upon the very Presence [60] or Operation of any Object or Event, which are occasioned by some Impression
on our Bodies;" then we may denote by the Word *Affection,* those *Plea-*
sures or *Pains* not thus excited, but "resulting from some *Reflection*
upon, or *Opinion* of our Possession of any Advantage, or from a certain
Prospect of future pleasant Sensations on the one hand, or from a like

21. See Cicero, *Tusculan Disputations,* IV.6–12.

Reflection or *Prospect* of evil or painful Sensations on the other, either to our selves or others."*

Passion.   When more violent *confused Sensations* arise with the *Affection,* and are attended with, or prolonged by bodily Motions, we call the whole by the Name of *Passion,* especially when accompanied with some *natural Propensities,* to be hereafter explained.

Division by Malebranche.   If this use of these Words be allowed, the Division of MALEBRANCHE is very natural. Good Objects excite *Love;* evil Objects *Hatred:* each of these is subdivided, as the Object is *present* and *certain,* or *doubtfully expected,* or *certainly removed.* To these three Circumstances correspond three Modifications of the original Affections; *viz. Joy, Desire* and *Sorrow.* Good present, raises Joy of Love, or *Love of Joy:* Good in suspense, [62] the *Love of Desire;* Good lost, *Love of Sorrow.* Evil [61] present, raises *Aversion of Sorrow;* Evil expected, *Aversion* or *Hatred of Desire;* and Evil removed, *Aversion of Joy.* The *Joy of Love,* and the Joy of Hatred, will possibly be found nearly the same sort of Sensations, tho upon different Occasions; the same may be said of the *Sorrow of Aversion:* and thus this Division will amount to the same with that of the Stoicks.[22]

Desire and Aversion. Joy and Sorrow.   PERHAPS it may be more easy to conceive our *Affections* and Passions in this manner. The Apprehension of Good, either to our selves or others, as attainable, raises *Desire:* The like Apprehension of Evil, or of the Loss of Good, raises *Aversion,* or Desire of removing or preventing it. These two are the proper *Affections,* distinct from all *Sensation:* We may

* See above, *Sect.* 2. *Art.* 1.
[[This footnote was added in the third edition.]]
22. At *De la Recherche de la Vérité,* V.9 Malebranche presents his account of love and aversion which roughly corresponds to Hutcheson's description. But Hutcheson misinterprets Malebranche's theory of the passions, perhaps intentionally, in two important ways. First, Malebranche's main point in V.9 is to emphasize that love is primary and that even aversion assumes love as it is a privation of the good. In accord with his Augustinianism and Cartesianism, Malebranche's opposition is not as sharply binary as Hutcheson presents it. Second, Malebranche distinguishes between desire as a general passion (V.7) and love as a particular passion (V.9).

call both *Desires* if we please. The Reflection upon the Presence or certain Futurity of any Good, raises the Sensation of Joy, which is distinct from those immediate Sensations which arise from the Object itself.* A like Sensation is raised, when we reflect upon the Removal or Prevention of Evil which once threatned our selves or others. The *Reflection* upon the Presence of Evil, or the certain Prospect [63] of it, or of the Loss of Good, is the Occasion of the Sensation of *Sorrow,* distinct from [62] those *immediate Sensations* arising from the Objects or Events themselves.

These Affections, *viz. Desire, Aversion, Joy and Sorrow,* we may, after MALEBRANCHE, call *spiritual* or *pure Affections;* because the purest Spirit, were it subject to any Evil, might be capable of them. But beside these Affections, which seem to arise necessarily from a rational Apprehension of Good or Evil, there are in our Nature violent *confused Sensations,* connected with *bodily Motions,* from which our *Affections* are denominated *Passions.*

Affections may be distinguished from Passions.

We may further observe something in our Nature, determining us very frequently to Action, distinct both from *Sensation* and *Desire;* if by Desire we mean a distinct Inclination to something apprehended as Good either publick or private, or as the Means of avoiding Evil: *viz.* a certain *Propensity of Instinct* to Objects and Actions, without any Conception of them as Good, or as the Means of preventing Evil. These Objects or Actions are generally, tho not always, in effect the *Means* of some Good; but we are determined to them even without this Conception of them. Thus, as we [64] observed above,† the *Propensity to Fame* [63] may continue after one has lost all notion of *Good,* either publick or private, which could be the Object of a distinct Desire. Our *particular Affections* have generally some of these *Propensities* accompanying them; but these Propensities are sometimes without the Affections or distinct Desires,

Affections attended with undesigning Propensities. Anger.

---

* See *Sect.* 2. *Art.* 1.
[[This footnote was added in the third edition.]]
† *Sect.* 1. near the End.

and have a stronger Influence upon the Generality of Men, than the Affections could have alone. Thus in Anger, beside the Intention of removing the uneasy Sensation from the Injury received; beside the Desire of obtaining a Reparation of it, and Security for the future, which are some sort of *Goods* intended by Men when they are calm, as well as 5 during the Passion, there is in the passionate Person a Propensity to occasion *Misery* to the Offender, a Determination to *Violence,* even where there is no *Intention* of any Good to be obtained, or Evil avoided by this Violence. And 'tis principally this Propensity which we denote by the Name *Anger,* tho other Desires often accompany it. 10

So also our *Presence* with the distressed is generally necessary to their relief; and yet when we have no Hopes nor Intention of relieving them, we shall find a *Propensity* to [65] run to such Spectacles of Pity. Thus also, beside the calm *Desire* of the Happiness of a Person beloved, we have a strong Propensity to their *Company,* to the very [64] *Sight* of 15 them, without any Consideration of it as a Happiness either to our selves or to the Person beloved. The sudden Appearance of great Danger, determines us to shriek out or fly, before we can have any distinct Desires, or any Consideration that a Shriek or Flight are proper means of Relief. These *Propensities,* along with the Sensations above- 20 mentioned, when they occur without rational Desire, we may call *Passions,* and when they happen along with Desires, denominate them *passionate.* This part of our Constitution is as intelligible as many others universally observed and acknowledged; such as these, that Danger of falling makes us stretch out our Arms; noise makes us wink; that a 25 Child is determined to suck; many other Animals to rise up and walk; some to run into Water, before they can have any Notion of Good to be obtained, or Evil avoided by these means.

Love and Hatred. Envy. It may perhaps be convenient to confine *Love* and *Hatred* to our Sentiments toward Moral Agents; *Love* denoting "*Desire* of the Happiness 30 of another, generally attended with some *Approbation* of him as innocent at least, or being of a mixed [66] Character, where Good is generally prevalent:" And *Hatred* "denoting Disapprobation by our *Sense,* with the Absence of Desire of their [65] Happiness." *Benevolence* may 35 denote only "the Desire of another's Happiness;" and *Malice,* "the Desire of their Misery," abstractly from any Approbation or Condemnation by our *Moral Sense.* This sort of Malice is never found in our Nature, when we are not transported with Passion. The Propensities of Anger and Envy have some Resemblance of it; yet Envy is not an ultimate Desire of another's Misery, but only a subordinate Desire of it, as the Means of advancing our selves, or some Person more beloved than the Person envied.

Fear, as far as it is an *Affection,* and not an undesigning Propensity, is "a Mixture of *Sorrow* and *Aversion,* when we apprehend the Probability of Evil, or the Loss of Good befalling our selves, or those we love:" There is more or less of Sorrow, according to the apprehended Degrees of Probability. Hope, if it be any way an Affection, and not an Opinion, is "a Mixture of *Desire* and *Joy,* upon the probability of obtaining Good, and avoiding Evil." Both these Passions may have some *Propensities* and *Sensations* attending them, distinct from those of the other Affections.

Fear.
Hope.

[67] The confused Use of the Names, *Love, Hatred, Joy, Sorrow, Delight,* has made [*66*] some of the most important Distinctions of our Affections and Passions, to be overlooked. No Modifications of Mind can be more different from each other, than a *private Desire,* and a publick; yet both are called *Love.* The *Love of Money,* for Instance, the *Love of a generous Character,* or a *Friend:* The *Love of a fine Seat,* and *the Love of a Child.* In like manner, what can be more different than the *Sorrow for a Loss befallen our selves,* and *Sorrow for the Death of a Friend?* Of this Men must convince themselves by Reflection.

Confused Use of Names,

There is also a considerable Difference even among the *selfish Passions,* which bear the same general Name, according to the different *Senses* which constitute the Objects good or evil. Thus the Desire of *Honour,* and the Desire of *Wealth,* are certainly very different sorts of Affections, and accompanied with different Sensations: The *Sorrow* in like manner for our Loss by a *Shipwreck,* and our *Sorrow* for having done a *base Action,* or *Remorse:* Sorrow for our being subject to the *Gout* or *Stone,* and Sorrow for our being *despised* and *condemned,* or *Shame:*

Sorrow for the Damage done by a *Fire,* and that Sorrow which arises upon an [68] apprehended *Injury* from a Partner, or any other of our Fellows, which we call *Anger.* Where we [67] get some special distinct *Names,* we more easily acknowledge a Difference, as it may appear in *Shame* and *Anger;* but had we other *Names,* appropriated in the same manner, we should imagine, with good ground, as many distinct *Passions.* The like Confusion is observable about our Senses.*

To say that the *Sensation* accompanying all sorts of Joy is pleasant, and *that* accompanying Sorrow uneasy, will not argue that there is no farther Diversity. Pains have many differences among themselves, and so have Pleasures, according to the different *Senses* by which they are perceived. To enumerate all these *Diversities,* would be difficult and tedious. But some Men have piqued themselves so much upon representing "all our Affections as *selfish;* as if each Person were in his whole Frame only a *seperate System* from his Fellows, so that there was nothing in his Constitution leading him to a *publick Interest,* further than he apprehended it subservient to his own private Interest; and this Interest made nothing else, than the gratifying our *external Senses* and *Imagination,* or obtaining the Means of it:" that thereby the Wisdom [69] and Goodness of [68] the AUTHOR of our Nature is traduced, as if he had given us the strongest *Dispositions* toward what he had in his Laws prohibited; and directed us, by the Frame of our Nature, to the meanest and most contemptible Pursuits; as if *what* all good Men have represented as the *Excellence* of our Nature, were a *Force* or *Constraint* put upon it by *Art* or *Authority.* It may be useful to consider our Affections and Passions more particularly, as "they are excited by something in our Frame different from *Self-Love,* and tend to something else than the private Pleasures of the *external Senses or Imagination.*" This we may do under the following Heads, by shewing

1. How our Passions arise from the *Moral Sense,* and *Sense of Honour.*

2. How our Passions tend toward the *State of others,* abstractly from any Consideration of their *Moral Qualities.*

---

* *Treat.* I. *Sect.* I. *Art.* 10.

3. How the *publick Passions* are diversified by the *Moral Qualities* of the Agents, when they appear to our Moral Sense as virtuous or vicious.

4. How the publick Passions are diversified by the *Relations* of several Agents to each other, when we consider at once their *State,* as to Happiness or Misery, and [*69*] their past as well as present *Actions* towards each other.

5. How all these Passions may be complicated with the *selfish.* Under each of these Heads we may find the six Passions of *Malebranche,* or [*70*] the four of *Zeno;* with many other Combinations of them.

False Representations of our Nature rectified.

III. 1. The Passions about our own Actions occasioned by the *Moral Sense.* When we form the Idea of a *morally good Action,* or see it represented in the *Drama,* or read it in *Epicks* or *Romance,* we feel a *Desire* arising of doing the like. This leads most Tempers into an imagined Series of *Adventures,* in which they are still acting the generous and virtuous Part, like to the Idea they have received. If we have executed any good Design, we feel inward *Triumph of Joy:* If we are disappointed thro our own *Negligence,* or have been diverted from it by some *selfish View,* we shall feel a Sorrow called *Remorse.*

1. Passions about our own Actions. The Passion of Heroism in Castle building. Moral Joy or Self-Approbation. Remorse.

When the Idea is in like manner formed of any *morally evil Action,* which we might possibly accomplish, if we reflect upon the Cruelty or pernicious Tendency of it, there arises *Reluctance,* or Aversion: If we have committed such a Crime, upon like Reflection we feel the Sorrow called *Remorse:* If we have resisted the Temptation, [*70*] we feel a secret *Joy* and *Self-Approbation,* for which there is no special Name.

Reluctance.

We might enumerate six other Passions from the Sense of *Honour,* according as we [*71*] apprehend our Actions, or any other Circumstances, shall affect the *Opinions* which others form concerning us. When any Action or Circumstance occurs, from which we imagine Honour would arise, we feel *Desire;* when we attain it, *Joy;* when we are disappointed, *Sorrow.* When we first apprehend any Action or Circumstance as *dishonourable,* we feel *Aversion* arising; if we apprehend our selves involved

Modesty. Shame.

in it, or in danger of being tempted to it, we feel a Passion we may call *Modesty* or *Shame;* when we escape or resist such Temptations, or avoid what is dishonourable, we feel a *Joy,* for which there is no special Name.

Ambition.
Pride.

We give the Name *Ambition* to a violent Desire of Honour, but gener-   5
ally in a bad Sense, when it would lead the Agent into *immoral Means* to gratify it. The same Word often denotes the *Desire of Power. Pride* denotes sometimes the same Desires of Honour and Power, with Aversion to their contraries; sometimes *Pride* denotes Joy upon any apprehended *Right* or *Claim* to Honour; generally it is taken in a bad Sense,   10
when one claims that to which he has no Right.

Shame for
others.

[71] Men may feel the Passion of *Shame* for the dishonourable Actions of others, when any part of the Dishonour falls upon *themselves;* [72] as when the Person dishonoured is one of their *Club,* or *Party,* or *Family.*   15
The general Relation of *human Nature* may produce some uneasiness upon the Dishonour of another, tho this is more owing to our *publick Sense.*

2. Publick
Passions
abstractly.
Goodwill.
Compassion.
Pity.
Congratula-
tion.

IV. 2. The second Class are the *publick Passions* about the *State of others,*   20
as to Happiness or Misery, abstractly from their *Moral Qualities.* These Affections or Passions extend to all perceptive Natures, when there is no real or imagined Opposition of Interest. We naturally *desire* the absent Happiness of others; *rejoice* in it when obtained, and *sorrow* for it when lost. We have *Aversion* to any impending Misery; we are *sorrowful* when it   25
befals any Person, and *rejoice* when it is removed. This Aversion and Sorrow we often call Pity or Compassion; the Joy we may call *Congratulation.*

Since our Moral Sense represents *Virtue* as the greatest Happiness to the Person possessed of it, our publick Affections will naturally make us desire the *Virtue of others.* When the Opportunity of a great Action oc-   30
curs to any Person against whom we are [72] no way prejudiced, we *wish* he would attempt it, and desire his good Success. If he succeeds, we feel *Joy;* if he is disappointed, [73] or quits the Attempt, we feel *Sorrow.* Upon like Opportunity of, or Temptation to a base Action, we

have *Aversion* to the Event: If he resists the Temptation, we feel *Joy;* if he yields to it, *Sorrow.* Our Affections toward the *Person* arise jointly with our Passions about this Event, according as he acquits himself virtuously or basely.

V. 3. The Passions of the third Class are our *publick Affections,* jointly with *moral Perceptions* of the Virtue or Vice of the Agents. When Good appears attainable by a Person of *Moral Dignity,* our Desire of his Happiness, founded upon *Esteem* or *Approbation,* is much stronger than *that* supposed in the former Class. The Misfortune of such a Person raises stronger *Sorrow, Pity,* or *Regret,* and *Dissatisfaction* with the Administration of the World, upon a light View of it, with a Suspicion of the *real Advantage* of Virtue. The Success of such a Character raises all the contrary Affections of *Joy* and *Satisfaction* with Providence, and *Security* in Virtue. When Evil threatens such a Character, we have strong *Aversion* to it, with *Love* toward the Person: His escaping the Evil raises *Joy, Confidence* in [73] Providence, with *Security* in Virtue. If the Evil befals him, we feel the contrary Passions, *Sorrow, Dissatisfaction* with Providence, [74] and *Suspicion* of the Reality of Virtue. 3. Publick Passions with moral Perceptions. Regret.

Hence we see how unfit such Representations are in *Tragedy,* as make the perfectly Virtuous miserable in the highest degree. They can only lead the Spectators into *Distrust* of Providence, *Diffidence* of Virtue; and into such Sentiments, as some Authors, who probably mistake his meaning, tell us *Brutus* express'd at his Death, "That the Virtue he had pursued as a solid Good, proved but an empty Name." But we must here remember, that, notwithstanding all the frightful Ideas we have inculcated upon us of the *King of Terrors,* yet an *honourable Death* is far from appearing to a generous Mind, as the greatest of Evils. The *Ruin of a Free State,* the *Slavery of a generous Spirit,* a *Life upon shameful Terms,* still appear vastly greater Evils; beside many other exquisite *Distresses* of a more private nature, in comparison of which, an honourable Death befalling a favourite Character, is looked upon as a Deliverance. Which of them fit for the Drama.

Passions toward moral evil Agents. No disinterested or ultimate Malice in Men. Anger.

Under this Class are also included the Passions employed about the Fortunes of Characters, apprehended as *morally Evil.* Such Characters do raise *Dislike* in any [74] Observer, who has a moral Sense: But *Malice,* or the *ultimate Desire* of their Misery, does [75] not necessarily arise toward them. Perhaps our Nature is not capable of desiring the Misery 5 of any Being calmly, farther than it may be necessary to the Safety of the innocent: We may find, perhaps, that there is no Quality in any Object which would excite in us *pure disinterested Malice,* or calm Desire of Misery for its own sake.* When we apprehend any Person as *injurious* to our selves, or to any innocent Person, especially to a Person 10 beloved, the Passion of *Anger* arises toward the Agent. By *Anger* is generally meant "a Propensity to occasion Evil to another, arising upon apprehension of an Injury done by him:" This violent Propensity is attended generally, when the Injury is not very sudden, with *Sorrow* for the Injury sustained, or threatned, and *Desire* of repelling it, and mak- 15 ing the Author of it *repent* of his Attempt, or *repair* the Damage.

Its Effects.

This Passion is attended with the most violent *uneasy Sensations,* and produces as great Changes in our Bodies as any whatsoever. We are precipitantly led by this Passion, to apprehend the *injurious* as [75] *directly* 20 *malicious,* and designing the Misery of others without farther Intention. While the Heat of this Passion continues, we seem naturally to pursue the Misery [76] of the injurious, until they relent, and convince us of their better Intentions, by expressing their Sense of the Injury, and offering Reparation of Damage, with Security against future Offences. 25

Now as it is plainly necessary, in a System of Agents *capable of injuring* each other, that every one should be made *formidable* to an Invader, by such a violent Passion, till the Invader shews his Reformation of Temper, as above, and no longer; so we find it is thus ordered in our Constitution. Upon these Evidences of Reformation in the Invader, our 30 Passion naturally abates; or if in any perverse Temper it does not, the *Sense of Mankind* turns against him, and he is looked upon as cruel and inhumane.

* *See Sect. 5. Art. 5. of this Treatise.*

In considering more fully the Passions about the Fortunes of evil Characters, distinct from *Anger,* which arises upon a fresh Injury, we may first consider the evil Agents, such as a sudden View sometimes represents them, *directly evil* and *malicious;* and then make proper Abatements, for *what* the worst of Men come short of this compleatly evil Temper. As Mathematicians [76] suppose perfect *Hardness* in some Bodies, and *Elasticity* in others, and then make Allowances for the imperfect Degrees in natural Bodies.

[77] The Prospect of Good to a Person apprehended as *entirely malicious,* raises *Aversion* in the Observer, or *Desire* of his Disappointment; at least, when his Success would confirm him in any evil Intention. His Disappointment raises *Joy* in the Event, with *Trust* in Providence, and *Security* in Virtue. His Success raises the contrary Passions of *Sorrow, Distrust,* and *Suspicion.* The *Prospect of Evil,* befalling an evil Character, at first, perhaps, seems grateful to the Observer, if he has conceived the Passion of *Anger;* but to a sedate Temper, no Misery is farther the Occasion of *Joy,* than as it is necessary to some prepollent Happiness in the whole. The *escaping* of Evil impending over such a Character, by which he is confirmed in Vice, is the Occasion of *Sorrow,* and *Distrust* of Providence and Virtue; and the Evil befalling him raises *Joy,* and *Satisfaction* with Providence, and *Security* in Virtue. We see therefore, that the *Success of evil Characters,* by obtaining Good, or avoiding Evil, is an unfit Representation in *Tragedy.*

Joy of Hatred. Sorrow of Hatred.

[77] Let any one reflect on this Class of Passions, especially as they arise upon Occasions which do not affect himself, and he will see how little of *Self-Love* there is in them; and yet they are frequently as violent as any Passions [78] whatsoever. We seem conscious of some *Dignity* in these Passions above the selfish ones, and therefore never conceal them, nor are we ashamed of them. These *complicated Passions* the Philosophers have confusedly mentioned, under some general Names, along with the simple selfish Passions. The *Poets* and *Criticks* have sufficiently shown, that they felt these Differences, however it did not concern them to explain them. We may find Instances of them in all Dramatick Performances, both Antient and Modern.

Passions about mixed Characters.
Envy, Sorrow, Joy. Pity.

The *Abatements* to be made for what human Nature comes short of the highest Degrees either of Virtue or Vice, may be thus conceived: When the Good in any *mixed Character* surpasses the Evil, the Passions arise as toward the *Good;* where the Evil surpasses the Good, the Passions arise as toward the *Evil,* only in both Cases with less Violence. And further, the Passions in both Cases are either *stopped,* or turned the contrary way, by want of due *Proportion* between the *State* and *Character.* Thus an imperfect good Character, [78] in pursuit of a Good too great for his Virtue, or to the exclusion of more worthy Characters, instead of raising *Desire* of his Success, raises *Aversion;* his Success raises *Envy,* or a Species of *Sorrow,* and his Disappointment *Joy.* [79] An imperfectly evil Character, threatned by an Evil greater than is necessary to make him relent and reform, or by a great Calamity, which has no direct tendency to reform him, instead of raising *Desire* toward the Event, raises *Aversion;* his escaping it raises *Joy,* and his falling under it raises *Pity,* a Species of Sorrow.

The best Plots in Tragedy.

There is another Circumstance which exceedingly varies our Passions of this Class, when the Agents themselves, by their *own Conduct,* procure their Misery. When an imperfect good Character, by an evil Action, procures the highest Misery to himself; this raises these complicated Passions, *Pity* toward the Sufferer, *Sorrow* for the State, *Abhorrence* of Vice, *Awe* and *Admiration* of Providence, as keeping strict Measures of Sanctity and Justice. These Passions we may all feel, in reading the *Oedipus* of *Sophocles,* when we see the Distress of that Prince, occasioned by his superstitious Curiosity about his future Fortunes; his rash Violence of Temper, in Duelling without Provocation, and in pronouncing Execrations on Persons unknown. [79] We feel the like Passions from the Fortunes of *Creon* in the *Antigone;* or from the Fates of *Pyrrhus* and *Orestes,* in the *Andromache of Racine;* or our *Distressed Mother.* We heartily [80] pity these Characters, but without repining at Providence; their Misery is the Fruit of their own Actions. It is with the justest Reason, that *Aristotle** prefers such Plots to all others

---

* *Aristotle Poetic,* Chap. 13.
[[Aristotle, *Poetics,* 1453a1–12.]]

for *Tragedy,* since these Characters come nearest to those of the Spectators, and consequently will have the strongest Influence on them. We are generally conscious of some good Dispositions, mixed with many Weaknesses: few imagine themselves capable of attaining the *height* of perfectly good Characters, or arriving to their high Degrees of Felicity; and fewer imagine themselves capable of sinking into the Baseness of perfectly *evil Tempers,* and therefore few dread the Calamities which befal them.

There is one farther Circumstance which strengthens this Class of Passions exceedingly, that is, the *greatness of the Change of Fortune* in the Person, or the *Surprize* with which it comes. As this gives the Person a more *acute Perception* either of Happiness or Misery, so it [*80*] strengthens our *Passions,* arising from Observation of his State. Of this the Poets are very sensible, who so often represent to us the former Prosperity of the Person, for whom they [81] would move our pity; his *Projects,* his *Hopes,* his *half-executed Designs.* One left his *Palace unfinished,* another his *betrothed Mistress,* or *young Wife;* one promised himself *Glory,* and a fortunate *old Age;* another was heaping up *Wealth,* boasted of his *Knowledge,* was honoured for his *fine Armour,* his *Activity,* his *Augury.*

How these Passions are raised high and complicated.

Ἀλλ' οὐκ οἰωνοῖσιν ἐρύσσατα κῆρα μέλαιναν.
οὐδε τί οἱ τόγ' ἐπήρκεσε λυγρον ὄλεθρυν.—Homer.[23]

Sed non Augurio potuit depellere pestem; Sed non Dardanice medicari cuspidis ictum Invaluit.—Virg.[24]

23. The passages from Homer are *Iliad* II.859, "but he did not ward off black death with bird omens," and II.873, "fool, and this did not protect him from grievous destruction." Along with the passages from Virgil directly following them, they are common examples used to illustrate the human failure to ward off fate.

24. Here Hutcheson quotes two distinct passages from Virgil's *Aeneid:* "But the augury was unable to drive away ruin" (IX.328) and "But he was not able to heal the cut of the Dardan blade" (VII.756–57).

The Joy is in like manner increased upon the Misfortunes of evil Characters, by representing their former *Prosperity, Pride* and *Insolence.*

This Sorrow or Joy is strangely diversified or complicated, when the Sufferers are *multiplied,* by representing the Persons attached to the principal Sufferer, and setting before us their *Affections, Friendships,* 5 *tender Solicitudes, care in Education, succour in former Distresses;* this every [*81*] one will find in reading the Stories of *Pallas, Camilla, Nisus,* and *Euryalus;*[25] or in general, any Battle of *Homer* or *Virgil.* What there [82] is in Self-Love to account for these Effects, let all Mankind judge.

10

4. Publick Passions and Relations of Agents.

VI. The Passions of the fourth Class arise from the same *moral Sense* and *publick Affections,* upon observing the Actions of Agents some way *attached* to each other, by prior Ties of Nature or good Offices, or disengaged by *prior Injuries;* when these *Relations* are known, the moral Qualities of the Actions appear considerably different, and our Passions 15

Contrastes and Complications of Passions.

are much diversified by them: there is also a great *Complication* of different Passions, and a sort of *Contraste,* or assemblage of opposite Passions toward the several Persons concerned. The most moving *Peripeties,* and *Remembrances,* in *Epick* and *Dramatick* Poetry, are calculated to raise these complicated Passions; and in *Oratory* we study to do the 20 same.

Thus strong Sentiments of *Gratitude,* and vigorous Returns of good Offices observed, raise in the Spectator the highest *Love* and *Esteem* toward both the *Benefactor,* and even the *Person obliged,* with *Security* and *Delight* in Virtue.—*Ingratitude,* or returning bad Offices designedly, 25 raises the greatest *Detestation* against [*82*] the Ungrateful; and *Love* with *Compassion* toward the [83] Benefactor, with *Dejection* and *Diffidence* in a virtuous Course of Life.—*Forgiving of Injuries,* and much more *returning Good for Evil,* appears wonderfully great and beautiful to our

30

25. Pallas, Camilla, Nisus, and Euryalus were all heroes of the Trojan War celebrated in Virgil's *Aeneid.* In describing them, Virgil emphasized the approbation that spectators had for them as well as their sympathetic ties to friends and family in order to amplify the pathos of their deaths (cf. IX.423–37, X.491–5, XI.532–96).

moral Sense: it raises the strongest *Love* toward the Forgiver, *Compassion* for the Injury received; toward the Injurious, if *relenting,* some degree of *Good-will,* with *Compassion;* if not relenting, the most violent *Abhorrence* and *Hatred.*—Mutual *good Offices* done designedly between morally *good Agents,* raise *Joy* and *Love* in the Observer toward both, with *delight* in Virtue.—*Mutual Injuries* done by evil Agents designedly, raise *Joy* in the Events, along with *Hatred* to the Agents, with *Detestation* of Vice.—*Good Offices* done designedly by *good Agents* toward *Evil,* but not so as to encourage, or enable them to further Mischief, raise *Love* toward the *good Agent; Displicence,* with some *Good-will* toward the evil Agent.—*Good Offices* designedly done mutually among *evil Agents,* if these Offices do not promote their evil Intentions, diminish our Dislike and Hatred, and introduce some *Compassion* and *Benevolence.*—*Good Offices* from *good Agents,* to *Benefactors unknown* to the Agent, or to their unknown Friends or Posterity, increase *Love* toward both; and raise great *Satisfaction* and *Trust* in [83] *Providence,* with [84] *Security* in Virtue, and *Joy* in the Event.—*Undesigned evil Returns* in like Case with the former, raise *Sorrow* in the Observer upon account of the Event, *Pity* toward both, with *Suspicion* of Providence and Virtue.—An *undesigned Return of Evil* to an evil Agent from a good one, whom he had injured, raises *Joy* upon account of the Event, and *Trust* in Providence.—*Undesigned evil Offices mutually done* to each other by evil Agents, raise *Joy* in the Event, *Abhorrence* of Vice, and *Satisfaction* with Providence.—*Undesigned good Offices* done by good Agents toward the evil, by which they are further excited or impowered to do evil, raise *Pity* toward the good Agent, *Indignation* and *Envy* toward the Evil, with *Distrust* in Providence.—*Undesigned good Offices* done by good to evil Agents, by which they are not excited or enabled to do further mischief, raise *Envy* or *Indignation* toward the evil Agent, if the Benefit be great; if not, they scarce raise any new Passion distinct from that we had before, of *Love* toward the one, and *Hatred* or *Dislike* toward the other.

These Passions might have been diversified, according to *Malebranche's* Division, as the Object or Event was *present,* or in *suspense,* or *certainly removed:* And would appear in different Degrees of [84]

Strength, according [85] as the Persons concerned were more nearly attached to the Observer, by *Nature, Friendship,* or *Acquaintance.*[26]

5. Publick Passions join'd with the selfish.

VII. The Passions of the last Class, are those in which any of the former Kinds are complicated with *selfish Passions,* when our own Interest is concerned. It is needless here to repeat them over again: Only this may be noted in general, that, as the Conjunction of selfish Passions will very much increase the Commotion of Mind, so the Opposition of any *selfish Interests,* which appear of great Importance, will often conquer the *publick Desires* or Aversions, or those founded upon the Sense of *Virtue* or *Honour;* and this is the Case in vicious Actions done against *Conscience.*

These Complications of Passions are often not reflected on by the Person who is acted by them, during their Rage: But a judicious Observer may find them by Reflection upon himself, or by Observation of others; and the Representation of them never fails to affect us in the most lively manner.

—Aestuat ingens
Imo in Corde Pudor, mixtoque Insania Luctu,
Et Furiis agitatus Amor, & conscia Virtus.—Virg.[27]

[85/86] In all this tedious Enumeration, let any one consider, "How few of our Passions can be any way deduced from *Self-Love,* or desire of private Advantage: And how improbable it is, that Persons in the Heat of Action, have any of those *subtle Reflections,* and *selfish Intentions,* which some Philosophers invent for them: How great a part of the Commotions of our Minds arise upon the *moral Sense,* and from *publick Affections* toward the good of others. We should find, that without these Principles in our Nature, we should not feel the one half at least

26. See Malebranche, *De la Recherche,* V. 7–9.
27. Virgil, *Aeneid,* X.870–72. Dryden renders it "Love, anguish, wrath, and grief, to madness wrought//Despair, and secret shame, and conscious thought//Of inborn worth, his lab'ring soul oppress'd." The third line is thought now to be spurious, but was common to eighteenth-century editions.

of our present *Pleasures* or *Pains;* and that our Nature would be almost reduced to *Indolence.*"

An accurate Observation of the several distinct *Characters* and *Tempers* of Men, which are constituted by the various Degrees of their *natural Sagacity,* their *Knowledge,* their *Interests,* their *Opinions,* or *Associations* of Ideas, with the *Passions* which are prevalent in them, is a most useful and pleasant Entertainment for those, who have Opportunities of large Acquaintance and Observation. But our present Purpose leads only to consider the first general [87] *Elements,* from the various Combinations [*86*] of which, the several *Tempers* and *Characters* are formed.

How Characters and Tempers of Men are formed.

This account of our Affections will, however, prepare the way for discerning considerable Evidences for the *Goodness of the Deity,* from the Constitution of our Nature; and for removing the Objections of voluptuous luxurious Men, against the Rules of Virtue laid down by Men of Reflection. While no other Ideas of *Pleasure* or *Advantage* are given us, than those which relate to the external Senses; nor any other *Affections* represented as natural, save those toward private Good: it may be difficult to persuade many, even of those who are not Enemies to Virtue from *Inclination,* of the Wisdom of the Deity, in making the *Biass* of our Nature opposite to the Laws he would give us; and making all *Pleasure,* the most natural Character of Good, attend the *prohibited Actions,* or the *indifferent* ones; while *Obedience* to the Law must be a *constrained* Course of Action, inforced only by *Penalties* contrary to our *natural Affections* and *Senses. Nature* and *Grace* are by this Scheme made very opposite: Some would question whether they could have the same Author. Whereas, if the preceding Account be just, we see no [88] such Inconsistency: "Every Passion [*87*] or Affection in its *moderate Degree* is innocent, many are directly *amiable,* and *morally good:* we have *Senses* and *Affections* leading us to *publick Good,* as well as to *private;* to *Virtue,* as well as to external Pleasure."

The Order of Nature partly vindicated.

SECTION IV

*How far our several Affections and Passions are
under our Power, either to govern them when raised, or to
prevent their arising: with some general Observations
about their Objects.*

Affections and
Passions
depend
much upon
Opinions.

[88/89] I. From what was said above it appears, that our Passions are
not so much in our *Power,* as some seem to imagine, from the *Topicks*
used either to raise or allay them. We are so constituted by Nature, that,
as soon as we form the Idea of certain Objects or Events, our *Desire* or
Aversion will arise toward them; and consequently our Affections must   5
very much depend upon the *Opinions* we form, concerning any thing
which occurs to our Mind, its *Qualities, Tendencies,* or *Effects.* Thus the
Happiness of every sensitive Nature is desired, as soon as we remove all
Opinion or *Apprehension* of *Opposition of Interest* between this Being
and others. The *Apprehension* of morally good Qualities, is the neces-   10
sary Cause of *Approbation,* by our moral Sense, and of stronger [90]
Love. The Cause of *Hatred,* is the *Apprehension* [89] of the opposite
Qualities. *Fear,* in like manner, must arise from *Opinion of Power,* and
Inclination to hurt us: *Pity* from the Opinion of another's *undeserved
Misery: Shame* only arises from *Apprehension* of *Contempt* from others: 15
Joy, in any Event, must arise from an Opinion of its Goodness. Our
selfish Passions in this, do not differ from our *publick ones.*

This may shew us some Inconsistency in Topicks of Argument, often
used to inculcate *Piety* and *Virtue.* Whatever Motives of Interest we
suggest, either from a present or future *Reward,* must be ineffectual, un-   20
til we have first laboured to form *amiable Conceptions* of the *Deity,* and
of our *Fellow Creatures.* And yet in many Writers, even in this Cause,
"Mankind are represented as *absolutely evil,* or at best as *entirely selfish;*
nor are there any nobler Ideas of the DEITY suggested. It is grown a
fashionable Topick, to put some *sly selfish Construction* upon the most   25
generous human Actions; and he passes for the *shreudest Writer,* or *Or-
ator,* who is most artful in these Insinuations."

II. The Government of our Passions must then depend much upon our *Opinions:* [91] But we must here observe an obvious Difference among our Desires, *viz.* that [*90*] "some of them have a *previous,* painful, or uneasy Sensation, antecedently to any *Opinion* of Good in the Object; nay, the Object is often chiefly esteemed good, only for its *allaying this Pain* or Uneasiness; or if the Object gives also positive Pleasure, yet the *uneasy Sensation* is previous to, and independent of this *Opinion* of Good in the Object." These Desires we may call *Appetites.* "Other Desires and Aversions necessarily presuppose an *Opinion* of Good and Evil in their Objects; and the Desires or Aversions, with their concomitant uneasy Sensations, are produced or occasioned by this *Opinion* or *Apprehension.*" Of the former kind are *Hunger* and *Thirst,* and the Desires between the *Sexes;* to which Desires there is an uneasy Sensation *previous,* even in those who have little other Notion of Good in the Objects, than allaying this *Pain* or *Uneasiness.* There is something like to this in the Desire of *Society,* or the Company of our fellow Creatures. Our Nature is so much formed for this, that altho the *Absence of Company* is not immediately painful, yet if it be long, and the Person be not employed in something which tends to *Society* at last, or which is designed to fit him for Society, an uneasy *Fretfulness, Sullenness,* and *Discontent,* [92] will grow upon him by degrees, which Company alone [*91*] can remove. He shall not perhaps be sensible always, that it is the Absence of Company which occasions his Uneasiness: A painful Sensation dictates nothing of it self; it must be therefore some *Reflection* or *Instinct,* distinct from the Pain, which suggests the Remedy. Our Benevolence and Compassion pre suppose indeed some *Knowledge* of other sensitive Beings, and of what is good or evil to them: But they do not arise from any previous *Opinion,* that "the Good of others tends to the Good of the Agent." They are *Determinations of our Nature,* previous to our Choice from Interest, which excite us to Action, as soon as we know other sensitive or rational Beings, and have any Apprehension of their Happiness or Misery.

In other Desires the Case is different. No Man is distressed for want of *fine Smells, harmonious Sounds, beautiful Objects, Wealth, Power,* or *Grandeur,* previously to some Opinion formed of these things as good,

Appetites and Affections distinguished.

or some *prior Sensation* of their Pleasures. In like manner, *Virtue* and *Honour* as necessarily give us Pleasure, when they occur to us, as Vice and Contempt give us Pain; but, antecedently to some *Experience* or *Opinion* of this Pleasure, there is no previous uneasy Sensation in their Absence, as there [93] is in the Absence of the Objects of *Appetite.* The 5 Necessity [92] of these Sensations previous to our Appetites, has been considered already.* The Sensations accompanying or subsequent to our other Desires, by which they are denominated *Passions,* keep them in a just Balance with our *Appetites,* as was before observed.

But this holds in general, concerning all our Desires or Aversions, 10 that according to the *Opinion* or *Apprehension* of Good or Evil, the Desire or Aversion is increased or diminished: Every *Gratification* of any Desire gives at first Pleasure; and Disappointment Pain, proportioned to the Violence of the Desire. In like manner, the *escaping* any Object of Aversion, tho it makes no permanent Addition to our Happiness, 15 gives at first a pleasant *Sensation,* and relieves us from Misery, proportioned to the Degree of *Aversion* or *Fear.* So when any Event, to which we had an Aversion, befals us, we have at first Misery proportioned to the Degree of Aversion. So that some Pain is subsequent upon all *Frustration* of Desire or Aversion, but it is previous to those Desires only, 20 which are called *Appetites.*

[93/94] III. Hence we see how impossible it is for one to judge of the *Degrees* of Happiness or Misery in others, unless he knows their *Opinions,* their *Associations* of Ideas, and the *Degrees* of their Desires and Aversions. We see also of how much Consequence our *Associations* of 25 Ideas and *Opinions* are to our Happiness or Misery, and to the Command of our Passions.

---

* *Sect. 2. Art. 6.*

For tho in our *Appetites* there are uneasy Sensations, previous to any
Opinion, yet our very Appetites may be strengthened or weakened, and
variously alter'd by *Opinion,* or *Associations* of Ideas. Before *their* Inter-
vention, the bodily Appetites are easily satisfied: Nature has put it in
almost every one's power, so far to gratify them, as to support the Body,
and remove Pain. But when *Opinion,* and *confused Ideas,* or *Fancy*
comes in, and represents some particular kinds of Gratifications, or
great Variety of them, as of great Importance; when Ideas of *Dignity,*
Grandure, Magnificence, Generosity, or any other *moral Species,* are
joined to the Objects of Appetites, they may furnish us with endless
Labour, Vexation, and Misery of every kind.

> Associations of Ideas and Opinions increase or diminish the strength of our Desires.

As to the other Desires which pre suppose some *Opinion* or *Appre-*
hension of [94] Good, [95] previous to any Sensation of uneasiness; they
must still be more directly influenced by *Opinion,* and *Associations* of
Ideas. The higher the *Opinion* or *Apprehension* of Good or Evil is, the
stronger must the *Desire* or *Aversion* be; the greater is the Pleasure of
Success at first, and the greater the Pain of *Disappointment.* Our publick
Desires are influenced in the same manner with the private: what we
conceive as Good, we shall desire for those we love, as well as for our
selves; and that in proportion to the *Degree of Good* apprehended in it:
whatever we apprehend as Evil in any degree to those we love, to that
we shall have proportionable Aversion.

The common Effect of these *Associations* of Ideas is this, "that they
raise the Passions into an extravagant Degree, beyond the proportion
of real Good in the Object: And commonly beget some secret Opinions to justify the Passions. But then the *Confutation* of these false
Opinions is not sufficient to break the *Association,* so that the *Desire*
or *Passion* shall continue, even when our Understanding has suggested
to us, that the Object is not good, or not proportioned to the Strength
of the Desire." Thus we often may observe, that Persons, who by reasoning have laid aside all Opinion of [95] *Spirits being in the* [96] *dark*
more than in the light, are still uneasy to be alone in the dark.* Thus

---

*Ac veluti pueri trepidant, atque omnia caecis
In tenebris metuunt, sic nos in luce timemus

the *luxurious,* the *extravagant Lover,* the *Miser,* can scarce be supposed
to have *Opinions* of the several Objects of their Pursuit, proportioned
to the Vehemence of their Desires; but the constant *Indulgence* of any
Desire, the frequent *Repetition* of it, the *diverting* our Minds from all
other Pursuits, the Strain of *Conversation* among Men of the same   5
Temper, who often haunt together, the *Contagion* in the very Air and
Countenance of the passionate, beget such wild *Associations* of Ideas,
that a sudden *Conviction of Reason* will not stop the Desire or Aversion, any more than an Argument will surmount the *Loathings* or
Aversions, acquired against certain Meats or Drinks, by Surfeits or   10
emetick Preparations.

The *Luxurious* are often convinced, when any Accident has revived
a *natural Appetite,* of the superior Pleasures in a plain Dinner, with a
sharp Stomach:† but [*96/97*] this does not reform them; they have got
all the Ideas of *Dignity, Grandure, Excellence,* and *Enjoyment of Life*   15
joined to their Table. Explain to a Miser the Folly of his Conduct, so
that he can alledg nothing in his Defence; yet he will go on,

> Ut locuples moriatur egenti vivere fato.—Juv.²⁸

Interdum nihilo quae sunt metuenda magis.—Luc   20

[["Just as children are agitated, and fear all things lurking in the dark, so sometimes in the daylight we fear things no more [deserving] of fear," Lucretius, *De
Rerum Natura,* II.55–58.]]

†—Leporem sectatus, equove   25
Lassus ab in domito, vel si Romana fatigat
Militia assuetum Graecari—
Cum labor extuderit fastidia
—Cum sale panis
Latrantem stomachum bene leniet—Hor.   30

[[Horace, *Satire* 2.2, 8–11, 15, 17–18. "After chasing a rabbit, or coming away
tired from a horse that is hard to control, or if the Roman and Greek military drills
exhaust you . . . when work has hammered away your pickiness then bread and salt
will calm your grumbling stomach quite well."]]   35

28. Juvenal, *Satire,* 14, 137: "to live in need in order that you may die wealthy."

He has likewise all Ideas of *Good,* of *Worth,* and *Importance* in Life confounded with his Coffers.

A romantick Lover has in like manner no Notion of Life without his *Mistress,* all *Virtue* and *Merit* are summed up in his *inviolable Fidelity.* The *Connoisseur* has all Ideas of valuable *Knowledge, Gentlemanlike Worth* and *Ability* associated with his beloved Arts. The Idea of *Property* comes along with the Taste, and makes his Happiness impossible, without *Possession* of what he admires. A plain Question might confute the *Opinion,* but will not break the *Association:* "What Pleasure has the Possessor more than others, to whose Eyes they are exposed as well as his?"

Our *publick Desires* are affected by confused Ideas, in the same manner with our private Desires. What is apprehended [97] as [98] Good, thro' an Association of foreign Ideas, shall be pursued for *those we love,* as well as what is really good for them. Our *benevolent Passions* in the nearer Ties, are as apt to be too violent as any whatsoever: this we may often experience in the *Love of Offspring, Relations, Parties, Cabals.* The Violence of our Passion makes us sometimes incapable of pursuing effectually their Good, and sinks us into an useless State of Sorrow upon their Misfortunes. *Compassion* often makes the Evil greater to the Spectator than to the Sufferer; and sometimes subjects the Happiness of a Person of great Worth, to every Accident befalling one entirely void of it.

The Desire of Virtue, upon extensive impartial Schemes of publick Happiness, can scarce be too strong; but, upon *mistaken or partial Views* of publick Good, this Desire of Virtue may often lead Men into very pernicious Actions. One may conceive a sort of *Extravagancy,* and *effeminate Weakness* even of this Desire; as when Men are dissatisfied with themselves for *Disappointments* in good Attempts, which it was not in their Power to accomplish; when some *heroick Tempers* shew no Regard to private Good; when the Pursuit of the lovely Form is so passionate, that the Agent [99] does not relish his *past Conduct* [98] by agreeable Reflection, but like the Ambitious,

Nil actum reputat si quid superesset agendum.—Lucan.[29]

But the most pernicious *Perversions* of this Desire are "some *partial Admirations* of certain moral Species, such as *Fortitude, Propagation of true Religion, Zeal for a Party;* while other Virtues are overlooked, and the very *End* to which the admired Qualities are subservient is forgotten. Thus some *Phantoms* of Virtue are raised, wholly opposite to its true Nature, and to the sole End of it, *the publick Good.*"

Honour, in like manner, has had its foolish Associations, and the true Nature of it has been overlooked, so that the Desire of it has run into *Enthusiasm,* and pernicious *Madness.* Thus, "however our Desires, when our *Opinions* are true, and the Desire is proportioned to the *true Opinion,* are all calculated for good, either publick or private; yet *false Opinions,* and *confused Ideas,* or too great a *Violence* in any of them, above a due Proportion to the rest, may turn the best of them into destructive Follies."

Malicious or cruel Tempers, how they arise.

[*99*/100] This is probably the Case in those Affections which some suppose *natural,* or at least incident to our Natures, and yet *absolutely evil:* Such as *Rancour,* or *disinterested Malice, Revenge, Misanthropy.* We indeed find our Nature determined to disapprove an *Agent* apprehended as evil, or malicious, thro' *direct Intention;* we must desire the Destruction of such a Being, not only from Self-Love, but from our Benevolence to others. Now when we rashly form Opinions of *Sects,* or *Nations,* as absolutely evil; or get associated Ideas of *Impiety, Cruelty, Profaneness,* recurring upon every mention of them: when, by repeated Reflection upon Injuries received, we strengthen our Dislike into an *obdurate Aversion,* and conceive that the Injurious are *directly malicious;* we may be led to act in such a manner, that Spectators, who are unacquainted with our *secret Opinions,* or *confused Apprehensions of others,*

---

29. Lucan, *De Bello Civili,* II.657, is the closest line. The quote describes Caesar's ceaseless ambition. It is skillfuly captured in Nicholas Rowe's translation of 1718: "[but he, with empire fired and vast desires,]/ to all and nothing less than all aspires," in Sarah Annes Brown and Charles Martindale (eds.), *Lucan, The Civil War: Translated as Lucan's Pharsalia by Nicholas Rowe* (London: Everyman, 1998).

may think we have *pure disinterested Malice* in our Nature; a very *Instinct* toward the Misery of others, when it is really only the *overgrowth* of a just natural Affection, upon false Opinions, or confused Ideas; even as our *Appetites,* upon which our natural Life depends, may acquire accidental *Loathings* at the most wholesom Food. Our Ideas and Opinions of Mankind are often very rashly formed, [101] but our *Affections* [*100*] are generally suited to our *Opinions.* When our Ideas and Opinions of the moral Qualities of others are just, our Affections are generally regular and good: But when we give loose Reins to our *Imagination* and *Opinion,* our Affections must follow them into all Extravagance and Folly; and inadvertent Spectators will imagine some *Dispositions* in us wholly useless, and absolutely and directly *evil.*

Now the *Gratification* of these destructive Desires, like those of all the rest, gives at first some *Pleasure,* proportioned to their Violence; and the *Disappointment* gives proportioned *Pain.* But as to the *Continuance* of these Pleasures or Pains, we shall find hereafter great Diversity.

From this view of our Desires, we may see "the great Variety of *Objects, Circumstances, Events,* which must be of Importance to the Happiness of a Creature, furnished with such a *Variety of Senses* of Good and Evil, with equally various *Desires* corresponding to them: especially considering the strange *Combinations of Ideas,* giving Importance to many Objects, in their own Nature indifferent."

IV. We must in the next Place enquire "how far these several *Desires* must [101] necessarily [102] arise, or may be prevented by our Conduct."

How far the several Desires must necessarily arise in us.

The Pleasures and Pains of the *external Senses* must certainly be perceived by every one who comes into the World; the one raising some Degree of Desire, and the other Aversion: the *Pains of Appetites* arise yet more certainly than others, and are previous to any *Opinion.* But then it is very much in our power to keep these Sensations *pure* and *unmixed* with any foreign Ideas: so that the plainest Food and Raiment, if sufficiently nourishing and healthful, may keep us easy, as well as the *rarest* or most *expensive.* Nay the Body, when accustomed to the simpler

1. That of external pleasures.

Sorts, is easiest in the Use of them: And we are raised to an higher Degree of *Chearfulness,* by a small Improvement in our Table, than it is possible to bring a *pampered Body* into, by any of the Productions of Nature. Whatever the Body is once accustomed to, produces no considerable Change in it.   5

2. The Desires of the Pleasures of the Imagination. The Pleasures of the *Imagination,* or of *the internal Sense of Beauty,* and *Decency,* and *Harmony,* must also be perceived by us. The *Regularity, Proportion* and *Order* in external Forms, will as necessarily strike the Mind, as any Perceptions of the external Senses. But then, as we have   10 no uneasiness [103] of *Appetite,* previous to the [*102*] Reception of those grateful Ideas, we are not *necessarily* made miserable in their Absence; unless by some fantastick *Habit* we have raised very violent Desires, or by a long Pursuit of them, have made our selves incapable of other Enjoyments.   15

Again, the Sense and Desire of *Beauty* of several kinds is entirely abstracted from *Possession* or *Property;* so that the finest *Relish* of this kind, and the strongest subsequent *Desires,* if we admit no foolish Conjunctions of Ideas, may almost every where be gratified with the Prospects of *Nature,* and with the Contemplation of the more curious *Works of*   20 *Art,* which the Proprietors generally allow to others without Restraint. But if this Sense or Desire of Beauty itself be accompanied with the Desire of *Possession* or *Property;* if we let it be guided by *Custom,* and receive *Associations* of foreign Ideas in our Fancy of *Dress, Equipage, Furniture, Retinue;* if we relish only the Modes of the *Great,* or the Marks of *Dis-*   25 *tinction* as beautiful; if we let such Desires grow strong, we must be very *great* indeed, before we can have any Pleasure by this Sense: and every Disappointment or Change of Fortune must make us miserable. The like Fate may attend the Pursuit of *speculative Sciences, Poetry, Musick,* or [104] *Painting;* to excel in these things is granted but to few. [*103*] A   30 violent Desire of *Distinction* and *Eminence* may bring on Vexation and Sorrow for the longest Life.

The Pleasures and Pains of the *publick Sense* will also necessarily arise in   3. The publick Desires.
us. Men cannot live without the *Society* of others, and their *good Offices;*
they must observe both the *Happiness* and *Misery,* the *Pleasures* and
Pains of their Fellows: *Desire* and *Aversion* must arise in the Observer.
Nay farther, as we cannot avoid more near Attachments of Love, either
from the Instinct between the *Sexes,* or that toward *Offspring,* or from
Observation of the *benevolent Tempers* of others, or their particular *Vir-*
tues and *good Offices,* we must feel the Sensations of *Joy* and *Sorrow,*
from the State of others even in the stronger Degrees, and have the publick Desires in a greater Height. All we can do to prevent the *Pains* of
general Benevolence, will equally lessen the *Pleasures* of it. If we restrain
our *publick Affection* from growing strong, we abate our Pleasures from
the good Success of others, as much as we lessen our Compassion for
their Misfortunes: If we confine our Desires to a small *Circle* of Acquaintance, or to a *Cabal* or *Faction,* we contract our Pleasures as much
as we do our Pains. The Distinction of Pleasures and Pains into *real*
[105] and *imaginary,* or rather into *necessary* and *voluntary,* [104] would
be of some use, if we could correct the *Imaginations* of others, as well as
our own; but if we cannot, we are sure, whoever thinks himself miserable, is really so; however he might possibly, by a better Conduct of his
Imagination, have prevented this Misery. All we can do in this affair, is
to enjoy a great Share of the Pleasures of the *stronger Ties,* with fewer
Pains of them, by confining the stronger Degrees of Love, or our
Friendships, to Persons of *corrected Imaginations,* to whom as few of the
uncertain Objects of Desire are necessary to Happiness as is possible.
Our Friendship with such Persons may probably be to us a much
greater Source of Happiness than of Misery, since the Happiness of
such Persons is more probable than the contrary.

Since there is nothing in our Nature determining us to *disinterested*
Hatred toward any Person; we may be secure against all the Pains of
Malice, by preventing false *Opinions* of our Fellows as absolutely evil,
or by guarding against *habitual Anger,* and rash *Aversions.*

The *moral Ideas* do arise also necessarily in our Minds. We cannot
avoid observing the *Affections* of those we converse with; [106] their *Ac-*
tions, their *Words,* their *Looks* betray them. We are conscious of [105] our

own Affections, and cannot avoid Reflection upon them sometimes: the kind and generous Affections will appear amiable, and all Appearance of Cruelty, Malice, or even very selfish Affections, will be disapproved, and appear odious. Our *own Temper,* as well as that of others, will appear to our moral Sense either lovely or deformed, and will be   5
the Occasion either of Pleasure or Uneasiness. We have not any proper *Appetite* toward Virtue, so as to be uneasy, even antecedently to the Appearance of the lovely Form; but as soon as it appears to any Person, as it certainly must very early in Life, it never fails to raise *Desire,* as Vice does raise *Aversion.* This is so rooted in our Nature, that no *Education,*   10
false Principles, depraved Habits, or even *Affectation* itself can entirely root it out. LUCRETIUS and HOBBES shew themselves in innumerable Instances struck with some *moral Species;* they are full of Expressions of *Admiration, Gratitude, Praise, Desire of doing Good;* and of *Censure, Disapprobation, Aversion to some Forms of Vice.*   15

Since then there is no avoiding these Desires and Perceptions of *Morality,* all we can do to secure our selves in the possession of Pleasures of this kind, without Pain, consists in "a vigorous Use of our Reason, to [107] discern what Actions really [*106*] tend to the publick Good in the *whole,* that we may not do *that* upon a partial View of Good, which   20
afterwards, upon a fuller Examination, we shall condemn and abhor our selves for; and withal, to fix our *Friendships* with Persons of like Dispositions, and just Discernment." Men of partial Views of publick Good, if they never obtain any better, may be easy in a very pernicious Conduct, since the *moral Evil* or *Deformity* does not appear to them.   25
But this is seldom to be hop'd for in any partial Conduct. Those who are injured by us fail not to complain; the Spectators, who are disengaged from our partial Attachments, will often take the Freedom to express their Sentiments, and set our Conduct in a full Light: This must very probably occasion to us *Shame* and *Remorse.* "It cannot therefore   30
be an indifferent Matter, to an Agent with a moral Sense, what *Opinions* he forms of the Tendency of Actions; what partial *Attachments* of Love he has toward *Parties* or *Factions.* If he has true Opinions of the Tendencies of *Actions;* if he carefully examines the real Dignity of *Persons*

and *Causes,* he may be sure that the Conduct which he now approves he shall always approve, and have delight in Reflection upon it, however it be censured by others. But if he takes up at hazard *Opinions* of Actions; [108] if [*107*] he has a foolish *Admiration* of particular Sects, and as foolish *Aversions* and Dislike to others, not according to any real Importance or Dignity, he shall often find occasion for *Inconstancy* and *Change* of his Affections, with *Shame* and *Remorse* for his past Conduct, and an inward *Dislike* and *Self-Condemnation.*"

What most deeply affects our Happiness or Misery, are the Dispositions of those Persons with whom we voluntarily contract some *nearer Intimacies* of Friendship: If we act wisely in this Point, we may secure to our selves the greatest Pleasures with the fewest Pains, by attaching our selves to Persons of real Goodness, good Offices toward whom are useful to the World. The Ties of *Blood* are generally very strong, especially toward *Offspring;* they need rather the Bridle than the Spur, in all Cases wherein the Object is not recommended to a singular Love by his good Qualities. We may, in a considerable measure, restrain our *natural Affection* toward a worthless Offspring, by setting our *publick Affections* and our *moral Sense* against it, in frequent Contemplation of their Vices, and of the Mischief which may arise to Persons of more worth from them, if we give them any Countenance in their Vices.

[*108*/109] The regulating our Apprehensions of the *Actions of others,* is of very great Importance, that we may not imagine Mankind worse than they really are, and thereby bring upon our selves a Temper full of *Suspicion, Hatred, Anger* and *Contempt* toward others; which is a constant State of Misery, much worse than all the Evils to be feared from *Credulity.* If we examine the true *Springs* of human Action, we shall seldom find their Motives worse than *Self-Love.* Men are often subject to *Anger,* and upon sudden *Provocations* do Injuries to each other, and that only from Self-Love, without Malice, but the greatest part of their Lives is employed in Offices of *natural Affection, Friendship, innocent Self-Love,* or *Love of a Country.* The little *Party-Prejudices* are generally founded upon Ignorance, or false Opinions, rather apt to move *Pity* than *Hatred.* Such Considerations are the best Preservative against *An-*

ger, *Malice,* and *Discontent* of Mind with the Order of Nature. "When you would make yourself chearful and easy (says the Emperor*) consider the *Virtues* of your several Acquaintances, the *Industry* and *Diligence* of one, the *Modesty* of another, the *Generosity* or [*109*] *Liberality* of a [110] third; and in some Persons some other Virtue. There is nothing so delightful, as the Resemblances of the *Virtues* appearing in the Conduct of your Contemporaries as frequently as possible. Such Thoughts we should still retain with us."

When the *moral Sense* is thus assisted by a sound Understanding and Application, our own Actions may be a constant Source of solid Pleasure, along with the Pleasures of *Benevolence,* in the highest Degree which our Nature will admit, and with as few of its Pains as possible.

How far our Sense of Honour is in our power. As to the Desires of *Honour,* since we cannot avoid observing or hearing of the Sentiments of others concerning our Conduct, we must feel the Desire of the *good Opinions* of others, and Aversion to their *Censures* or *Condemnation:* since the one necessarily gives us Pleasure, and the other Pain. Now it is impossible to bring all Men into the same Opinions of particular Actions, because of their different Opinions of *publick Good,* and of the *Means* of promoting it; and because of *opposite Interests;* so that it is often impossible to be secure against all Censure or Dishonour from some of our Fellows. No one is so much Master of *external Things,* as to make his honourable Intentions successful; and yet [110] *Success* [111] is a Mark by which many judge of the Goodness of Attempts. Whoever therefore suffers his Desire of *Honour* or *Applause* to grow violent, without Distinction of the *Persons* to whose Judgment he submits, runs a great hazard of Misery. But our natural Desire of Praise, to speak in the Mathematical Style, is in a compounded Proportion of the *Numbers* of Applauders, and their *Dignity.* "He therefore who makes *Distinction* of Persons justly, and acts wisely for the *publick Good,* may secure himself from much uneasiness upon injudicious Censure, and may obtain the Approbation of those whose Esteem alone is valuable, or at least far over-ballances the Censure of others."

*Marcus Antoninus, *Lib.* vi. *C.* 48.

The *Desire of Wealth* must be as necessary as any other Desires of our Nature, as soon as we apprehend the usefulness of Wealth to gratify all other Desires. While it is desired as the *Means* of something farther, the Desire tends to our Happiness, proportionably to the good Oeconomy of the *principal Desires* to which it is made subservient. It is in every man's power, by a little Reflection, to prevent the Madness and Enthusiasm with which Wealth is insatiably pursued, even for itself, without any direct Intention of using it. The Consideration of the small Addition often [*111*] made by Wealth to the Happiness of the Possessor, may check [112] this Desire, and prevent that *Insatiability* which sometimes attends it.

The Desire of Wealth and Power.

Power in like manner is desired as the Means of gratifying other *original Desires;* nor can the Desire be avoided by those who apprehend its usefulness. It is easy to prevent the *Extravagance* of this Desire, and many of its consequent Pains, by considering "the *Danger* of affecting it by injurious Means, supporting it by *Force,* without consent of the Subject, and employing it to *private Interest,* in opposition to publick Good." No Mortal is easy under such Subjection; every Slave to such a Power is an *Enemy:* The Possessor must be in a continual State of *Fear, Suspicion* and *Hatred.*

There is nothing in our Nature leading us necessarily into the *fantastick Desires;* they wholly arise thro' our *Ignorance* and *Negligence;* when, thro' want of Thought, we suffer foolish *Associations* of Ideas to be made, and imagine certain trifling Circumstances to contain something *honourable and excellent* in them, from their being used by Persons of *Distinction.* We know how the *Inadvertencies, Negligences, Infirmities,* and even *Vices,* either of great or ingenious Men, have been affected, [*112*] and imitated by those who were incapable of [113] imitating their Excellencies. This happens often to young Gentlemen of plentiful Fortunes, which set them above the Employments necessary to others, when they have not cultivated any relish for the Pleasures of the *Imagination,* such as *Architecture, Musick, Painting, Poetry, Natural Philosophy, History:* When they have no farther Knowledge of these things, than stupidly to praise what they hear others praise: When they have

The Occasion of fantastick Desires.

neglected to cultivate their *publick Affections,* are bantered a long time from *Marriage* and *Offspring;* and have neither themselves Minds fit for *Friendships,* nor any intimate Acquaintance with such as are fit to make Friends of: When their *moral Sense* is weakened, or, if it be strong in any points, these are fixed at random, without any *regular Scheme:* When thro' Ignorance of *publick Affairs,* or want of *Eloquence* to speak what they know, they despair of the *Esteem* or *Honour* of the Wise: When their Hearts are too gay to be entertained with the dull Thoughts of increasing their *Wealth,* and they have not Ability enough to hope for *Power;* such poor empty Minds have nothing but Trifles to pursue; any thing becomes agreeable, which can supply the Void of Thought, or prevent the sullen Discontent which must grow upon a Mind conscious of no *Merit,* and expecting [*113*] the *Contempt* of its Fellows; as a *Pack of Dogs,* [114] an *Horse,* a *Jewel,* an *Equipage,* a *Pack of Cards,* a *Tavern;* any thing which has got any confused Ideas of *Honour, Dignity, Liberality,* or *genteel Enjoyment of Life* joined to it. These fantastick Desires any Man might have banished at first, or entirely prevented. But if we have lost the *Time* of substituting better in their stead, we shall only change from one sort to another, with a perpetual Succession of *Inconstancy* and *Dissatisfaction.*

> —Cui si vitiosa Libido
> Fecerit Auspicium—
> Iidem eadem possunt horam durare probantes.—Hor. Ep. 1.³⁰

V. The End of all these Considerations, is to find out the most effectual way of advancing the Happiness of Mankind; in order to which, they may perhaps appear of considerable Consequence, since Happiness consists in "the highest and most durable Gratifications of, either all our *Desires,* or, if all cannot be gratify'd at once, of those which tend to the greatest and most durable *Pleasures,* with exemption either from

---

30. Horace, *Epistles,* I.1. This is an inversion of Horace's text, 85–86, "but if a morbid whim has given him the omen," followed by 82, "can the same person persist for one hour in liking the same things?"

all *Pains* and Objects of *Aversion,* or at least from those which are the most grievous." The following general Observations may be premised concerning their Objects.

5 [*114*/115] 1. "It is plainly impossible that any Man should pursue the Gratifications of all these *Desires* at once, with Prudence, Diligence, and Vigor, sufficient to obtain the highest Pleasures of each kind, and to avoid their opposite Pains." For, not to mention the *Narrowness* of the Powers of our Minds, which makes them incapable of a Multiplicity of 10 Pursuits at once; the very *Methods* of obtaining the highest Gratification of the several Senses and Desires, are directly inconsistent with each other. For example, the violent Pursuit of the Pleasures of the *external Senses,* or *Sensuality,* is opposite to the Pleasures of the *Imagination,* and to the Study of the ingenious *Arts,* which tend to the Ornament of Life: 15 These require Labour and Application, inconsistent with the *Voluptuousness* of the external Senses, which by itself would engross the whole Application of our Minds, thro' vain Associations of Ideas.

Again: The violent Pursuits of either of the former kinds of Pleasures, is often directly inconsistent with *publick Affections,* and with our 20 *moral Sense,* and *Sense of Honour.* These Pleasures require a quite different Temper, a Mind little set upon selfish Pleasures, strongly possessed with Love for [116] others, and Concern for their [*115*] Interests capable of Labour and Pain. However our desire of Honour be really *selfish,* yet we know it is never acquired by Actions appearing selfish; but by such 25 as appear publick-spirited, with neglect of the Pleasures of the external Senses and Wealth. *Selfishness* is generally attended with *Shame;** and hence we conceal even our *Desire of Honour* itself, and are ashamed of *Praise* in our own Presence, even when we are doing beneficent Actions, with design to obtain it. The Pursuits of *Wealth* and *Power* are often 30 directly opposite to the Pleasures of all the other kinds, at least for the present, however they may be intended for the future Enjoyment of them.

* *Treat.* II. *Sect.* 5. *Art.* 7.

The full Pursuit of all kinds of Pleasure is impossible.

No Certainty of Success in any Pursuit, save that of Virtue.

2. "There is no such *Certainty* in human Affairs, that a Man can assure himself of the perpetual Possession of these Objects which gratify any one Desire," except that of *Virtue* itself: which, since it does not depend upon external Objects and Events,* but upon our own *Affections* and *Conduct,* we may promise to our selves that we shall always enjoy. But then Virtue consists in Benevolence, or Desire of the publick Good: *The Happiness of others* is [117] very uncertain, so [*116*] that our publick Desires may often be disappointed; and every Disappointment is uneasy, in proportion to the Degree of Desire. And therefore, however the *Admiration* and fixed *Pursuit of Virtue* may always secure one stable and constant Pleasure of *Self-Approbation,* yet this Enjoyment presupposes a *Desire of publick Good,* subject to frequent Disappointments, which will be attended with Uneasiness proportioned to the Degree of publick Desire, or the *Virtue* upon which we reflect. There seems therefore no possibility of securing to our selves, in our present State, an *unmixed Happiness* independently of all other Beings. Every Apprehension of Good raises desire, every Disappointment of Desire is uneasy; every Object of Desire is uncertain except Virtue, but the *Enjoyment of Virtue* supposes the Desire of an uncertain Object, *viz.* the *publick Happiness.* To secure therefore independently of all other Beings invariable and pure Happiness, it would be necessary either to have the *Power* of directing all Events in the Universe, or to root out all *Sense of Evil,* or Aversion to it, while we retained our *Sense of Good,* but without previous Desire, the Dissappointment of which could give Pain. The *rooting out of all Senses and Desires,* were it practicable, would cut off all Happiness as well as Misery: The removing [118] or stopping a part of them, might indeed be [*117*] of consequence to the Happiness of the *Individual* on some occasions, however pernicious it might be to the *Whole.* But 'tis plain, we have not in our power the modelling of our *Senses or Desires,* to form them for a private Interest: They are fixed for us by the AUTHOR of our Nature, subservient to the Interest of the *System;* so that each Individual is made, previously to his own Choice, a Member

---

* *Treat.* II. *Sect.* 3. last Paragraph.

of a *great Body,* and affected with the Fortunes of the Whole, or at least of many Parts of it; nor can he break himself off at pleasure.

This may shew the Vanity of some of the lower rate of Philosophers of the *Stoick Sect,* in boasting of an undisturbed Happiness and Serenity, independently even of the DEITY, as well as of their Fellow-Creatures, wholly inconsistent with the *Order* of Nature, as well as with the Principles of some of their great Leaders: for which, Men of Wit in their own Age did not fail to ridicule them.

The Mistakes of the Stoicks about compleat Happiness.

That must be a very fantastick Scheme of Virtue, which represents it as a *private sublimely selfish Discipline,* to preserve our selves wholly unconcerned, not only in the [119] Changes of Fortune as to our *Wealth* or *Poverty, Liberty* or *Slavery, Ease* or *Pain,* but even in all *external Events* [*118*] whatsoever, in the Fortunes of our dearest *Friends* or *Country,* solacing ourselves that we are easy and undisturbed. If there be any thing amiable in human Nature, the Reflection upon which can give us pleasure, it must be kind *disinterested Affections* towards our Fellows, or towards the *whole,* and its AUTHOR and Cause. These Affections, when reflected upon, must be one constant Source of Pleasure in *Self-Approbation.* But some of these very Affections, being toward an uncertain Object, must occasion Pain, and directly produce one sort of Misery to the virtuous in this Life. 'Tis true indeed, it would be a much greater Misery to want such an amiable Temper, which alone secures us from the basest and most detestable State of *Self-Condemnation* and *Abhorrence.* But, allowing such a Temper to be the necessary Occasion of one sort of Happiness, even the greatest we are capable of, yet it may also be the Occasion of no inconsiderable Pains in this Life.

That this *affectionate Temper* is true Virtue, and not that *undisturbed Selfishness,* were it attainable, every one would readily own who saw them both in Practice. Would any honest Heart relish such a Speech [120] as this from a *Cato* or an *Aemilius Paulus?* "I foresee the Effects of this Defeat, my *Fellow-Creatures,* my *Countrymen,* my [*119*] honourable *Acquaintances;* many a generous gallant *Patriot* and *Friend, Fathers, Sons,* and *Brothers, Husbands* and *Wives,* shall be inslaved, tortured, torn from each other, or in each other's sight made subject to the *Pride, Av-*

arice, Petulancy, or *Lust* of the Conqueror. I have, for my *own Pleasure,* to secure agreeable *Reflections,* laboured in their Defence. I am unconcerned in their Misfortunes; their *bodily Tortures,* or more exquisite *Distresses of Mind* for each other, are to me indifferent. I am entirely absolute, compleat in myself; and can behold their Agonies with as much   5
Ease or Pleasure, as I did their Prosperity." This is the plain Language of some boasting *Refiners* upon Virtue; Sentiments as disagreeable as those of *Catiline.*

The Desire of Virtue is toward an Object ἐκ τῶν ἐφ᾽ ἡμῖν, or *in our power,* since all Men have naturally *kind Affections,* which they may in-   10
crease and strengthen; but these kind Affections tend toward an *uncertain Object,* which is not in our power. Suppose the *Stoick* should alledg, "Vice is the only Evil, and Virtue the only Good." If we have *Benevolence* to others, we must [121] wish them to be virtuous, and must have compassion toward the vicious: thus still we may be subjected to   15
Pain or Uneasiness, [*120*] by our *very Virtue;* unless we suppose, *what* no Experience can confirm, that Men may have strong Desires, the Disappointment of which will give no *Uneasiness,* or that Uneasiness is no Evil. Let the *Philosopher* regulate his own Notions as he pleases about Happiness or Misery; whoever imagines himself unhappy, is so in real-   20
ity; and whoever has *kind Affections* or Virtue, must be uneasy to see others really unhappy.

But tho a pure unmixed Happiness is not attainable in this Life, yet all their Precepts are not rendered useless.

Est quoddam prodire tenus, si non datur ultra.—Hor. Ep. 1[31]   25

3. The full
Sense of Good
may be pre-
served, with-
out the Pains
of Desire, in
many Cases.

3. For we may observe, thirdly, that "the *Sense of Good* can continue in its full Strength, when yet we shall have but *weak Desires.*" In this case we are capable of enjoying all the Good in any Object, when we obtain it, and yet exposed to no great Pain upon *Disappointment.* This may be   30
generally observed, that "the *Violence of Desire* does not proportionably enliven the Sensation of Good, when it is obtained; nor does *diminish-*

---

31. Horace, *Epistles,* I.32, "It is worthwhile to take a few steps forward, even if we may not go still further."

ing the Desire weaken the Sensation, tho it will diminish the [122] *Uneasiness of Disappointment,* or the *Misery of contrary Evils.*" Our high Expectations of Happiness from [*121*] any Object, either thro' the *Acuteness* of our Senses, or from our *Opinions* or *Associations* of Ideas, never fail to increase Desire: But then the *Violence of Desire* does not proportionably enliven our *Sensation* in the Enjoyment. During the first confused Hurry of our Success, our *Joy* may perhaps be increased by the Violence of our *previous Desire,* were it only by allaying the great Uneasiness accompanying the Desire itself. But this Joy soon vanishes, and is often succeeded by *Disgust* and *Uneasiness,* when our *Sense* of the Good, which is more fixed in Nature than our *Fancy* or *Opinions,* represents the Object far below our Expectation. Now he who examines all *Opinions* of Good in Objects, who prevents or corrects *vain Associations* of Ideas, and thereby prevents *extravagant Admirations,* or *enthusiastick Desires,* above the real Moment of Good in the Object, if he loses the *transient Raptures* of the first Success, yet he enjoys all the *permanent Good* or Happiness which any Object can afford; and escapes, in a great measure, both the uneasy Sensations of the more *violent Desires,* and the *Torments of Disappointment,* to which Persons of irregular Imaginations are exposed.

[123] This is the Case of the *Temperate* and the *Chaste,* with relation to the Appetites; of the Men of *Moderation* and *Frugality,* [*122*] and *corrected Fancy,* with regard to the Pleasures of *Imagination;* of the *Humble* and the *Content,* as to *Honour, Wealth* or *Power.* Such Persons upon good Success, want only the first *transitory Ecstacies;* but have a full and lively *Sense* of all the lasting Good in the Objects of their Pursuit; and yet are in a great measure secure against both the Uneasiness of *violent Desire,* and the *Dejection* of Mind, and *abject Sorrow* upon Disappointment, or upon their being exposed to the contrary Evils.

Further, Persons of *irregular Imaginations* are not soon reformed, nor their Associations of Ideas broke by every *Experience* of the Smallness of the Good in the admired Object. They are often rather set upon *new Pursuits* of the same kind, or of greater *Variety* of like Objects. So their experience of *Disappointment,* or of contrary Evils, does not soon correct their Imaginations about the Degrees of Good or Evil. The Loss of

Good, or the Pressure of any Calamity, will continue to torment them, thro' their *vain Notions* of these Events, and make them insensible of the real Good which they might still enjoy in their present [124] State. Thus the *Covetous* have smaller Pleasure in any given *Degree of Wealth;* the *Luxurious* from a *splendid Table;* the *Ambitious* from any given [*123*]   5 *Degree of Honour or Power,* than Men of more moderate Desires: And on the other hand, the Miseries of *Poverty, mean Fare, Subjection, or Contempt,* appear much greater to them, than to the moderate. Experience, while these confused Ideas remain, rather increases the Disorder: But if just *Reflection* comes in, and tho late, applies the proper Cure, by   10 correcting the *Opinions* and the *Imagination,* every Experience will tend to our Advantage.

The same way may our *publick Desires* be regulated. If we prevent confused Notions of Good, we diminish or remove many Anxieties for our *Friends* as well as our selves. Only this must be remembered, that   15 weakening our *publick Affections,* necessarily weakens our *Sense* of publick Good founded upon them, and will deprive us of the Pleasures of the *moral Sense,* in reflecting on our Virtue.

4. Laying our account to meet with Evil, often lessens our Misery.

4. We may lastly remark, "That the *Expectation* of any Pain, or the fre-   20 quent *Consideration* of the Evils which may befal us, or the Loss of Good we now enjoy, before these Events actually threaten [125] us, or raise any *Consternation* in our Minds by their Approach, does not diminish our *Joy* upon escaping Evil, or our *Pleasure* upon the arrival of any [*124*] Good beyond Expectation: But this previous Expectation   25 generally diminishes our *Fear,* while the Event is in suspence, and our *Sorrow* upon its arrival;" Since thereby the Mind examines the *Nature* of the Event, sees how far it is necessarily Evil, and what Supports under it are in its power: This *Consideration* may break vain Conjunctions of foreign Ideas, which occasion our greatest Fears in Life, and even in   30 Death itself. If, indeed, a *weak Mind* does not study to correct the *Imagination,* but still dwells upon its possible Calamities, under all their *borrowed Forms* of Terror; or if it industriously aggravates them to itself, this previous Consideration may embitter its whole Life, without arming it against the smallest Evil.   35

This Folly is often occasioned by that Delight which most Men find in the *Pity of others* under Misfortunes; those especially, who are continually indulged as the *Favourites of Families* or *Company,* being long enured to the Pleasure arising from the perpetual *Marks of Love* toward them from all their Company, and from their tender *Sympathy* in Distress: this often leads them even to *feign Misery* to obtain Pity, [126] and to raise in themselves the most dejected Thoughts, either to procure *Consolation,* or the Pleasure of observing the *Sympathy* of others. This *peevish* or *pettish* [125] *Temper,* tho it arises from something sociable in our Frame, yet is often the Fore-runner of the greatest Corruption of Mind. It disarms the Heart of its natural *Integrity;* it induces us to throw away our true *Armour,* our *natural Courage,* and cowardly to commit our selves to the vain Protection of others, while we neglect our own Defence.

SECTION V

A Comparison of the Pleasures and Pains of the several Senses, as to Intenseness and Duration.

[*126/*127] I. Having considered how far these Desires must necessarily affect us, and when they are the Occasions of Pleasure or Pain; since by the first general *Observation,* the Pursuits of their several Pleasures, and the avoiding their several Pains, may often be inconsistent with each other; let us next examine, which of these several Pleasures are *the most valuable,* so as to deserve our Pursuit, even with neglect of the others; and which of these Pains are *most grievous,* so as to be shunned even by the enduring of other Pains if necessary.

"The *Value* of any Pleasure, and the *Quantity* or *Moment* of any Pain, is in a compounded Proportion of the *Intenseness* and *Duration.*" In examining the Duration of Pleasure, we must include not only the Constancy of the *Object,* but even of our *Fancy;* for a Change in either of these will put an end to it.

The difficulty
in comparing
the several
Pleasures, as
to Intenseness.

[*127*/128] To compare these several Pleasures and Pains as to their *Intenseness*, seems difficult, because of the Diversity of *Tastes,* or *Turns of Temper* given by *Custom* and *Education,* which make strange *Associations of Ideas,* and form *Habits;* from whence it happens, that, tho all the several kinds of original Senses and Desires seem equally natural, yet some are led into a constant Pursuit of the Pleasures of one kind, as the only Enjoyment of Life, and are indifferent about others. Some pursue, or seem to pursue only the Pleasures of the *external Senses,* and all other Pursuits are made subservient to them: Others are chiefly set upon the Pleasures of *Imagination* or *internal Senses; social* and *kind Affections* employ another sort, who seem indifferent to all private Pleasure: This last Temper has generally joined with it an high *moral Sense,* and *Love of Honour.* We may sometimes find an high *Sense of Honour* and desire of *Applause,* where there is indeed a *moral Sense,* but a very weak one, very much perverted, so as to be influenced by *popular Opinion,* and made subservient to it: In this *Character* the Pleasures of the external Senses, or even of the Imagination, have little room, except so far as they may produce *Distinction.* Now upon comparing the several Pleasures, perhaps the Sentence of the *Luxurious* [129] would be quite opposite [*128*] to that of the *Virtuous.* The *Ambitious* would differ from both. Those who are devoted to the *internal Senses* or *Imagination,* would differ from all the three. The *Miser* would applaud himself in his Wealth above them all. Is there therefore no disputing about Tastes? Are all Persons alike happy, who obtain the several Enjoyments for which they have a Relish? If they are, the Dispute is at an end: A Fly or Maggot in its proper haunts, is as happy as a *Hero,* or *Patriot,* or *Friend,* who has newly delivered his *Country* or *Friend,* and is surrounded with their grateful *Praises.* The *Fly* or *Maggot* may think so of itself; but who will stand to its Judgment, when we are sure that it has experienced only one sort of Pleasure, and is a stranger to the others? May we not in like manner find some Reasons of *appealing* from the Judgment of certain Men? Or may not some *Characters* be found among Men, who alone are capable of judging in this matter?

II. It is obvious that "those alone are capable of judging, who have experienced all the several *kinds of Pleasure,* and have their *Senses* acute and fully exercised in them all." Now a high Relish for *Virtue,* or a strong *moral Sense,* with [130] its concomitant *publick Sense and Affec-*
5 *tions,* and a *Sense of Honour,* was never alledged to impair our *external Senses,* or [129] to make us incapable of any pleasure of the *Imagination; Temperance* never spoiled a *good Palate,* whatever *Luxury* may have done; a generous affectionate publick Spirit, reflecting on itself with delight, never vitiated any Organ of *external Pleasure,* nor weakened their
10 Perceptions. Now all virtuous Men have given *Virtue* this Testimony, that its Pleasures are superior to any other, nay to all others jointly; that a friendly generous *Action* gives a *Delight* superior to any other; that other Enjoyments, when compared with the Delights of *Integrity, Faith, Kindness, Generosity,* and *publick Spirit,* are but trifles scarce worth any
15 regard.*

The Pleasures of a moral Kind proved superior, by the Testimony of the Virtuous.

Nay, we need not confine our Evidence to the Testimony of the *perfectly Virtuous.* The *vicious Man,* tho no fit judge, were he entirely aban-doned, since he loses his *Sense* of the Pleasures of the *moral Kind,* or at
20 least has not experienced them fully, yet he generally retains so much of human Nature, and of the *Senses* and *Affections* of our [131] Kind, as sometimes to experience even *moral Pleasures.* There is scarce any Mortal, who is wholly insensible to all *Species of Morality.*

By the Testimony of the Vicious.

[130] A Luxurious *Debauchee* has never perhaps felt the *Pleasures* of a
25 wise publick-spirited Conduct, of an entirely upright, generous, social,

*See this Argument in *Plato de Repub.* Lib. IX. And Lord *Shaftesbury's* Inquiry concerning Virtue.
[[Plato, *Republic* 586d–e. Plato's argument in this passage concerns the superiority of the pleasures of the highest part of the soul. "How much the social pleasures
30 are superior to any other may be known by visible tokens and effects. . . . But more particularly still may this superiority be known from the actual prevalence and ascendancy of this sort of affection over all besides. . . . No joy, merely of sense, can be a match for it," Shaftesbury, "Inquiry Concerning Virtue," II.2.1. (*Characteristicks,* II.59)]]

and affectionate Life, with the Sense of his own *moral Worth,* and mer-
ited *Esteem* and *Love;* this course of Life, because unknown to him, he
may despise in comparison of his *Pleasures.* But if in any particular Affair, a *moral Species,* or *Point of Honour* has affected him, he will soon
despise his sensual Pleasures in comparison of the Moral. Has he a Per-   5
son whom he calls his *Friend,* whom he loves upon whatever fantastick
Reasons, he can quit his *Debauch* to serve him, nay can run the Hazard
of *Wounds* and *Death* to rescue him from Danger? If his *Honour* be concerned to resent an *Affront,* will he not quit his Pleasures, and run the
hazard of the greatest bodily Pain, to shun the Imputation of *Cowardice*   10
or *Falshood?* He will scorn one who tells him, that "a *Lyar,* or a *Coward,*
may be happy enough, while he has all things necessary to *Luxury.*" 'Tis
in vain to alledge, "that there is no disputing about *Tastes:*" To every
Nature there are certain *Tastes* assigned by the great AUTHOR [132] of
all. To the *human Race* there are assigned a *publick Taste,* a *moral one,*   15
and a *Taste for Honour.* These Senses they cannot extirpate, more than
their *external Senses:* [131] They may pervert them, and weaken them by
false *Opinions,* and foolish *Associations* of Ideas; but they cannot be
happy but by keeping them in their natural State, and gratifying them.
The Happiness of an *Insect* or *Brute,* will only make an *Insect* or *Brute*   20
happy. But a Nature with further *Powers,* must have further *Enjoyments.*

Nay, let us consider the different *Ages* in our own Species. We once
knew the time when an *Hobby-Horse,* a *Top,* a *Rattle,* was sufficient
Pleasure to us. We grow up, we now relish *Friendships, Honour, good
Offices, Marriage, Offspring, serving a Community or Country.* Is there no   25
difference in these Tastes? We were happy before, are we no happier
now? If not, we have made a foolish Change of Fancy. An Hobby-
Horse is more easily procured than an *Employment;* a Rattle kept in order with less trouble than a *Friend;* a Top than a *Son.* But this Change
of Fancy does not depend upon our *Will.* "Our Nature determines us   30
to certain Pursuits in our several Stages; and following her Dictates, is
the only way to our Happiness. Two States may both be [133] happy,
and yet the one infinitely preferable to the other: Two Species may both
be *content,* and yet the Pleasures of the one, greater beyond all comparison, than those of the other." The *virtuous Man,* who has [132] as true   35

a Sense of all external Pleasure as any, gives the preference to *moral Plea-sures*. The Judgment of the *Vicious* is either not to be regarded, because of his Ignorance on one side; or, if he has experience of *moral Sentiments* in any particular Cases, he agrees with the *Virtuous*.

III. Again, we see in fact, that in the virtuous Man, *publick Affections*, a *moral Sense*, and *Sense of Honour*, actually overcome all other Desires or Senses, even in their full Strength. Here there is the fairest Combate, and the Success is on the side of Virtue.

Experience proves the same.

There is indeed an obvious Exception against this Argument. "Do not we see, in many Instances, the *external Senses* overcome the *moral?*" But the Reply is easy. A constant Pursuit of the Pleasures of the external Senses can never become agreeable, without an Opinion of *Innocence*, or the *Absence* of moral Evil; so that here the moral Sense is not engaged in the Combat. [134] Do not our* luxurious Debauchees, among their Intimates, continually defend their Practices as *innocent?* Transient Acts of Injustice may be done, contrary to the moral Sentiments of the [*133*] Agent, to obtain relief from some pressing Evil, or upon some violent Motion of *Appetite;* and yet even in these cases, Men often argue them-selves into some *moral Notions* of their *Innocence*. But for a continued Course of Life disapproved by the Agent, how few are the Instances? How avowedly miserable is that State, wherein all *Self-Approbation*, all *consciousness of Merit or Goodness* is gone? We might here also alledge, what universal Experience confirms, "that not only an Opinion of *In-nocence* is a necessary Ingredient in a Course of *selfish Pleasures*, so that there should be no Opposition from the moral Sense of the Agent; but that some *publick Affections*, some *Species of moral Good*, is the most powerful *Charm* in all sensual Enjoyments." And yet, on the other hand, "*Publick Affections, Virtue, Honour*, need no Species of sensual Pleasure to recommend them; nor even an Opinion or Hope of Ex-emption from external Pain. These powerful Forms can appear amia-ble, and engage our Pursuit thro' the rugged [135] Paths of *Hunger, Thirst, Cold, Labour, Expences, Wounds and Death*."

* *Treat.* II. *Sect.* 4. *Art.* 4. last Paragraph.

Thus, when a Prospect of external Pleasure, or of avoiding bodily Pain, engages Men into Actions really evil, the *moral Sense* of the Agent is not really overcome [*134*] by the *external Senses.* The Action or Omission does not appear morally evil to the Agent. The *Temptation* seems to extenuate, or wholly excuse the Action. Whereas when a *Point of* 5 *Honour,* or a *moral Species,* makes any one despise the Pleasures or Pains of the *external Senses,* there can be no question made of a real Victory. The external Senses represent these Objects in the same manner, when they are conquered. None denies to the Virtuous their *Sense of Pain, Toil or Wounds.* They are allowed as lively a Sense as others, of all *exter-* 10 *nal Pleasure* of every kind. The Expences of *Generosity, Humanity, Charity* and *Compassion* are allowed, even when yielded to Virtue, to be known to the full. But the moral Sense, weak as it often is, does not yield even to known *external Pleasure, Ease or Advantage:* but, where there is a depraved *Taste,* and a weak *Understanding,* private Advantage, 15 or the avoiding of some external Evil, may make Actions appear *inno-cent,* which are not; and then the moral Sense gives no Opposition. All the Conquest [136] on such Occasions is only this, that private external *Advantage* surmounts our Aversion to *Dishonour,* by making us do Actions which *others* will censure, but we esteem *innocent.* In these Cases 20 we generally fear only the Reproach of a *Party,* [*135*] of whom we have conceived an unfavourable Opinion.*

Nay farther: It was before observed, that "fantastick *Associations* of Ideas do not really increase the Pleasure of *Enjoyment,* however they increase the previous *Desire.* The want of such Associations does not abate 25 the external *Pain,* tho it diminishes the previous *Fear,* or takes away some farther *Fears* which may attend the Pain." So that a Man of the most correct Imagination does feel and know all the *Good* in external Pleasure, and all the *Evil* in Pain. "When therefore the *moral Sense,* and *publick Affections,* overcome all *sensual Pleasure,* or *bodily Pain,* they do 30 it by their own Strength, without *foreign Aids. Virtue* is never blended with *bodily Pleasure,* nor *Vice* with *bodily Pain* in our Imaginations. But

* *Sect.* 4. *Art.* 3.

when the external Senses seem to prevail against the moral Sense, or publick Affections, it is continually by *Aid* borrowed from the *moral* [137] *Sense, and publick Affections* themselves, or from our Sense of Honour." The Conquest is over a weakned moral Sense, upon partial views of Good, not by external Pleasure alone, but [*136*] by some *moral Species,* raised by a false Imagination.

Set before Men in the clearest Light all external Pleasures, but strip them of their borrowed Notions of *Dignity, Hospitality, Friendship, Generosity, Liberality, Communication of Pleasure;* let no regard be had to the *Opinions* of others, to *Credit,* to avoiding *Reproach,* to *Company:* Separate from the Pursuit of Wealth all Thoughts of a *Family, Friends, Relations, Acquaintance;* let Wealth be only regarded as the Means of private Pleasure of the *external Senses,* or of the *Imagination,* to the Possessor alone; let us divide our confused Ideas,* and consider things barely and apart from each other: and in opposition to these Desires, set but the weakest *moral Species,* and see if they can prevail over it. On the other hand, let us examine as much as we please, a *friendly, generous, grateful, or publick spirited Action;* divest it of all external Pleasure, still

* See *Marcus Antoninus,* Lib. III. c. II. and often elsewhere.
[[This footnote was added in the third edition. In his edition of *Aurelius,* Hutcheson renders the passage: "This also should be observed, that such things as ensue upon what is well constituted by nature, have also something graceful and attractive. Thus, some parts of a well baked loaf will crack and become rugged. What is thus cleft beyond the design of the baker, looks well, and invites the appetite. So when figs are at the ripest, they begin to crack. Thus in full ripe olives, their approach to putrefication gives the proper beauty to the fruit. Thus, the laden'd ear of corn hanging down, the stern brow of the lyon, and the foam flowing from the mouth of the wild boar, and many other things, considered apart, have nothing comely; yet because of their connexion with things natural, they adorn them, and delight the spectator. Thus, to one who has a deep affection of soul, and penetration into the constitution of the whole, scarce any thing connected with nature will fail to recommend itself agreeably to him. Thus, the real vast jaws of savage beasts will please him, no less than the imitations of them by painters or statuaries. With like pleasure will his chaste eyes behold the maturity and grace of old age in man or woman, and the inviting charms of youth. Many such things will he experience, not credible to all, but only those who have the genuine affection of soul toward nature and its works," James Moor and Francis Hutcheson (trans.), *The Meditations of the Emperor Marcus Aurelius Antoninus,* 76–77.]]

it will appear the more lovely; the longer we fix our Attention [138] to it, the more we admire it. What is it which we feel in our own Hearts, determining as it were our Fate as to Happiness or Misery? What sort of Sensations are the most lively and delightful? In what sort of Possessions does the highest Joy and Self-Satisfaction consist? Who has ever felt the Pleasure of a generous [137] friendly *Temper*, of *mutual Love*, of *compassionate Relief and Succour* to the distressed; of having *served a Community*, and render'd Multitudes happy; of a strict *Integrity*, and *thorow Honesty*, even under external Disadvantages, and amidst Dangers; of Congratulation and publick Rejoycing, in the Wisdom and Prosperity of Persons beloved, such as Friends, Children, or intimate Neighbours? Who would not, upon Reflection, prefer that *State of Mind*, these *Sensations of Pleasure*, to all the Enjoyments of the *external Senses*, and of the *Imagination* without them?*

Our Judgments in the Case of others proves the same. IV. The truth, in a Question of this nature, one might expect would be best known by the Judgment of *Spectators*, concerning the Pursuits of others. Let them see one entirely employed in Solitude, with the most exquisite Tastes, Odors, [139] Prospects, Painting, Musick; but without any *Society*, *Love* or *Friendship*, or any Opportunity of doing a kind or generous *Action;* and see also a† Man employed in protecting the Poor and Fatherless, receiving the Blessings of those who were ready to perish, and making the Widow to sing for [138] Joy; a Father to the Needy, an Avenger of Oppression; who never despised the Cause of his very Slave, but considered him as his Fellow-Creature, formed by the same Hand; who never eat his Morsel alone, without the Orphan at his Ta-

---

* See this Subject fully treated, in the second Part of Lord *Shaftesbury's Inquiry concerning Virtue.*

† See the Character of *Job*, Ch. xxxi. See also *Treat.* II. *Sect.* 6.

[[The general tenor of the passage from Job emphasizes the blameworthiness of those who act wickedly towards their communities. It concludes: "If my land has cried out against me, and its furrows have wept together; if I have eaten its yield without payment, and caused the death of its owners; let thorns grow instead of wheat, and foul weeds instead of barley'" (*The Holy Bible: New Revised Standard Version* (Oxford: Oxford University Press, 1989), 527).]]

ble, nor caused the Eyes of the Poor to fail; who never suffered the Naked to perish, but warmed them with the Fleece of his Sheep; who never took advantage of the Indigent in Judgment, thro' Confidence in his own Power or Interest; Let this Character be compared with the former; nay, add to this latter some considerable *Pains* of the *external Senses,* with *Labour* and kind *Anxiety:* which of the two would a Spectator chuse? Which would he admire, or count the happier, and most suitable to human Nature? Were he given to *Castle-building,* or were he advising a *Son,* or a *Friend,* which of these States would he chuse or recommend? Such a Trial would [140] soon discover the Prevalence of the *moral Species* above all Enjoyments of Life.

V. There are a sort of Pleasures opposite to those of the publick Sense, arising from the Gratification of *Anger* or *Hatred.* To compare these Pleasures with those of Benevolence, we must observe what holds universally of all Mankind. The Joy, and Gaiety, and Happiness of any Nature, of which we have formed no previous Opinion, [139] either favourable or unfavourable, nor obtained any other Ideas than merely that it is *sensitive,* fills us with Joy and Delight: The apprehending the Torments of any such sensitive Nature, gives us Pain. The Poets know how to raise delight in us by such *pastoral Scenes,* they feel the Power of such *pleasing Images:* they know that the human Heart can dwell upon such Contemplations with *delight;* that we can continue long with Pleasure, in the View of *Happiness* of any Nature whatsoever. When we have received unfavourable Apprehensions of any Nature, as *cruel* and *savage,* we begin indeed from our very publick Affections, to desire their Misery as far as it may be necessary to the Protection of others.

But that the Misery of another, for its *own sake,* is never grateful, we may all find by making this Supposition: "That had we the [141] most savage Tyger, or Crocodile, or some greater Monster of our own Kind, a *Nero,* or *Domitian,* chained in some Dungeon; that we were perfectly assured they should never have power of doing farther *Injuries;* that no Mortal should ever know their Fate or Fortunes, nor be influenced by them; that the *Punishments* inflicted on them would never restrain others by way of example, nor any *Indulgence* shown be discovered; [140]

Little Happiness in malicious Pleasures.

that the first Heat of our *Resentment* were allayed by Time"—No Mortal, in such a Case, would incline to torture such wretched Natures, or keep them in continual Agonies, without some prospect of *Good* arising from their Sufferings. What farther would the fiercest Rage extend to, if once the Tyrant, thus eternally confined from Mischief, began himself to feel *Remorse* and *Anguish* for his Crimes? Nay, did he continue without Reflection on his past Life, so as neither to betray Remorse nor Approbation, were Mankind well secured against his Temper, who would delight to load him with *useless Misery?*

If the Misery of others then be not grateful for itself, whence arises the Pleasure of *Cruelty* and *Revenge?* The Reason is plainly this: Upon apprehending *Injury* to our selves or others, NATURE wisely determines [142] us to study *Defense,* not only for the present, but for the future. *Anger* arises with its most *uneasy Sensations,* as every one acknowledges. *The Misery* of the Injurious allays this furious Pain. Our Nature scarce leads to any farther Resentment, when once the Injurious seems to us fully seized with *Remorse,* so that we fear no farther Evils from him, or when all his Power is gone. Those who continue their *Revenge* further, are prepossessed with [*141*] some *false Opinion* of Mankind, as worse than they really are; and are not easily inclined to believe their hearty Remorse for Injuries, or to think themselves secure. Some *Point of Honour,* or *Fear* of Reproach, engages Men in cruel Acts of Revenge: But this farther confirms, that the *Misery of another* is only grateful as it allays, or secures us against a furious Pain; and cannot be the Occasion, by itself, of any Satisfaction. Who would not prefer *Absence of Injury* to *Injury revenged?* Who would not chuse an untainted *Reputation, for Courage* gained in a just War, in which, without *Hatred* or *Anger,* we acted from Love of our Country, rather than the Fame acquired by asserting our questioned Courage with furious *Anger* in a *Duel,* and with continued *Hatred* toward the Person conquered? Who can dwell upon a *Scene of Tortures,* tho practis'd upon the vilest Wretch; or can delight either [143] in the Sight or Description of *Vengeance,* prolonged beyond all necessity of *Self-Defense,* or *publick Interest?* "The Pleasure of Revenge then is to the Pleasures of Humanity and Virtue, as the flaking the burning, and constantly recurring Thirst of a Fever, to the natural Enjoyments of grateful Food in Health."

VI. Were we to compare, in like manner, the *Pains* of the publick and moral Sense, and of the Sense of Honour, with [*142*] other *Pains of the external Senses,* or with the greatest external Losses, we should find the former by far superior. And yet nothing is more ordinary, than to find Men, who will allow "the *Pleasures* of the former Classes superior to any other, and yet look upon *external Pain* as more intollerable than any." There are two Reasons for this Mistake. 1. "They compare the most *acute Pains* of the external Senses with some *smaller Pains* of the other Senses." Whereas, would they compare the strongest of both Kinds, they would find the Ballance on the other side. How often have Parents, Husbands, Friends, Patriots, endured the greatest *bodily Pains,* to avoid the Pains of their *publick* and *moral Sense,* and *Sense of Honour?* How do they every day suffer Hunger, Thirst, and Toil, to prevent like Evils to those they love? [*144*] How often do Men endure, for their *Party* or *Faction,* the greatest external Evils, not only when they are un avoidable, but, when by counter-acting their *publick* or *moral Sense,* or *Sense of Honour,* they could extricate themselves? Some Crimes appear so horrid, some Actions so cruel and detestable, that there is hardly any Man but would rather suffer *Death,* than be conscious of having done them.

[*143*] The second Cause of Mistake in this Matter, is this, "The avoiding moral Evil by the Sufferance of *external Pain,* does not diminish the *Sense* of the Pain; but on the other hand, the *Motive* of avoiding grievous Pain, really diminishes the *moral Evil* in the Action done with that design." So that in such Instances we compare *external Pain* in its full strength, with a *moral Pain* of the lighter sort, thus alleviated by the Greatness of the *Temptation.** To make a just Comparison, it should be thus: "Whether would a Man chuse to be tortured to Death, or to have,

Moral Evil compared with other Evils, appears greater. Causes of Mistake.

* *Treat.* II. *Sect.* 7, 9. *Cor.* 3.
[[The reference is incorrect. The proper reference is to T2 VII.7 Cor. 3. See n 11.]]

without any *Temptation* or *Necessity,* tortured another, or a dear Friend, or Child to Death?" Not whether a Man will betray his Friend or Country, for fear of Tortures, but "whether it be better voluntarily, and under no fear, to betray a Friend, or our Country, than to suffer [145] Tortures, or the Pain of the Gout or Stone equal to Tortures?" Upon such Comparisons as these, we should find some other Pains and Misery superior to any *external Pain.* When we judge of the *State of others,* we would not be long in suspense which of these Evils to [*144*] chuse as the lightest for those whom we* most regarded.

Publick Affections compared with our Desire of Virtue. VII. We have hitherto only compared on the one side the *publick and moral Sense,* and the *Sense of Honour* jointly, with the *external Senses,* the *Pleasures of Imagination,* and *external Advantage* or *Disadvantage* jointly. The reason of joining them thus must be obvious, since, to a Mind not prepossessed with any *false Apprehensions* of things, the former three Senses and Desires really concur, in exciting to the same Course of Action; for promoting the publick Good, can never be opposite to *private Virtue;* nor can the *Desire of Virtue* ever lead to any thing pernicious to the Publick: Had Men also true Opinions, *Honour* could only be obtained by *Virtue,* or serving the Publick.

But since there may be some *corrupt partial Notions of Virtue,* as when Men have inadvertently engaged themselves into [146] some Party or Faction pernicious to the Publick, or when we mistake the *Tendencies* of Actions, or have some Notions of the DEITY,† as requiring

---

* *Treat.* II. *Sect.* 6. *Art.* 1.

† Such mistaken Notions of Religion, and of some particular moral Species, have produced these monstrous Decisions or Apothegms; viz. "*Some Actions are not lawful, tho they were necessary not only to universal temporal Happiness, but to the eternal Salvation of the whole World, or to avoid universal eternal Misery.*"

"*Fiat Justitia & ruat Caelum.*"

Whereas the only Reason why some Actions are looked upon as universally and necessarily Evil, is only this, "that in our present Constitution of Nature, they cannot possibly produce any *good,* prepollent to their *evil Consequences.*" Whatever

some Actions [*145*] apprehended pernicious to the publick, as *Duties* to himself; in such cases there is room to compare our *publick Sense or Desires* with our *moral*, to see which is prevalent. The Pleasures of these Senses, in such cases, need not be compared; the following either the one or the other will give little Pleasure: The Pain of the counteracted *Sense* will prevent all *Satisfaction*. This State is truly deplorable, when a Person is thus distracted between two noble Principles, his *publick Affections*, and *Sense of Virtue*. But it may be inquired, which of these Senses, when counteracted, would occasion the *greater Pain?* Perhaps nothing [147] can be answered *universally* on either side. With Men of *recluse contemplative Lives*, who have dwelt much upon some *moral Ideas*, but without large *extensive View* of publick Good, or without engaging themselves to the full in the *publick* [*146*] *Affections*, and common *Affairs of Life:* The *Sense of Virtue*, in some partial confined View of it, would probably prevail; especially since these partial Species of Virtue have always some sort of *kind Affection* to assist them. With *active Men*, who have fully exercised their *publick Affections*, and have acquired as it were an *Habit* this way, 'tis probable the *publick Affections* would be prevalent. Thus we find that active Men, upon any *publick Necessity*, do always break thro' the *limited narrow Rules* of Virtue or Justice, which are publickly received, even when they have scarce any *Scheme of Principles* to justify their Conduct: Perhaps, indeed, in such cases, their *moral Sense* is brought over to the Side of their *Affections*, tho their *speculative Opinions* are opposite to both.

Action would do so, in the *whole of its Effects* must necessarily be *good*. This Proposition is *Identick*.

[[The phrase means, "Do what is right even if it brings down the heavens." It apparently has no classical sources but was a common legal expression. Martin Luther had a well-known variant in his Second Sermon on Psalm 110 (37, 138, 7): "Fiat justitia et pereat mundus." Although Hutcheson is condemning the quotation as fanatical and inhumane, and associating it with an extremist Augustineanism, the quotation has become synonymous with doing what is right whatever the cost as opposed to what is politic.]]

The Moral Sense compared with the Sense of Honour.

VIII. It is of more consequence to compare the *publick and moral Senses,* in opposition to the *Sense of Honour.* Here there may be direct Opposition, since Honour is conferred according to the moral Notions [148] of those who confer it, which may be contrary to those of the *Agent,* and contrary to what he thinks conducive to the publick Good.

To allow the Prevalence of *Honour,* cannot with any Person of just Reflection, [*147*] weaken the Cause of Virtue, since Honour presupposes* a *moral Sense,* both in those who desire it, and those who confer it. But it is enough for some *Writers,* who affect to be wondrous shrewd in their Observations on human Nature, and fond of making all the World, as well as themselves, *a selfish Generation,* incapable of any real *Excellence* or *Virtue,* without any *natural Disposition* toward a *publick Interest,* or toward any *moral Species;* to get but a "Set of different *Words* from those commonly used, yet including the same *natural Dispositions,*† or presupposing them," however an inadvertent Reader may not observe it; and they are sufficiently furnished to shew, that there is no real *Virtue,* that all is but *Hyppocrisy, Disguise, Art,* or *Interest.* "To be *honoured, highly esteemed, valued, praised,* or on the contrary, to be *despised, undervalued, censured* or *condemned;* to be *proud* or *ashamed,* are Words without any meaning, if we take away a *moral* [149] *Sense.*" Let this Sense be as *capricious, inconstant, different* in different Persons as they please to alledge, "a *Sense of Morality* there must be, and *natural* it must be, if the *Desire of Esteem, Pride* or *Shame* be natural."

[*148*] To make this comparison between the *publick* and *moral* Senses on the one hand, and that of *Honour* on the other, 'tis to be observed, that all *Aversion to Evil* is stronger than *Desire of positive Good.* There are many sorts of positive Good, without which any one may be easy, and enjoy others of a different kind: But Evil of almost any *kind,* in a high Degree, may make Life intolerable. The *avoiding of Evil* is

---

*See *Treat.* II. *Sect.* 5. *Art.* 4.
† Ibid.

always allowed a more extenuating Circumstance in a *Crime,* than the *Prospect of positive Good:* to make therefore just Comparisons of the Prevalence of several Desires or Senses, their several *Goods* should be opposed to each other, and their *Evils* to each other, and not the *Pleasures* of one compared with the *Pains* of another.

Publick *Affections,* in their nearer Ties, frequently overcome not only the Pleasures of *Honour,* but even the *Pains of Shame.* This is the most common Event in Life, [150] that for some apprehended Interest of *Offspring, Families, Friends,* Men should neglect Opportunities of gaining *Honour,* and even incur *Shame* and *Contempt.* In Actions done for the Service of a *Party,* there can be no comparison, for *Honour* is often a Motive on both sides.

[*149*] 'Tis also certain, that the *Fear of Shame,* in some Instances, will overcome all other Desires whatsoever, even *natural Affection,* Love of *Pleasure, Virtue, Wealth,* and even of *Life* itself. This Fear has excited Parents to the Murder of their Offspring; has persuaded Men to the most dangerous Enterprizes; to squander away their *Fortunes,* to counteract their *Duty,* and even to throw away their *Lives,* The Distraction and Convulsion of Mind observable in these *Conflicts* of Honour, with Virtue and publick Affection, shews how *unnatural* that State is, wherein the strongest *Principles of Action,* naturally designed to co-operate and assist each other, are thus set in Opposition.

'Tis perhaps impossible to pronounce any thing universally concerning the Superiority of the Desire of *Honour* on the one hand, or that of the Desire of *Virtue* and *publick Good* on the other. *Habits* or [151] *Custom* may perhaps determine the Victory on either side. Men in high Stations, who have long indulged the Desire of *Honour,* and have formed the most frightful Apprehensions of *Contempt* as the worst of Evils; or even those in lower Stations, who have been long enured to value *Reputation* in any particular, and dread *Dishonour* in that point, may have *Fear of Shame* superior [*150*] to all Aversions. Men, on the contrary, who have much indulged *good Nature,* or reflected much upon the Excellency of *Virtue* itself, abstracted from *Honour,* may find Affections of this kind prevalent above the Fear of Shame.

To compare the *moral Sense* with the Sense of *Honour,* we must find cases where the Agent condemns an Action with all its present Circumstances as evil, and yet fears *Infamy* by omitting it, without any unequal Motives of other kinds on either side: Or when one may obtain *Praise* by an Action, when yet the Omission of it would appear to himself as considerable a Virtue, as the *Praise* to be expected from the Action would represent the Action to be. The common Instances, in which some, who pretend deep Knowledge of *human Nature,* triumph much, have not these necessary Circumstances. When a Man condemns *Duelling* in his private Sentiments, and yet practices it, we have indeed a considerable [152] Evidence of the Strength of this *Desire of Honour,* or *Aversion to Shame,* since it surpasses the Fear of Death. But here on one hand, besides the *Fear of Shame,* there is the *Fear of constant Insults,* of losing all the *Advantages* depending upon the Character of Courage, and sometimes even some *Species of Virtue* and *publick Good,* in restraining an insolent [*151*] Villain: On the other hand is the *Fear of Death.* The *moral Sense* is seldom much concerned: for however Men may condemn *voluntary Duelling;* however they may blame the *Age* for the Custom, or censure the *Laws* as defective, yet generally, in their present Case, Duelling appears a necessary Piece of *Self-Defence* against opprobrious Injuries and Affronts, for which the Law has provided no Redress, and consequently leaves Men to the natural Rights *of Self-Defence* and *Prosecution of Injuries.* The Case seems to them the same with that of *Thieves* and *Night-Robbers,* who may be put to Death by private Persons, when there is no hope of overtaking them by Law. These are certainly the Notions of those who condemn *Duelling,* and yet practise it.

It is foreign to our present Purpose, to detect the Fallacy of these Arguments, in defence of *Duels,* as they are commonly practiced among us; when Men from a [153] sudden Anger, upon some trifling or imaginary *Affronts* the despising of which would appear honourable in every wise Man's Eyes, expose themselves, and often their dearest Friends to Death, and hazard the Ruin of their own Families, as well as that of their Adversary; tho the *Success* in such Attempts can have no tendency

Duels no proper Instances.

to justify them [152] against the dishonourable *Charge,* or to procure any Honour from Men of worth.

The magnified Instance of *Lucretia** is yet less to our purpose. Some talk, as if "she indeed would rather have died than consented to the Crime; but the *Crime* did not appear so great an Evil as the *Dishonour;* to the Guilt she submitted to avoid the Shame." Let us consider this renowned Argument. Was there then no Motive on either side, but *Fear of Shame,* and a *Sense of Duty?* If we look into the Story, we shall find, that to persuade her to consent, there conspired, beside the *Fear of Shame,* and of *Death,* which she little regarded, the Hope of *noble Revenge,* or rather of *Justice* on the Ravisher, and the whole Tyrant's Family; nay, the Hopes of a [154] *nobler Fame* by her future Conduct; the *Fear* of suffering that contumely by *force,* which she was tempted to consent to, and that in such a manner as she could have had no Redress. All these Considerations concurred to make her consent. On the other side, there was only the *moral Sense* of a Crime thus extenuated by the most grievous *Necessity,* and by hopes of *doing Justice* to her Husband's Honour, and *rescuing her Country:* Nay, [153] could she not have at once saved her *Character* and her *Life* by consenting; when in that virtuous Age she might have expected *Secrecy* in the Prince, since boasting of such Attempts would have been dangerous to the greatest Man in *Rome?*

It is not easy to find just Room for a Comparison even in fictitious Cases, between these two *Principles.* Were there a Person who had no Belief of any DEITY, or of any reality in *Religion,* in a Country where his *secular Interest* would not suffer by a Character of *Atheism;* and yet

*Livy, *Lib.* I. *c.* 57.

[[Hutcheson is citing Livy's famous account of the rape of Lucretia, her suicide, the consequent overthrow of the Tarquins by Brutus, and the establishment of the Roman Republic. He is likely also opposing Lucretia as *causa proxima* of the establishment of the Roman republic to St. Augustine's well-known condemnation of Lucretia's suicide (and opposition between the behavior of pagan and Christian women) in the *City of God,* I.19.]]

he knew that the Profession of zealous Devotion would tend to his *Honour:* If such a Person could have any Sense of *Morality,* particularly an Aversion to *Dissimulation,* then his *Profession of Religion* would evidence the Superiority of the *Sense of Honour;* [155] and his *Discovery* of his Sentiments, or *Neglect* of Religion, would evidence the Ballance to be on the other side. I presume in *England* and *Holland,* we have more Instances of the latter than the former. 'Tis true, our Gentlemen who affect the Name of *Freedom,* may have now their Hopes of *Honour* from their own *Party,* as well as others.

The Adherence to any particular *Religion* by one in a strange Country, where it was dishonourable, would not be allowed a [*154*] good Instance of the Prevalence of a *moral Species;* it is a very common thing indeed, but here are *Interests* of another Life, and Regard to a *future Return* to a Country where this Religion is in repute.

The Pleasures of Imagination greater than those of external Senses.

IX. The Pleasures of the *internal Senses,* or of the Imagination, are allowed by all, who have any tolerable Taste of them, as a much superior Happiness to those of the *external Senses,* tho they were enjoyed to the full.

Other Comparisons might be made but with less use, or certainty in any general Conclusions, which might be drawn from them.

[156] The Pleasures of *Wealth* or *Power,* are proportioned to the Gratifications of the *Desires* or *Senses,* which the Agent intends to gratify by them: So that, for the Reasons above offered, Wealth and Power give greater Happiness to the *Virtuous,* than to those who consult only *Luxury* or *external Splendor.* If these Desires are grown *enthusiastick* and *habitual,* without regard to any other end than *Possession,* they are an endless Source of Vexation, without any real *Enjoyment;* a perpetual *Craving,* without *Nourishment* or *Digestion;* and they may surmount all other Affections, [*155*] by Aids borrowed from other Affections themselves.

The *fantastick Desires* are violent, in proportion to the Senses from which the *associated Ideas* are borrowed. Only it is to be observed, that however the Desires may be violent, yet the obtaining the *Object desired* gives little Satisfaction; the *Possession* discovers the Vanity and Deceit, and the *Fancy* is turned toward different Objects, in a perpetual Succession of inconstant Pursuits.

X. These several kinds of Pleasure or Pain are next to be compared as to their *Duration.* Here we are not only to consider [157] the *Certainty* of the Objects occasioning these Sensations, but the *Constancy* of our Relish or Fancy.

A Comparison of the several Pleasures as to Duration.

1. The Objects necessary to remove the Pains of *Appetite,* and to give as grateful *external Sensations* as any others, to a Person of a *correct Imagination,* may be universally secured by common Prudence and Industry. But then the *Sensations* themselves are short and transitory; the *Pleasure* continues no longer than the *Appetite,* nor does it leave any thing behind it, to supply the *Intervals* of Enjoyment. When the Sensation is past, we are no happier for it, there is no pleasure in [156] *Reflection;* nor are past Sensations any security against, or support under either *external Pain,* or any other sort of evil incident to us. If we keep these Senses pure, and unmixed with *foreign Ideas,* they cannot furnish Employment for Life: If *foreign Ideas* come in, the Objects grow difficult and uncertain, and our *Relish* or *Fancy* full of Inconstancy and Caprice.

[158] 2. In like manner, the Pleasures of the *Imagination* may be enjoyed by all, and be a sure Foundation of Pleasure, if we abstract from *Property,* and keep our Imagination pure. Such are the Pleasures in the Observation of *Nature,* and even the Works of *Art;* which are ordinarily exposed to view. But as these give less Pleasure the more *familiar* they grow, they cannot sufficiently employ or entertain Mankind, much less can they secure us against, or support us under the *Calamities of Life,* such as *Anger, Sorrow, Dishonour, Remorse,* or *external Pain.* If the *monstrous* or *trifling Taste* take place, or the Ideas of *Property,* they may indeed give sufficient Employment, but they bring along with them little Pleasure, frequent *Disgusts, Anxieties,* and *Disappointments,* in the acquiring and retaining their Objects.

[157] 3. The *publick Happiness* is indeed, as to external Appearance, a very uncertain Object; nor is it often in our power to remedy it, by changing the Course of *Events.* There are perpetual Changes in Mankind from Pleasures to Pains, and often from Virtue to Vice. Our *pub-*

lick Desires must therefore frequently subject us to *Sorrow;* and the Pleasures of the *publick Sense* must [159] be very inconstant. 'Tis true
indeed, that a general *Good-will* to our kind, is the most constant Inclination of the Mind, which grows upon us by Indulgence; nor are we
ever dissatisfied with the *Fancy:* the *Incertainty* therefore is wholly ow-   5
ing to the *Objects.* If there can be any Considerations found out to make
it probable, that in the Whole all Events tend to Happiness, this implicit Hope indeed may make our *publick Affections* the greatest and
most constant Source of Pleasure. Frequent *Reflection* on this, is the best
Support under the Sorrow arising from particular evils, befalling our   10
Fellow-Creatures. In our *nearer Attachments* brought upon our selves,
we may procure to our selves the greatest Enjoyments of this kind, with
considerable *Security* and *Constancy,* by chusing for our *Friends,* or *dearest Favourites,* Persons of just Apprehensions of Things, who are subjected only to the *necessary Evils* of Life, and can enjoy all [*158*] the cer-   15
tain and constant Good. And in like manner, our Attachment to a
Country may be fixed by something else than the *Chance of our Nativity.*
The Enjoyments of the publick Sense cannot indeed secure us against
bodily *Pains* or *Loss;* but they are often a considerable Support under
them. Nothing can more allay *Sorrow* and *Dejection* of Mind for private   20
Misfortunes, than good [160] Nature, and Reflection upon the *Happiness* of those we love.

4. The *moral Sense,* if we form *true Opinions* of the Tendencies of
Actions, and of the *Affections* whence they spring, as it is the Fountain
of the most *intense Pleasure,* so "it is in itself *constant,* not subject to   25
Caprice or Change. If we resolutely incourage this Sense, it grows more
acute by frequent *Gratification,* never cloys, nor ever is surfeited. We
not only are sure never to want *Opportunities* of doing good, which are
in every one's power in the highest Degree;* but each good Action is
Matter of pleasant *Reflection* as long as we live. These Pleasures cannot   30
indeed wholly secure us against all kinds of *Uneasiness,* yet they never
tend naturally to increase them. On the contrary, their general [*159*]

---

* *Treat.* 2. *Sect.* 3. last Paragraph.

Tendency is to lead the virtuous Agent into all Pleasures, in the highest
Degree in which they are consistent with each other. Our *external Senses*
are not weakned by Virtue, our *Imaginations* are not impaired; the *temperate Enjoyment* of all external Pleasures is the highest. A virtuous Conduct is generally the most prudent, even as to outward *Prosperity.*
Where Virtue costs us much, its own [161] *Pleasures* are the more sublime. It directly advances the Pleasures of the *publick Sense,* by leading
us to promote the publick Happiness as far as we can; and *Honour* is its
natural and ordinary Attendant. If it cannot remove the *necessary Pains*
of Life, yet it is the best Support under them. These moral Pleasures do
some way more nearly affect us than any other: They make us delight
in our *selves,* and relish our very *Nature.* By these we perceive an *internal
Dignity* and *Worth;* and seem to have a Pleasure like to that ascribed
often to the DEITY, by which we enjoy our own *Perfection,* and that of
every other Being."

It may perhaps seem too *metaphysical* to alledge on this Subject, that
other *Sensations* are all dependent upon, or related by the Constitution
of our Nature, to something different from our *selves;* to a [160] *Body*
which we do not call *Self,* but something belonging to this *Self.* That
other *Perceptions* of *Joy* or *Pleasure* carry with them Relations to *Objects,*
and *Spaces* distinct from this *Self;* whereas "the Pleasures of Virtue are
the very *Perfection of this* SELF, and are immediately perceived as such,
independent of external Objects."

Our Sense of *Honour* may afford very constant Pleasures by good
Oeconomy: If [162] our *moral Sense* be not perverted; if we form just
Apprehensions of the *Worth of others,* Honour shall be pleasant to us in
a compound Proportion of the *Numbers* and *Worth* of those who confer
it. If therefore we cannot approve our selves to all, so as to obtain *universal Honour* among all to whom we are known, yet there are still Men
of just Thought and Reflection, whose *Esteem* a virtuous Man may procure. Their *Dignity* will compensate the Want of *Numbers,* and support
us against the Pains of *Censure* from the Injudicious.

The Inconstancy of the Pleasures of *Wealth* and *Power* is well known,
and is occasioned, not perhaps by Change of Fancy, for these Desires
are found to continue long enough, since they tend toward the *universal*

Means of gratifying all other Desires; but by the Uncertainty of *Objects*
[*161*] or *Events* necessary to gratify such continually increasing Desires
as these are, where there is not some fixed View different from the
Wealth or *Power* itself. When indeed they are desired only as the Means
of gratifying some other well-regulated *Desires,* we may soon obtain   5
such a Portion as will satisfy us. But if once the *End* be forgotten, and
Wealth or Power become grateful *for themselves,* no farther Limits are
to be expected: the Desires are insatiable, nor is there any [163] considerable *Happiness* in any given *Degree* of either.

10

The Durations
of the several
Pains
considered.
XI. Were we to consider the *Duration* of the several Pains, we may find
it generally as the Duration of their Pleasures. As to the external Senses,
the old *Epicurean* Consolation is generally just: "Where the Pain is violent, it shortens our *Duration;* when it does not shorten our *Duration,*
it is generally either *tolerable,* or admits of frequent *Intermissions;*" and   15
then, when the external Pain is once past, no Mortal is the worse for
having endured it. There is nothing uneasy in the *Reflection,* when we
have no present *Pain,* or fear no *Return* of it.

The *internal Senses* are not properly *Avenues of Pain.* No *Form* is necessarily the Occasion of positive Uneasiness.   20

[*162*] The Pains of the *moral Sense* and Sense of *Honour,* are almost
perpetual. *Time,* the Refuge of other Sorrows, gives us no *Relief* from
these. All other Pleasures are made insipid by these Pains, and Life itself
an uneasy Burden. Our very *Self,* our Nature is disagreeable to us. 'Tis
true, we do not always observe the Vicious to be uneasy. The *Deformity*   25
of *Vice* often does not appear to those who continue in a Course of [164]
it. Their Actions are under some Disguise of *Innocence,* or even of *Virtue*
itself. When this Mask is pulled off, as it often happens, nor can any vicious Man prevent its happening, Vice will appear as a *Fury,* whose Aspect no Mortal can bear. This we may see in one *Vice,* which perhaps has   30
had fewer false or fantastick Associations of favourable Ideas than any,
viz. Cowardice, or such a selfish Love of Life, and Aversion to Death, or
to the very Hazard of it, as hinders a Man from serving his Country or
his Friend, or supporting his own Reputation. How few of our gay Gen-

tlemen can bear to be reputed *Cowards,* or even secretly to imagine themselves void of *Courage?* This is not tolerable to any, how negligent soever
they may be about other Points in Morality. Other *Vices* would appear
equally odious and despicable, and bear as horrid an Aspect, were they
equally stript of the *Disguises of* [*163*] *Virtue.* A vicious Man has no other
Security against the Appearances of this terrifying *Form,* than *Ignorance*
or *Inadvertence.* If *Truth* break in upon him, as it often must, when any
Adversity stops his intoxicating Pleasures, or Spectators use *Freedom* with
his Conduct, he is render'd perpetually miserable, or must fly to the only
Remedy which Reason would suggest, all possible *Reparation* of Injuries,
and a new Course of Life, the Necessity of which [165] is not superseded
by any *Remedy* suggested by the *Christian Revelation.*

    The Pains of the *publick Sense* are very lasting. The *Misery* of others,
either in past or present Ages, is matter of very uneasy *Reflection,* and
must continue so, if their State appears in the whole *absolutely Evil.*
Against this there is no Relief but the Consideration of a "*good governing* Mind, ordering all for good in the whole, with the Belief of a *future
State,* where the particular seeming Disorders are rectified." A firm Per-
suasion of these Things, with strong *publick Affections* interesting us
strongly in this *Whole,* and considering this *Whole* as one great *System,*
in which all is wisely ordered for good, may secure us against these
Pains, by removing the Opinion of any *absolute Evil.*

    [*164*] The Pains arising from foolish *Associations of moral Ideas,* with
the Gratifications of *external Senses,* or with the Enjoyment of Objects
of *Beauty* or *Grandeur,* or from the Desires of *Property,* the Humour of
Distinction, may be as constant as the Pains of the *Senses* from which
these Ideas are borrowed. Thus what we gain by these Associations is
very little. "The *Desires* of Trifles are often made very strong and uneasy;
the *Pleasures of Possession* very [166] small and of short Continuance,
only till the Object be familiar, or the *Fancy* change: But the *Pains of
Disappointment* are often very lasting and violent. Would we guard
against these Associations, every real *Pleasure* in Life remains, and we
may be easy without these things, which to others occasion the greatest
Pains."

Gemmas, Marmor, Ebur, Tyrrhena Sigilla, Tabellas,
Argentum, vestes Getulo Murice tinctas,
Est qui non habet, est qui nec curat habere.—Hor.[32]

SECTION VI

*Some general Conclusions concerning the best
Management of our Desires. With some Principles
necessary to Happiness.*

[*165*/167] We see therefore, upon comparing the several kinds of Pleasures and Pains, both as to *Intention* and *Duration,* that "the whole Sum
of Interest lies upon the Side of *Virtue, Publick-spirit,* and *Honour.* That
to *forfeit* these Pleasures in whole, or in part, for any other *Enjoyment,*
is the most foolish Bargain; and on the contrary, to secure them with
the *Sacrifice* of all others, is the *truest Gain.*"

Constant Discipline necessary. There is one general *Observation* to be premised, which appears of the
greatest Necessity for the just *Management* of all our Desires; *viz.* that
we should, as much as possible, in all Affairs of Importance to our selves
or others, prevent the *Violence* of their *confused Sensation,* and stop their
Propensities from breaking out into Action, till we have fully examined
the real *Moment* of the Object, either of our Desires [*166*] or Aversions.[168] The only way to affect this is, "a constant *Attention* of Mind,
an habitual *Discipline* over our selves, and a fixed *Resolution* to stop all
Action, before a calm *Examination* of every Circumstance attending it;
more particularly, the real *Values* of external Objects, and the *moral
Qualities* or *Tempers* of rational Agents, about whom our Affections
may be employed." This Power we may obtain over our selves, by a frequent Consideration of the great *Calamities,* and pernicious Actions, to

32. Horace, *Epistles,* II.2, 180–182, "Gems, marble, ivory, Tyrrhenium images,
tablets, silver, clothes colored Gaetulian purple, there are some who do not have
these things: there are some who do not care to have them."

which even the *best of our Passions* may lead us, when we are rashly hurried into Action by their Violence, and by the *confused Sensations,* and
fantastick Associations of Ideas which attend them: Thus we may raise
an *habitual Suspicion* and *Dread* of every *violent Passion,* which, recurring along with them continually, may in some measure counter-ballance their *Propensities* and *confused Sensations.* This *Discipline* of our
Passions is in general necessary. The *unkind* or *destructive Affections,* our
Anger, Hatred, or *Aversion* to rational Agents, seem to need it most; but
there is also a great Necessity for it, even about the *tender* and *benign*
Affections, lest we should be hurried into *universal* and *absolute Evil,* by
the Appearance of *particular Good:* And consequently it must be of the
highest Importance to all, to strengthen as much [*167*] as possible, by
frequent Meditation and Reflection, the calm [169] Desires either private or publick, rather than the particular Passions, and to make the
calm universal Benevolence superior to them.

That the necessary *Resignation* of other Pleasures may be the more easy, **Resignation**
we must frequently suggest to our selves these Considerations above **of sensual**
mentioned. "*External Pleasures* are short and transitory, leave no agree- **Pleasures.**
able *Reflection,* and are no manner of *Advantage* to us when they are
past; we are no better than if we had wanted them altogether."
     In like manner, "past Pains give us no unpleasant *Reflection,* nor are
we the worse for having endured them. If they are violent, our Existence
will probably be short; if not, they are tolerable, or allow long Intervals
of Ease." Let us join to these a *stoical Consideration;* "that *external Pains*
give us a noble Opportunity of *moral Pleasures* in Fortitude, and *Sub-*
mission to the Order of the whole, if we bear them resolutely; but if we
fret under them, we do not alleviate the Suffering, but rather increase it
by *Discontent* or *Sullenness.*" When *external Pains* must be endured voluntarily to avoid *moral Evil,* we must, as much as possible, present to
our selves [*168*] "the *moral Species* itself, [170] with the *publick Good* to
ensue, the *Honour* and *Approbation* to be expected from all good Men,
the DEITY, and our own Hearts, if we continue firm; and on the contrary, the *Remorse, Shame* and Apprehension of *future Punishments,* if
we yield to this Temptation."

How necessary it is to break off the vain Associations of *moral Ideas,* from the Objects of *external Senses,* will also easily appear. This may be done, by considering how trifling the *Services* are which are done to our Friends or Acquaintances, by *splendid Entertainments,* at an Expense, which, otherways employed, might have been to them of considerable   5 Importance. Men who are at ease, and of as *irregular Imaginations* as our selves, may admire and praise our *Magnificence;* but those who need more *durable Services,* will never think themselves much obliged. We cannot expect any *Gratitude* for what was done only to please our own *Vanity:* The *Indigent* easily see this, and justly consider upon the whole   10 how much they have profited.

If the Wealth of the *Luxurious* fails, he is the Object of *Contempt:* No body pities him nor honours him: his *personal Dignity* was placed by himself in his *Table,* [*169*] *Equipage* and *Furniture;* his Admirers placed [171] it also in the same: When these are gone all is lost.   15

—Non est melius quo insumere possis?
Cur eget indignus quisquam te Divite? quare
Templa ruunt antiqua Deûm? cur improbe carae
Non aliquid Patriae ex tanto emetiris acervo?   20
Uni nimirum tibi recte semper erunt res:
O magnus posthac inimicis Risus.—Hor.[33]

There is no Enjoyment of external Pleasure, which has more im- posed upon Men of late, by some confused *Species of Morality,* than   25 *Gallantry.* The sensible Pleasure alone must, by all Men who have the least Reflection, be esteemed at a very low rate: But the Desires of this kind, as they were by Nature intended to found the most constant un-

---

33. Horace, *Satires,* II.2, 102–7. "Is there nothing better to spend your surplus on? Why are any undeserving men in want while you are rich? Why are the ancient   30 temples of the Gods ruined? Why, wicked man, don't you dole out something from that great heap for the fatherland? Surely things will only go right for you. Oh what a great laugh your enemies will have someday." This is the satire from which Shaftes- bury takes the epigram for *Sensus Communis,* "hac urget Lupus, hac Canis" ["On the one side a wolf attacks, on the other a dog"] (Shaftesbury, *Characteristicks,* I:37).   35

interrupted *Friendship,* and to introduce the most venerable and lovely *Relations,* by *Marriages* and *Families,* arise in our Hearts, attended with some of the *sweetest Affections,* with a disinterested *Love* and *Tenderness,* with a most gentle and obliging Deportment, with something great and

5   heroick in our Temper. The Wretch who rises no higher in this Passion than the mean *sensual Gratification,* is abhorred by every one: But these sublimer Sensations and Passions do often so fill the Imaginations of the *Amorous,* that they are unawares led into [172] the [*170*] most contemptible and cruel Conduct which can be imagined. When for some

10 trifling transitory *Sensations,* which they might have innocently enjoyed along with the highest *moral Pleasures* in Marriage, they expose the very Person they love and admire to the deepest *Infamy* and *Sorrow,* to the *Contempt* of the World, to perpetual *Confusion, Remorse,* and *Anguish;* or, to what is worse, an *Insensibility* of all Honour or Shame, Virtue or

15 Vice, Good or Evil, to be the Scorn and Aversion of the World; and all this coloured over with the gay Notions of *Pleasantry, Genteelness, Politeness, Courage, high Enjoyment of Life.*

Would Men allow themselves a little Time to reflect on the *whole Effect* of such capricious Pursuits, the *Anguish* and *Distraction* of Mind

20 which these Sallies of Pleasure give to *Husbands, Fathers, Brothers;* would they consider how they themselves would resent such Treatment of a *Wife,* a *Child,* a *Sister;* how much deeper such Distresses are, than those trifling Losses or Damages, for which we think it just to bring the Authors of them to the Gallows; sure none but a thorow Villain could

25 either practice or approve the one more than the other.

[*171*/173] A wise Man in his Oeconomy, must do much even in Complaisance to the *Follies* of others, as well as his own *Conveniency,* to support that general *good Opinion* which must be maintained by those who would be publickly useful. His *Expences* must be some way suited to his

30 *Fortune,* to avoid the Imputation of *Avarice.* If indeed what is saved in *private Expences,* be employed in *generous Offices,* there is little danger of this Charge. Such a *Medium* may be kept as to be above *Censure,* and yet below any *Affectation of Honour* or *Distinction* in these matters. If one corrects his own *Imagination* in these things, he will be in no dan-

35 ger of doing any thing pernicious to please others. He is still in a State

fit to judge of the real *Importance* of every thing which occurs to him, and will gratify the false *Relish* of others, no farther than it is consistent with, and subservient to *some nobler Views.*

Conduct necessary about the Pleasures of Imagination.

II. To make the Pleasures of *Imagination* a constant Source of *Delight,* as they seem intended in the Frame of our Nature, with no hazard of *Pain,* it is necessary to keep the Sense free from foreign *Ideas of Property,* and the *Desire of Distinction,* as much as possible. If this can be done, we may receive Pleasure from every *Work of* [174] *Nature or Art* around us. We enjoy [172] not only the whole of *Nature,* but the united Labours of all about us. To prevent the Idea of *Property,* let us consider "how little the *Proprietor* enjoys more than the *Spectator:* Wherein is he the better or the happier?" The *Poet,* or the *Connoisseur,* who judges nicely of the Perfection of the Works of Art, or the Beauties of Nature, has generally a *higher Taste* than the Possessor. The *magnificent Palace,* the *grand Apartments,* the *Vistas,* the *Fountains,* the *Urns,* the *Statues,* the *Grottos* and *Arbours,* are exposed either in their own *Nature,* or by the Inclination of the *Proprietor,* to the Enjoyment of others. The *Pleasure of the Proprietor* depends upon the *Admiration* of others, he robs himself of his chief Enjoyment if he excludes *Spectators:* Nay, may not a Taste for Nature be acquired, giving greater Delight than the Observation of Art?

> Deterius Lybicis olet, aut nitet, Herba lapillis?
> Purior in vicis aqua tendit rumpere Plumbum,
> Quam que per pronum trepidat cum murmure rivum?
> Nempe inter varias nutritur Sylva Columnas,
> Laudaturque Domus, longos qua prospicit Agros.
> Naturam expellas surca licet, usque recurret.—Hor.[34]

34. Horace, *Epistles,* I.10.19–24. "Is the grass poorer in fragrance or beauty than Libyan mosaics? Is the water purer which in city-streets struggles to burst its leaden pipes than that which dances and purls adown the sloping brooks? Why amid your varied columns you are nursing trees, and you praise the mansion which looks out on distant fields. You may drive out Nature with a pitchfork, yet she will ever hurry back." H. R. Fairclough, trans., *Horace: Satires, Epistles, and Ars Poetica* (Cambridge,

Must an *artful Grove,* an *Imitation* of a Wilderness, or the more confined *Forms* or [175] *Ever-greens,* please more than the real *Forest,* [173] with the *Trees of God?* Shall a *Statue* give more Pleasure than the *human Face Divine?*

Where the *Humour of Distinction* is not corrected, our Equals become our Adversaries: The Grandeur of another is our *Misery,* and makes our Enjoyments insipid. There is only one way of making this Humour tolerable, but this way is almost inconsistent with the *Inclination* itself, *viz.* "continually to haunt with our Inferiors, and compare our selves with them." But if inconstant *Fortune,* or their own Merit do raise any of them to equal us, our *Pleasure* is lost, or we must sink ourselves to those who are still *Inferior,* and abandon the Society of every Person whose *Art* or *Merit* raises him. How poor a Thought is this!

The Pursuits of the *Learned* have often as much Folly in them as any others, when Studies are not valued according to their *Use in Life,* or the real Pleasures they contain, but for the *Difficulty* and *Obscurity,* and consequently the *Rarity* and *Distinction.* Nay, an abuse may be made of the most noble and manly Studies, even of *Morals, Politicks,* and *Religion* itself, if our Admiration and Desire terminate upon the *Knowledge* itself, and not upon [174] the Possession of [176] the *Dispositions* and *Affections* inculcated in these Studies. If these Studies be only matter of *Amusement* and *Speculation,* instead of leading us into a constant *Discipline* over our selves, to correct our Hearts, and to guide our Actions, we are not much better employed, than if we had been studying some useless Relations of *Numbers,* or Calculations of Chances.

There is not indeed any part of Knowledge which can be called entirely *useless.* The most *abstracted Parts of Mathematicks,* and the Knowledge of *mythological History,* or antient *Allegories,* have their own Pleasures not inferior to the more gay Entertainments of *Painting, Musick,* or *Architecture;* and it is for the Advantage of Mankind that some are found, who have a Taste for these Studies. The only Fault lies, in letting

---

Mass.: Harvard University Press, 1978). Shaftesbury quotes line 24 in "Miscellaneous Reflections," IV.2 (*Characteristicks,* III:132).

any of those *inferior* Tastes engross the whole Man to the Exclusion of the nobler Pursuits of *Virtue* and *Humanity.*

Concerning all these Pleasures of the Imagination, let us consider also "how little support they can give Men under any of the Calamities of Life," such as the Treachery or Baseness of a *Friend,* a *Wife,* a *Child,* 5 or the perplexing Intricacies [*175*] of our common Affairs, or the Apprehension of *Death.*

[177]
Re veraque Metus hominum, Curaeque sequaces   10
Nec metuunt sonitus Armorum, nec fera Tela;
Audacterque inter Reges, rerumque Potentes
Versantur, nec fulgorem reverentur ab auro,
Nec clarum vestis splendorem purpureaï
Quid dubitas quin omne sit hoc rationis egestas?—LUC.[35]   15

Ideas of III. Under this Head of our Internal Sense, we must observe one natu-
Divinity arise ral Effect of it, that it leads us into *Apprehensions of a* DEITY. Grandeur,
from the inter- Beauty, Order, Harmony, wherever they occur, raise an Opinion of a
nal Senses. MIND, of *Design,* and *Wisdom.* Every thing great, regular, or propor-   20
tioned, excites *Veneration,* either toward itself, if we imagine it animated, if not animated, toward some apprehended Cause. No Determination of our Mind is more *natural* than this, no Effect more
universal. One has better Reason to deny the Inclination between the
Sexes to be natural, than a Disposition in Mankind to *Religion.*   25

We cannot open our Eyes, without discerning *Grandeur and Beauty* every where. Whoever receives these Ideas, feels an inward *Veneration* arise. We may fall into a Thousand vain Reasonings: foolish limited

35. Lucretius, *De Rerum Natura,* II.48–53. This passage is part of the famous "Proem" to Book II, the *locus classicus* of the sort of Epicureanism that Hutcheson   30
sought to undermine: "If truly the fears of men, and the cares which follow them, neither shrink at the sound of arms, nor fierce weapons; and boldly hover among kings and rulers of the world, neither revere the glitter of gold, nor the brilliant splendor of a purple robe, why then do we doubt that all this is reason alone?"

Notions of DIVINITY may be formed, as attached to the particular *Places* or [*176*] *Objects,* which strike us in the most lively [178] manner. Custom, Prejudice of Sense or Education, may confirm some foolish Opinion about the *Nature* or *Cause* of these Appearances: But wherever a superior MIND, a governing INTENTION or DESIGN is imagined, there *Religion* begins in its most simple Form, and an inward *Devotion* arises. Our Nature is as much determined to this, as to any other Perception or Affection. How we manage these Ideas and Affections, is indeed of the greatest Importance to our Happiness or Misery.

The Apprehension of an universal MIND with Power and Knowledge, is indeed an agreeable Object of Contemplation. But we must form our Ideas of all intelligent Natures, with some Resemblance or Analogy to our selves: We must also conceive something correspondent to our *Affections* in the DIVINITY, with some *moral Apprehensions* of the Actions and Tempers of his Creatures. The *Order of Nature* will suggest many Confirmations of this. We must conclude some *Worship* acceptable, and some Expressions of *Gratitude* as our Duty. The Conceptions of the DEITY must be various, according to the different Degrees of *Attention* and *Reasoning* in the Observers, and their own Tempers and Affections. Imagining the divine MIND, as *cruel,* [*177*] *wrathful, or capricious,* must be a perpetual Source of Dread and Horror; and will be apt to raise a *Resemblance* of Temper in the Worshipper, with its attendant *Misery.* A contrary [*179*] Idea of the DIVINITY, as good, and kind, delighting in universal Happiness, and ordering all Events of the Universe to this End, as it is the most delightful Contemplation, so it fills the good Mind with a constant *Security* and *Hope,* amidst either publick Disorders, or private Calamities.

To find out which of these two Representations of the DEITY is the true one, we must consult the *Universe,* the Effect of his Power, and the Scene of his Actions. After what has been observed by so many ingenious Authors, both *Ancient* and *Modern,* one cannot be at a loss which Opinion to chuse. We may only on this occasion consider the Evidences of divine Goodness appearing in the *Structure of our own Nature,* and in the Order of our *Passions* and *Senses.*

Evidences of
the Goodness
of God in the
Frame of our
Senses and
Affections. It was observed above, how admirably our Affections are contrived for good in the *whole*. Many of them indeed do not pursue the *private Good* of the Agent; nay, many of them, in various Cases, seem to tend to his detriment, by concerning him violently in the Fortunes of *others*, in their [*178*] *Adversity*, as well as their Prosperity. But they all aim at *good*, either private or publick: and by them each particular Agent is [180] made, in a great measure, subservient to the *good of the whole*. Mankind are thus insensibly link'd together, and make one great *System*, by an invisible Union. He who *voluntarily* continues in this Union, and delights in employing his Power for his *Kind*, makes himself happy: He who does not continue this Union freely, but affects to break it, makes himself wretched; nor yet can he break the *Bonds of Nature*. His *publick Sense*, his *Love of Honour*, and the very *Necessities* of his Nature, will continue to make him depend upon his *System*, and engage him to serve it, whether he inclines to it or not. Thus we are formed with a View to a general good *End;* and may in our own Nature discern a universal Mind watchful for the whole.

The same is observable in the Order of our *external Senses*. The simple Productions of Nature, which are useful to any Species of Animals, are also *grateful* to them; and the pernicious or useless Objects are made disagreeable. Our external Sensations are no doubt often *painful*, when our Bodies are in a dangerous State; when they want supplies of Nourishment; when any thing external would be injurious to them. But if it appears, "that the *general Laws* [*179*] are wisely constituted, and that it is necessary to the Good of a System of [181] such Agents, to be under the Influence of *general Laws*, upon which there is occasion for *Prudence* and *Activity*;" the particular *Pains* occasioned by a necessary *Law* of Sensation, can be no Objection against the Goodness of the Author.

Now that there is no room for complaint, that "our external Sense of *Pain* is made too acute," must appear from the Multitudes we daily see so careless of preserving the Blessing of *Health*, of which many are so prodigal as to lavish it away, and expose themselves to external *Pains* for very trifling Reasons. Can we then repine at the friendly *Admonitions* of Nature, joined with some *Austerity*, when we see that they are scarce sufficient to restrain us from Ruin? The same may be said of the *Pains* of other kinds. *Shame* and *Remorse* are never to be called too severe, while so many are not sufficiently restrained by them. Our *Compassion* and friendly *Sense of Sorrow*, what are they else but the *Alarms* and *Exhortations* of a kind impartial *Father*, to engage his *Children* to relieve a distressed *Brother?* Our *Anger* itself is a necessary Piece of Management, by which every pernicious Attempt is made *dangerous* to its Author.

[*180*/182] Would we allow room to our Invention, to conceive what sort of *Mechanism,* what *Constitutions* of Senses or Affections a *malicious powerful Being* might have formed, we should soon see how few Evidences there are for any such Apprehension concerning the AUTHOR of this World. Our *Mechanism,* as far as we have ever yet discovered, is wholly contrived for good. No cruel *Device,* no *Art* or *Contrivance* to produce evil: No such *Mark* or *Scope* seems ever to be aimed at. How easy had it been to have contrived some necessary Engines of *Misery* without any use; some *Member* of no other service but to be matter of *Torment; Senses* incapable of bearing the surrounding Objects without Pain; Eyes pained with the *Light;* a Palate offended with the *Fruits* of the Earth; a Skin as tender as the Coats of the *Eye,* and yet some more furious Pain forcing us to bear these Torments? Human *Society* might have been made as uneasy as the Company of *Enemies,* and yet a perpetual more violent Motive of *Fear* might have forc'd us to bear it. *Malice, Rancour, Distrust,* might have been our natural Temper. Our *Honour* and *Self-Approbation* might have depended upon *Injuries;* and the *Torments* of others been made our *Delight,* which yet we could not have enjoyed thro' [183] perpetual *Fear.* Many such Contrivances we [*181*] may easily conceive, whereby an evil *Mind* could have gratified his *Malice* by our *Misery.* But how unlike are they all to the Intention or Design of the Mechanism of this World?

Our *Passions* no doubt are often matter of Uneasiness to our selves, and sometimes occasion Misery to *others,* when any one is indulged into a Degree of Strength beyond its *Proportion.* But which of them could we have wanted, without greater Misery in the whole? They are by Nature ballanced against each other, like the *Antagonist Muscles* of the Body; either of which separately would have occasioned *Distortion* and irregular *Motion,* yet jointly they form a Machine, most accurately subservient to the *Necessities, Convenience, and Happiness* of a *rational System.* We have a Power of *Reason* and *Reflection,* by which we may see what Course of Action will naturally tend to procure us the most valuable *Gratifications* of all our Desires, and prevent any intolerable or unnecessary *Pains,* or provide some support under them. We have Wisdom sufficient to form Ideas of *Rights, Laws, Constitutions;* so as to preserve large Societies in Peace and Prosperity, and promote a *general Good* amidst all the *private Interests.*

[*182*/184] If from the present Order of Nature, in which *Good* appears far superior to *Evil,* we have just Presumptions to conclude the DEITY to be benevolent, it is not conceivable "that any Being, who desires the Happiness of others, should not desire a *greater Degree* of Happiness to them rather than a less; and that consequently the whole *Series of Events* is the best possible, and contains in the whole the greatest possible *absolute Good:*" especially since we have no Presumption of any *private Interest,* which an *universal* MIND can have in view, in opposition to the greatest Good of the whole. Nor are the particular Evils occurring to our Observation, any just Objection against the perfect Goodness of the universal PROVIDENCE to us, who cannot know how far these Evils may be necessarily connected with the *Means* of the greatest possible absolute Good.

The Conduct
of our publick
Sense and
Affections.

IV. In managing our *publick Sense* of the State of others, we must beware of one common Mistake, *viz.* "apprehending every Person to be miserable in those Circumstances, which we imagine would make our selves miserable." We may easily find, that the *lower Rank* of Mankind, whose only Revenue is their bodily Labour, enjoy as much *Chearfulness, Contentment,* [*183*/185] *Health, Gaiety,* in their own way, as any in the highest Station of Life. Both their Minds and Bodies are soon fitted to their State. The *Farmer* and *Labourer,* when they enjoy the bare Necessaries of Life, are easy. They have often more *correct Imaginations,* thro' *Necessity* and *Experience,* than others can acquire by *Philosophy.* This Thought is indeed a poor Excuse for a base selfish *Oppressor,* who, imagining Poverty a great Misery, bears hard upon those in a low Station of Life, and deprives them of their natural *Conveniences,* or even of bare *Necessaries.* But this Consideration may support a compassionate Heart, too deeply touched with apprehended Miseries, of which the *Sufferers* are themselves insensible.

The Pains of this *Sense* are not easily removed. They are not allayed by the Distinction of Pains into *real* and *imaginary.* Much less will it remove them, to consider how much of human Misery is owing to their own *Folly* and *Vice.* Folly and Vice are themselves the most pityable Evils. It is of more consequence to consider, what Evidences there are "that the Vice and Misery in the World are smaller than we sometimes in our melancholy Hours imagine." There are no doubt many furious [186] Starts of Passion, in which [*184*] Malice may seem to have place in our Constitution; but how seldom, and how short, in comparison of Years spent in fixed kind Pursuits of the Good of a *Family,* a *Party,* a *Country?* How great a Part of human Actions flow directly from *Humanity* and *kind Affection?* How many censurable Actions are owing to the same Spring, only chargeable on *Inadvertence,* or an Attachment to too *narrow a System?* How few owing to any thing worse than *selfish* Passions above their Proportion?

Here Men are apt to let their Imaginations run out upon all the *Robberies, Piracies, Murders, Perjuries, Frauds, Massacres, Assassinations,* they have ever either heard of, or read in History; thence concluding all Mankind to be very wicked: as if a *Court of Justice* were the proper Place of making an Estimate of the *Morals* of Mankind, or an *Hospital* of the *Healthfulness* of a Climate. Ought they not to consider, that the Number of honest *Citizens* and *Farmers* far surpasses that of all sorts of Criminals in any State; and that the innocent or kind Actions of even Criminals themselves, surpass their Crimes in Numbers? That 'tis the *Rarity* of Crimes, in comparison of innocent or good Actions, [187] which engages our Attention to them, and makes them be recorded in History; while incomparably more honest, generous, [*185*] domestick Actions are overlooked, only because they are so common; as one great *Danger,* or one *Month's Sickness,* shall become a frequently repeated Story, during a long Life of Health and Safety.

The Pains of the *external Senses* are pretty frequent, but how short in comparison of the long Tracts of Health, Ease and Pleasure? How rare is the Instance of a Life, with one tenth spent in violent Pain? How few want absolute Necessaries; nay, have not something to spend on *Gaiety* and *Ornament?* The Pleasures of *Beauty* are exposed to all in some measure. These kinds of Beauty which require *Property* to the full Enjoyment of them, are not ardently desired by many. The Good of every 5 kind in the Universe, is plainly superior to the Evil. How few would accept of *Annihilation,* rather than Continuance in Life in the middle State of Age, Health and Fortune? Or what separated Spirit, who had considered human Life, would not, rather than perish, take the hazard of it again, by returning into a Body in the State of Infancy?   10

> [188]
> —Who would lose,
> For fear of Pain, this intellectual Being,
> These Thoughts which wander thro' Eternity,
> To perish rather, swallowed up and lost   15
> In the wide Womb of uncreated Night,
> Devoid of Sense and Motion—Milton's *Par. lost,* Book 2.[36]

[*186*] These Thoughts plainly shew a *Prevalence* of Good in the World. But still our publick Sense finds much matter of compassionate Sorrow among Men. The *Many* are in a tolerable good State; but who 20 can be unconcerned for the distressed *Few?* They are few in comparison of the whole, and yet a great *Multitude.*

What Parent would be much concerned at the Pains of breeding of *Teeth,* were they sure they would be short, and end well? Or at the Pain of a Medicine, or an Incision, which was necessary for the Cure, and 25 would certainly accomplish it? Is there then no *Parent* in NATURE, no *Physician* who sees what is necessary for the *Whole,* and for the good of each Individual in the whole of his Existence, as far as is consistent with the general Good? Can we expect, in this our *Childhood* of Existence, to understand all the Contrivance and Art of this Parent and Physician 30

36. John Milton, *Paradise Lost,* 146–51. This is from Belial's speech, as Satan and the fallen angels debate a plan to recover heaven. Belial uses this as a pretext not to attack heaven, lest by angering God the fallen angels would cease to exist.

of Nature? May not [189] some harsh Discipline be necessary to Good? May not many natural Evils be necessary to prevent future moral Evils, and to correct the Tempers of the Agents, nay to introduce moral Good? Is not *Suffering* and *Distress* requisite, before there can be room for generous Compassion, *Succour,* and *Liberality?* Can there be *Forgiveness, Returns of good for evil,* [*187*] unless there be some *moral Evil?* Must the *Whole* want the eternally delightful *Consciousness* of such *Actions* and *Dispositions,* to prevent a few transient Sensations of Pain, or natural Evil? May there not be some unseen Necessity for the greatest universal Good, that* there should be an *Order of Beings* no more perfect than we are, subject to Error and wrong Affections sometimes? May not all the present Disorders which attend this State of *prevalent Order,* be rectified by the *directing Providence* in a future Part of our Existence? This Belief of a DEITY, a PROVIDENCE, and a *future State,* are the only sure Supports to a good Mind. Let us then acquire and strengthen our Love and Concern for this *Whole,* and acquiesce in what the governing MIND, who presides in it, is ordering in the wisest Manner, tho not yet fully known to us, for its most universal Good

[190] A future State, firmly believed, makes the greatest Difficulties on this Subject to vanish. No particular *finite Evils* can be looked upon as intolerable, which lead to Good, infinite in *Duration.* Nor can we complain of the Conditions of Birth, if the present Evils of Life have [*188*] even a probable hazard of *everlasting Happiness* to compensate them; much more if it be placed in our power certainly to obtain it. Never could the boldest Epicurean bring the lightest Appearance of Argument against the *Possibility* of such a State, nor was there ever any thing tolerable advanced against its *Probability.* We have no Records of any Nation which did not entertain this Opinion. Men of Reflection in all Ages, have found at least probable Arguments for it; and the Vulgar have been prone to believe it, without any other *Argument* than their natural Notions of *Justice* in the *Administration of the World.* Present *Hope* is present

The Necessity of believing a future State.

* See the Archbishop of *Dublin, de Origine Mali.*

Good: and this very Hope has enlivened human Life, and given ease to generous Minds, under Anxieties about the publick Good.

This Opinion was interwoven with all Religions; and as it in many instances overballanced the Motives to Vice, so it removed Objections against *Providence.* The [191] good Influence of this Opinion, however it might not justify any *Frauds,* yet probably did more good than what might overballance many Evils flowing from even very *corrupt Religions.* How agreeable then must it be to every good Man, that this Opinion, were there even no more to be done, should be confirmed beyond question or doubt, by a well attested *divine* [189] *Revelation,* for the perpetual *Security* of the virtuous, and for the constant Support of the *kind and compassionate?* How gladly must every honest Heart receive it; and rejoice that even those who have neither *Leisure* nor *Capacity* for deep *Reflection,* should be thus convinced of it?

The Conduct of the unkind Affections. As to the Management of those Passions which seem *opposite* to the *Happiness* of others, such as *Anger, Jealousy, Envy, Hatred;* it is very necessary to represent to our selves continually, the most *favourable Conceptions* of others, and to force our Minds to examine the *real Springs* of the resented Actions. We may almost universally find, that "no Man acts from *pure Malice;* that the Injurious only intended some *Interest of his own,* without any *ultimate Desire* of our Misery; that he is more to be pitied for his own mean *selfish Temper,* for the want of true *Goodness,* and its attendant *Happiness,* than to be hated for his Conduct, which is really more pernicious to himself [192] than to others.* Our *Lenity, Forgiveness,* and *Indulgence* to the Weakness of others, will be constant Matter of *delightful Consciousness,* and *Self-Approbation;* [190] and will be as probably effectual in most cases, to obtain *Reparation* of Wrongs, from an hearty *Remorse,* and thorow *Amendment of the Temper* of the Injurious, as any Methods of Violence." Could we raise our Goodness even to an higher Pitch, and consider "the Injurious as our *Fellow-Members* in this great intellectual Body, whose Interest and Happiness it becomes us to promote, as much as we can consistently with that of

---

* See this Point handled with great Judgment, in *Plato's Gorgias.*
[[Plato, *Gorgias,* see particularly 477a–d.]]

others, and not to *despise, scorn,* or *cut them off,* because of every *Weak-ness, Deformity,* or *lighter Disorder;*" we might bring our selves to that divine Conduct, of even *returning good for evil.*

In like manner, our *Emulation, Jealousy,* or *Envy,* might be restrained in a great measure, by a constant *Resolution* of bearing always in our Minds the* *lovely Side* of every Character:† "The compleatly Evil are as rare as the perfectly Virtuous: There is something amiable almost in every one." Could we enure our selves [193] constantly to dwell on these things, we might often bear patiently the *Success of a Rival,* nay, some-times even rejoice in it, be more happy our [*191*] selves, and turn him into a real *Friend.* We should often find those *Phantoms* of Vice and Corruption which torment the *Jealous,* vanishing before the bright Warmth of a thorow *good Temper,* resolved to search for every thing *lovely and good,* and averse to think any *evil.*

V. In governing our *moral Sense,* and *Desires of Virtue,* nothing is more necessary than to study the *Nature* and *Tendency* of human Actions; and to extend our views to the *whole Species,* or to all *sensitive Natures,* as far as they can be affected by our Conduct. Our moral Sense thus regulated, and constantly followed in our Actions, may be the most constant Source

Conduct of the moral Sense, and Sense of Honour.

---

* Epictet. Enchir. *Cap.* 65.

[[Turco (*Saggio,* 255) notes that Hutcheson is citing Simplicius's commentary on *Enchiridion,* §65, which explicates Epictetus's, *Enchiridion,* §43. This must have been Hutcheson's primary edition of Epictetus, which is notable, as Simplicius often softens Epictetus's rather harsh Stoicism through his own Neoplatonic lens. "Every thing hath two handles, the one soft and manageable, the other such as will not endure to be touched. If then your Brother do you an Injury, do not take it by the hot and hard handle, by representing to your self all the aggravating Circumstances of the Fact; but look rather on the soft side, and extenuate it as much as possible, by considering the nearness of the Relation, and the long Friendship and Familiarity between you. Obligations to Kindness, which a single Provocation ought not to dissolve. And thus you will take the accident by its manageable handle." Epictetus *his Morals With* Simplicius *His Comment,* 379–80.]]

† Plato Phaedon.

[["[T]here are not many very good or very bad people, but the great majority are something between the two" *Phaedo,* 90a. (Hugh Tredennick and Harold Tar-rant [trans. & intro.] *Plato: The Last Days of Socrates* [London: Penguin, 1969], rev. ed.).]]

of the most *stable Pleasure*. The same Conduct is always the most probable Means of obtaining the *Pleasures of Honour*. If there be a Distinction
between *Truth* and *Falshood*, Truth must be stronger than Falshood: It
must be more probable that *Truth* will generally prevail; that the real *good
Tendency* of our Actions, and the Wisdom of our *Intentions* will be
known; and *Misrepresentations* or *partial Views* will vanish. Our Desire of
Honour is not confined to our present State. The Prospect of *future Glory*
is a strong Motive [194] of Action. And thus the *Time,* in which our
Character may have the hazard of obtaining Justice, has no other Limits
[*192*] than those of the *Existence of rational Natures*. Whereas, *partial Notions* of Virtue, and *partial Conduct,* have no other Foundation for
Self-Approbation, than our *Ignorance, Error,* or *Inadvertence;* nor for *Honour,* than the like *Ignorance, Error,* or *Inadvertence* of others.

   That we may not be engaged into any thing contrary to the publick
Good, or to the true Schemes of Virtue, by the Desire of *false Honour,*
or *Fear of false Shame,* it is of great use to examine the *real Dignity* of
those we converse with, and to confine our *Intimacies* to the truly virtuous and wise. From such we can expect no Honour, but according to
our sincere Pursuit of the *publick Good;* nor need we ever fear any
Shame in such a Course. But above all, did we frequently, and in the
most lively manner, present to ourselves that great, and wise, and good
MIND, which presides over the Universe, sees every *Action,* and knows
the true *Character* and *Disposition* of every Heart, approving nothing
but sincere Goodness and Integrity; did we consider that the time will
come, when we shall be as conscious of his *Presence,* as we are of our
own *Existence;* as sensible of his *Approbation* or [195] *Condemnation,* as
we are of the Testimony of our own Hearts; when we shall be engaged
in a *Society of Spirits,* stripped of these *Prejudices* [*193*] and *false Notions*
which so often attend us in Flesh and Blood, how should we despise
that Honour which is from Men, when opposite to the truest Honour
from GOD himself?

VI. Concerning the Desires of *Wealth* and *Power,* besides what was suggested above to allay their Violence, from considering the small Addition commonly made to the *Happiness* of the Possessor, by the greatest
Degrees of them, and the *Uncertainty* of their Continuance; if we have
obtained any share of them, let us examine their *true Use,* and what is
the best Enjoyment of them.

> —Quid asper
> Utile Nummus habet? Patriae carisque propinquis
> Quantum elargiri decet?—Persius.[37]

What *moral Pleasures,* what Delights of *Humanity,* what *Gratitude*
from Persons obliged, what *Honour,* may a wise Man of a generous
Temper purchase with them? How foolish is the Conduct of heaping
up Wealth for *Posterity,* when smaller Degrees might make them equally
happy! when great *Prospects* of this kind are the strongest *Temptations* to
them, to indulge *Sloth, Luxury,* [196] *Debauchery, Insolence, Pride,* and
Contempt of their Fellow-Creatures; [194] and to banish some noble
Dispositions, *Humility, Compassion, Industry, Hardiness of Temper and
Courage,* the Offspring of the sober rigid Dame *Poverty.* How often
does the *Example,* and almost direct *Instruction* of Parents, lead Posterity into the basest Views of Life!

> —Qui nulla exempla beati
> Pauperis esse putat—
> Cum dicis Juveni stultum qui donat amico,
> Qui paupertatem levat attollitque propinqui,
> Et spoliare doces & circumscribere—
> Ergo Ignem, cujus scintillas ipse dedisti,
> Flagrantem late, & rapientem cuncta videbis.—Juv. Sat. 14.[38]

37. Persius, *Satires,* III. 69–71, "Are shiny new coins more useful? How much
should be spent on our country and our near and dear?"

38. Juvenal, *Satires,* 14, "It is believed that there are no happy paupers" (120–121);
"When you tell a youth that it is stupid to give a present to a friend, or to help a
poor relative, you teach him to rob and cheat" (235–37); "Therefore the fire, whose
sparks you tended, you will now see blaze far and wide and seize everything it
meets" (244–45).

The Desires of
Wealth and
Power.

How powerfully might the Example of a wisely generous Father, at once teach his Offspring the true *Value* of Wealth or Power, and prevent their *Neglect* of them, or foolish *throwing* them away, and yet inspire them with a *generous Temper,* capable of the just *Use* of them!

Support against Death. Death is one Object of our *Aversion,* which yet we cannot avoid. It can scarcely be said, that "the *Desire of Life* is as strong as the Sum of all *selfish Desires.*" It may be so with those who enure themselves to no Pleasures but those of the *external Senses.* [197] But how often do we see [*195*] Death endured, not only from Love of *Virtue,* or *publick Affections,* in Heroes and Martyrs, but even from Love of *Honour* in lower Characters! Many Aversions are stronger than that to Death. *Fear of bodily Pain, fear of Dishonour,* which are selfish Aversions, do often surpass our Aversion to Death, as well as *publick Affections* to Countries or Friends. It is of the greatest Consequence to the *Enjoyment* of Life, to know its true *Value;* to strip Death of its borrowed Ideas of Terror; to consider it barely as the *Cessation of both the Pains and Pleasures we now feel,* coming frequently upon us with no more Pain than that of *Swooning,* with a noble Hazard, or rather a certain *Prospect* of superior Happiness to every *good Mind.* Death in this view must appear an inconsiderable Evil, in comparison of *Vice, Self-Abhorrence,* real *Dishonour,* the *Slavery of one's Country,* the *Misery of a Friend.*

The tender Regards to a *Family* and *Offspring,* are often the strongest Bands to restrain a generous Mind from submitting to Death. What shall be the Fate of a *Wife,* a *Child,* a *Friend,* or a *Brother,* when we are gone, are the frequent Subjects of grievous Anxiety. The Fortunes of such Persons often depend much upon us; and when [198] they do not, yet we are more anxious [*196*] about their State when we shall be absent.

> Ut assidens implumibus pullis avis,
> Serpentium allapsus timet
> Magis relictis, non ut adsit Auxilî
> Latura plus praesentibus.—Hor.[39]

39. Horace, *Epodes,* I.19–22, "just as the mother bird while guarding unfledged

Next to the Belief of a good PROVIDENCE, nothing can support Men more under such *Anxieties,* than considering how often the *Orphan* acquires a *Vigor* of Mind, *Sagacity* and *Industry,* superior to those who are enfeebled by the constant *Care* and *Services* of others. A wise Man would desire to be provided with Friends against such an Exigency; Persons of such Goodness, as would joyfully accept the *Legacy* of a *Child,* or indigent *Friend* committed to their Protection.

If Death were an *entire End* of the Person, so that no Thought or Sense should remain, all *Good* must cease at Death, but no *Evil* commence. The *Loss of Good* is Evil to us now, but will be no *Evil* to a Being which has lost all *Sense of Evil.* Were this the Case, the Consolation against Death would only be this, frequently to look upon *Life* and all its Enjoyments as granted to us only for a *short Term;* to employ this uncertain Time as much as we can in the Enjoyment [199] of the *noblest Pleasures;* [197] and to prevent Surprize at our Removal, by *laying our Account* for it.

But if we exist, and think after Death, and retain our *Senses* of Good and Evil, no Consolation against Death can be suggested to a *wicked Man;* but for the *virtuous,* there are the best Grounds of *Hope* and *Joy.* If the *Administration* of the whole be good, we may be sure "that *Order* and *Happiness* will in the whole prevail: Nor will *Misery* be inflicted any farther than is necessary for some prepollent Good." Now there is no Presumption, that the *absolute Misery* of any *virtuous* Person can be necessary to any good End: Such Persons therefore are the most likely to enjoy a State of perfect Happiness.

VII. To conclude: Let us consider that common Character, which when ascribed to any *State, Quality, Disposition,* or *Action,* engages our *Favour* and *Approbation* of it, *viz.* its being *natural.* We have many Suspicions about Tempers or Dispositions formed by *Art,* but are some way prepossessed in favour of what is *natural:* We imagine it must be advantageous and delightful to be in a natural State, and to live according to Nature. "This very Presumption in favour of what is natural, is a plain

What is the natural State of Men.

---

chicks/fears most the serpent's glide/when she has left the nest, although her presence/could not be any help to them," West, trans., *Horace.*

Indication that [200] the Order of Nature is good, and that Men are some [*198*] way convinced of it. Let us enquire then what is meant by it."

If by natural we mean "that which we enjoy or do, when we first begin to exist, or to think," it is impossible to know what *State, Temper,*   5 or *Actions,* are *natural.* Our *natural State* in this Sense differs little from that of a *Plant,* except in some accidental *Sensations of Hunger,* or of *Ease,* when we are well nourished.

Some elaborate Treatises of great Philosophers about *innate Ideas,* or Principles practical or speculative, amount to no more than this, "That   10 in the Beginning of our Existence we have no *Ideas* or *Judgments;*" they might have added too, no *Sight, Taste, Smell, Hearing, Desire, Volition.* Such Dissertations are just as useful for understanding *human Nature,* as it would be in explaining the *animal Oeconomy,* to prove that the Faetus is animated before it has *Teeth, Nails, Hair,* or before it can *eat,*   15 *drink, digest, or breathe:* Or in a *natural History of Vegetables,* to prove that *Trees* begin to grow before they have *Branches, Leaves, Flower, Fruit,* or *Seed:* And consequently that all these things were adventitious, or the Effect of Art.

[201] But if we call "that *State,* those *Dispositions* and *Actions, natu-*   20 *ral,* to [*199*] which we are inclined by some part of our Constitution, antecedently to any *Volition of our own;* or which flow from some *Principles* in our Nature, not brought upon us by our own *Art,* or that of others;" then it may appear, from what was said above, that "a State of *Good-will, Humanity, Compassion, mutual Aid, propagating and sup-*   25 *porting Offspring, Love of a Community or Country, Devotion, or Love and Gratitude to some governing Mind,* is our natural State," to which we are naturally inclined, and do actually arrive, as universally, and with as much uniformity, as we do to a certain *Stature* and *Shape.*

If by natural we understand "the *highest Perfection of the Kind,* to   30 which any Nature may be improved by cultivating its natural Dispositions or Powers;" as few arrive at this in the Growth of their *Bodies,* so few obtain it in their *Minds.* But we may see what this Perfection is, to which our *natural Dispositions* tend, when we improve them to the utmost, as far as they are consistent with each other, making the *weaker*   35 or *meaner* yield to the *more excellent* and *stronger.* Our several *Senses* and

Affections, publick and *private,* with our Powers [202] of *Reason* and *Reflection,* shew this to be the *Perfection* of our *Kind, viz.* "to know, [200] love, and reverence the great AUTHOR of all things; to form the most *extensive Ideas* of our own true Interests, and those of all other *Natures,* *rational* or *sensitive;* to abstain from all *Injury;* to pursue regularly and impartially the *most universal absolute Good,* as far as we can; to enjoy constant *Self-Approbation,* and *Honour* from wise Men; with *Trust in divine* PROVIDENCE, *Hope of everlasting Happiness,* and a full *Satisfaction* and *Assurance* of Mind, that the whole Series of *Events* is directed by an unerring *Wisdom,* for the greatest universal *Happiness* of the whole."

To assert that "Men have generally arrived to the *Perfection of their Kind* in this Life," is contrary to Experience. But on the other hand, to suppose "no Order at all in the *Constitution* of our Nature, or no *prevalent Evidences* of good Order," is yet more contrary to Experience, and would lead to a Denial of PROVIDENCE in the most important Affair which can occur to our Observation. We actually see such Degrees of *good Order,* of *social Affection,* of *Virtue* and *Honour,* as make the Generality of Mankind continue in a tolerable, nay, an *agreeable* State. However, in some [203] Tempers we see the *selfish Passions* by Habits grown too strong; [201] in others we may observe *Humanity, Compassion,* and *Good-nature* sometimes raised by Habits, as we say, to an Excess.

Were we to strike a *Medium* of the several Passions and Affections, as they appear in the whole Species of Mankind, to conclude thence what has been the natural Ballance previously to any Change made by Custom or Habit, which we see casts the Ballance to either side, we should perhaps find the *Medium* of the publick Affections not very far from a sufficient *Counter-ballance* to the *Medium* of the Selfish; and consequently the *Overballance* on either side in particular Characters, is not to be looked upon as the *original Constitution,* but as the *accidental Effect* of Custom, Habits, or Associations of Ideas, or other preternatural Causes: So that an universal *increasing* of the Strength of *either,* might in the whole be of little advantage. The raising universally the *publick Affections,* the Desires of *Virtue* and *Honour,* would make the *Hero of Cervantes,* pining with *Hunger* and *Poverty,* no rare Character.

The universal increasing of *Selfishness,* unless we had more accurate Understandings to discern our *nicest Interests,* would fill the World with universal *Rapine* and *War.* The Consequences of [204] either universally *abating,* or *increasing* the Desires between the *Sexes,* the *Love of Offspring,* or the several [202] *Tastes* and *Fancies* in other Pleasures, would perhaps be found more pernicious to the whole, than the present Constitution. What seems most truly wanting in our Nature, is greater *Knowledge, Attention* and *Consideration:* had we a greater Perfection this way, and were evil *Habits,* and foolish *Associations of Ideas* prevented, our *Passions* would appear in better order.

But while we feel in ourselves so much *publick Affection* in the various Relations of Life, and observe the like in others; while we find every one desiring indeed his *own Happiness,* but capable of discerning, by a little Attention, that not only his external *Conveniency,* or *worldly Interest,* but even the most immediate and lively *Sensations of Delight,* of which his Nature is susceptible, immediately flow from a *Publick Spirit, a generous, human, compassionate Temper,* and a suitable *Deportment;* while we observe so many Thousands enjoying a tolerable State of *Ease* and *Safety,* for each one whose Condition is made *intolerable,* even during our present *Corruption:* How can any one look upon this World as under the Direction of an *evil Nature,* or even question a perfectly *good* PROVIDENCE? How clearly does the [205] *Order of our Nature* point out to us our true *Happiness* and *Perfection,* and lead us to it as naturally as the several *Powers* of [203] the *Earth,* the *Sun,* and *Air,* bring *Plants* to their Growth, and the Perfection of their Kinds? We indeed are directed to it by our *Understanding* and *Affections,* as it becomes *rational* and *active Natures;* and *they* by *mechanick Laws.* We may see, that "*Attention* to the most *universal Interest* of all sensitive Natures, is the Perfection of each individual of Mankind:" That they should thus be like well-tuned *Instruments,* affected with every *Stroke* or *Touch* upon any one. Nay, how much of this do we actually see in the World? What *generous Sympathy, Compassion,* and *Congratulation* with each other? Does not even the flourishing State of the *inanimate Parts of Nature,* fill us with joy? Is not thus *our Nature* admonished, exhorted and commanded to cultivate *universal Goodness* and *Love,* by a *Voice heard thro' all the Earth, and Words sounding to the Ends of the World?*

Illustrations upon
the Moral Sense

[*205/207*] The Differences of Actions from which some are constituted *morally Good,* and others *morally Evil,* have always been accounted a very important Subject of Inquiry: And therefore, every Attempt to free this Subject from the usual Causes of Error and Dispute, the *Confusion of ambiguous Words,* must be excusable.

In the following Discourse, *Happiness* denotes pleasant *Sensation* of any kind, or a continued State of such *Sensations;* and *Misery* denotes the contrary *Sensations.*

Such Actions as tend to procure Happiness to the Agent, are called *privately useful:* and such Actions as procure Misery to the Agent, *privately hurtful.*

[*206*] Actions procuring Happiness to others may be called *publickly useful,* and the contrary Actions *publickly hurtful.* Some Actions may be both *publickly and privately useful,* and others both *publickly and privately hurtful.*

These different *natural Tendencies* of Actions are universally acknowledged; and in proportion to our *Reflection* upon human Affairs, we shall enlarge our Knowledge of these Differences.

When these *natural Differences* are known, it remains to be inquired into: 1st, "What *Quality* in any Action determines our *Election* of it rather than the contrary?" Or, if the Mind determines itself, "What *Motives* or *Desires* excite to an Action, rather than the contrary, or rather than to the *Omission?*" 2dly, "What *Quality* determines our *Approbation* of one Action, rather than of the contrary Action?"

Definitions.

Two Questions about Morality.

The Words *Election* and *Approbation* seem to denote simple Ideas known by *Consciousness;* which can only be explained by *synonimous Words,* or by concomitant or con[209]sequent Circumstances. *Election* is purposing to do an Action rather than its contrary, or than being inactive. *Appro[207]bation* of our own Action denotes, or is attended with a Pleasure in the *Contemplation* of it, and in *Reflection* upon the *Affections* which inclined us to it. *Approbation* of the Action of another is pleasant, and is attended with *Love* toward the Agent.*

The *Qualities* moving to *Election,* or *exciting to Action,* are different from those moving to *Approbation:* We often do Actions which we do not *approve,* and *approve* Actions which we *omit:* We often *desire* that an Agent had omitted an Action which we *approve;* and *wish* he would do an Action which we *condemn. Approbation* is employed about the Actions of *others,* where there is no room for our Election.

Now in our Search into the *Qualities* exciting either our *Election* or *Approbation,* let us consider the several *Notions* advanced of moral Good and Evil in both these Respects; and what *Senses, Instincts,* or *Affections,* [210] must be necessarily supposed to account for our *Approbation* or Election.

The Epicurean Opinion.

There are two Opinions on this Subject entirely opposite: The one that of the old *Epicureans,* as it is beautifully explained in the first Book of *Cicero, De* [208] *finibus;* which is revived by Mr. *Hobbes,* and followed by many better Writers: "That all the Desires of the *human Mind,* nay of all *thinking Natures,* are reducible to *Self-Love,* or *Desire of private Happiness:* That from this Desire all Actions of any Agent do flow."[40] Our *Christian Moralists* introduce other sorts of Happiness to be desired, but still " 'tis the *Prospect of private Happiness,* which, with some of them, is the sole *Motive of Election.*[41] And that, in like manner, what

---

*See *Treat.* II. *Sect.* 2. Parag. ult.

[[This note was added in the third edition. Much of T2 II, but not the final paragraph, concerns approbation toward an agent.]]

40. See, particularly, Cicero, *De Finibus,* 23b.

41. This is perhaps a reference to John Clarke, as Hutcheson would stop short of calling Pufendorf or Locke Epicureans, even though they share a similar theory of motivation.

determines any Agent to *approve* his own Action, is its *Tendency to his private Happiness* in the whole, tho it may bring *present Pain* along with it: That the *Approbation* of the Action of another, is from an Opinion of its Tendency to the Happiness of the *Approver*, either *immediately* or more *remotely:* That each Agent may discover it to be the surest way to promote his private Happiness, to do *publickly useful Actions,* and to abstain from those which are *publickly hurtful:* [211] That the neglecting to observe this, and doing *publickly hurtful Actions,* does mischief to the whole of Mankind, by hurting any one part; that every one has some little *damage* by this Action: Such an *inadvertent Person* might possibly be *pernicious* to any one, were he in his Neighbourhood; and the very *Example* [209] of such Actions may extend over the whole World, and produce some pernicious Effects upon any Observer. That therefore every one may look upon such Actions as *hurtful to himself,* and in this view does disapprove them, and hates the Agent. In the like manner, a *publickly useful Action* may diffuse some small *Advantage* to every Observer, whence he may *approve* it, and *love* the Agent."

This Scheme can never account for the principal Actions of human Life:* Such as the *Offices of Friendship, Gratitude, natural Affection, Generosity, publick Spirit, Compassion.* Men are conscious of no such Intentions or *acute Reflections* in these Actions. Ingenious speculative Men, in their straining to support an *Hypothesis,* may contrive a thousand *subtle selfish Motives,* which a kind generous Heart never dreamed of. In like manner, this Scheme can never account for [212] the sudden *Approbation,* and violent *Sense* of something amiable in Actions done in distant Ages and Nations, while the Approver has perhaps never thought of these distant *Tendencies* to his Happiness. Nor will it better account for our *want of Approbation* [210] toward *publickly useful Actions* done *casually,* or only with Intention of *private Happiness* to the Agent. And then, in these Actions reputed *generous,* if the Agent's Motive was only a view to his *own Pleasure,* how come we to approve them

Does not answer the Appearances.

---

* See *Treat.* III. *Sect.* 1.

more than his *enriching himself,* or his *gratifying his own Taste* with good Food? The whole *Species* may receive a like Advantage from both, and the Observer an equal Share.

Were our *Approbation* of Actions done in *distant Ages* and *Nations,* occasioned by this Thought, that such an Action done toward our selves would be useful to us, why don't we approve and love in like manner any Man who *finds a Treasure,* or *indulges* himself in any exquisite *Sensation,* since these Advantages or Pleasures might be conferred on *our selves;* and tend more to *our Happiness* than any Actions in distant Ages?

The *Sanctions of Laws* may make any Agent chuse the Action required, under the Conception of *useful* to himself, and lead [213] him into an Opinion of *private Advantage* in it, and of detriment in the contrary Actions; but what should determine any Person to approve the *Actions of others,* because of a Conformity to a [211] Law, if Approbation in any Person were only an Opinion of private Advantage?

The opposite Opinion does plainly. The other Opinion is this, "That we have not only *Self-Love,* but *benevolent Affections* also toward others, in various Degrees, making us desire their Happiness as an *ultimate End,* without any view to private Happiness: That we have a *moral Sense* or Determination of our Mind, to *approve* every *kind Affection* either in our selves or others, and all publickly useful Actions which we imagined do flow from such Affection, without our having a view to our *private Happiness,* in our Approbation of these Actions."

These two Opinions seem both intelligible, each consistent with itself. The former seems not to represent human Nature as it is; the other seems to do it.

Schemes seemingly different from both. There have been many *ways of speaking* introduced, which seem to signify something different from both the former Opinions. Such as these, that "Morality of Actions consists in *Conformity to Reason, or Difformity* [214] *from it:*" That "*Virtue* is acting according to the *absolute Fitness and Unfitness of Things,* or agreeably to the [212] *Natures* or *Relations* of Things," and many others in different Authors. To examine these is the

Design of the following Sections; and to explain more fully how the *Moral Sense* alledged to be in Mankind, must be presupposed even in these Schemes.

SECTION I

Concerning the Character of Virtue, agreeable to Truth or Reason.

[*213/215*] Since Reason is understood to denote our *Power of finding out true Propositions,* Reasonableness must denote the same thing, with *Conformity to true Propositions, or to Truth.*

Reasonableness in an Action is a very common Expression, but yet upon inquiry, it will appear very confused, whether we suppose it the Motive to *Election,* or the Quality determining *Approbation.*

There is one sort of *Conformity to Truth* which neither determines to the one or the other; *viz.* that *Conformity which is between every true Proposition and its Object.* This sort of Conformity can never make us *chuse* or *approve* one Action more than its contrary, for it is found in all Actions alike: Whatever *attribute* can be ascribed to a *generous kind Action,* the contrary *Attribute* may as *truly* be ascribed to a *selfish cruel Action:* Both Propositions are equally *true,* [216] and the two contrary Actions, the Objects of the two [*214*] *Truths* are equally *conformable* to their several Truths, with that sort of *Conformity* which is between a Truth and its Object. This *Conformity* then cannot make a Difference among Actions, or recommend one more than another either to *Election* or *Approbation,* since any Man may make as many Truths about Villany, as about Heroism, by ascribing to it *contrary Attributes.*

For Instance, these are *Truths* concerning the *Preservation* of *Property.* "It tends to the Happiness of human Society: It incourages Industry: It shall be rewarded by God." These are also *Truths* concerning *Robbery.* "It disturbs Society: It discourages Industry: It shall be punished by God." The former *three Truths* have the *Preservation of Property* for their

Conformity to Truth examined.

Object; the *latter three* have *Robbery.* And each Class of Truths hath that sort of *Conformity* to its Object, which is common to all Truths with their Objects. The *moral Difference* cannot therefore depend upon this *Conformity,* which is common to both.

The *Number* of Truths in both cases may be plainly the same; so that   5 a good Action cannot be supposed to agree to *more Truths* than an evil one, nor can an evil Action be disagreeable to any *Truth* or [*215*] *Compages* [217] *of Truths* made about it; for whatever Propositions do not agree with their Objects are not Truths.

If *Reasonableness,* the Character of Virtue, denote some other sort of   10 *Conformity* to Truth, it were to be wished that these Gentlemen, who make it the original Idea of moral Good, antecedent to any *Sense* or *Affections,* would explain it, and shew how it determines us antecedently to a Sense, either to *Election* or *Approbation.*

They tell us, "we must have some *Standard* antecedently to all *Sense*   15 or *Affections,* since we judge even of our Senses and Affections themselves, and approve or disapprove them: This Standard must be our *Reason,* Conformity to which must be the original Idea of moral Good."

                                                                            20

Reasons either justifying or exciting. But what is this *Conformity of Actions to Reason?* When we ask the Reason of an Action we sometimes mean, "*What Truth shews a Quality in the Action, exciting the Agent to do it?*" Thus, why does a *Luxurious* Man pursue *Wealth?* The Reason is given by this Truth, "Wealth is useful to purchase Pleasures." Sometimes for a Reason of Actions we shew the   25 *Truth expressing a Quality, engaging our Approbation.* Thus the *Reason* of hazarding [*216*] Life in just War, is, that "it tends to preserve our [218] honest Countrymen, or evidences publick Spirit:" The *Reason* for *Temperance,* and against *Luxury* is given thus, "Luxury evidences a selfish base Temper." The former sort of Reasons we will call *exciting,* and the   30 latter *justifying.** Now we shall find that all *exciting Reasons* presuppose *Instincts* and *Affections;* and the *justifying* presuppose a *Moral Sense.*

---

*Thus *Grotius* distinguishes the Reasons of War, into the *Justificae,* and *Suasoriae.* [[See Grotius, *De Jure Belli et Pacis,* II.1.1. Grotius makes his distinction with ref-

As to *exciting Reasons,* in every calm rational Action some *end* is desired or intended; no end can be intended or desired previously to some one of these Classes of Affections, *Self-Love, Self-Hatred,* or desire of private Misery, (if this be possible) *Benevolence* toward others, or *Malice:* All Affections are included under these; no *end* can be previous to them all; there can therefore be no *exciting Reason* previous to *Affection.*

We have indeed many confused Harangues on this Subject, telling us, "We have two Principles of Action, *Reason,* and *Affection,* or *Passion* (*i.e.* strong Affection): the *former* in common with [217] Angels, the *latter* with Brutes: No Action is wise, or good, or reasonable, to which we are not excited [219] by *Reason,* as distinct from all *Affections;* or, if any such Actions as flow from *Affections* be good, 'tis only by *chance,* or *materially* and not *formally.*" As if indeed *Reason,* or the Knowledge of the Relations of things, could excite to Action when we proposed no *End,* or as if *Ends* could be intended without *Desire or Affection.*

But are there not also exciting Reasons, even previous to any end, moving us to propose one end rather than another? To this *Aristotle* long ago answered, "that there are *ultimate Ends* desired without a view to any thing else, and *subordinate Ends* or Objects desired with a view to something else."[42] To *subordinate Ends* those *Reasons* or *Truths* excite, which shew them to be conducive to the *ultimate End,* and shew *one Object* to be more effectual than another: thus *subordinate Ends* may be called *reasonable.* But as to the *ultimate Ends,* to suppose *exciting Reasons* for them, would infer, that there is no *ultimate End,* but that we desire one thing for another in an infinite Series.

Thus ask a Being who desires *private Happiness,* or has *Self-Love?* "what [218] Reason [221] excites him to desire Wealth"? He will give this

Marginal notes:
Exciting Reasons suppose Affections.

No exciting Reasons for ultimate Ends.

erence to Polybius and Livy. Barbeyrac, in the commentary on his edition of Grotius (Jean Barbeyrac, *Le Droit de la Guere et de la Paix par Hugo Grotius* [Amsterdam: Pierre de Coup, 1724], 2v.), cites Polybius, *History,* III.6.]]

42. See *Nicomachean Ethics,* I.1. See also Gilbert Burnet (ed.), *Letters Between the Late Mr. Gilbert Burnet, and* Mr. *Hutchinson, Concerning The true Foundation of Virtue or Moral Goodness. Formerly Published in the London Journal* (London: W. Wilkins, 1735), 49–50.

Reason, that "Wealth tends to procure Pleasure and Ease." Ask his Reason for desiring Pleasure or Happiness: One cannot imagine what Proposition he could assign as his *exciting Reason*. This Proposition is indeed true, "There is an *Instinct* or *Desire* fixed in his Nature, determining him to pursue his Happiness;" but it is not this *Reflection* on his   5
own Nature, or this *Proposition* which excites or determines him, but the *Instinct itself*. This is a Truth, "*Rhubarb* strengthens the Stomach:" But 'tis not a *Proposition* which strengthens the Stomach, but the *Quality* in that Medicine. The Effect is not produced by *Propositions* shewing the *Cause*, but by the *Cause* itself.   10

In like manner, what *Reason* can a benevolent Being give, as exciting him to hazard his Life in just War? This perhaps, "such Conduct tends to the Happiness of his Country." Ask him, "why he serves his Country?" he will say, "His Country is a very valuable Part of Mankind." Why does he study the Happiness of Mankind? If his Affections be really   15
disinterested, he can give no *exciting Reasons* for it: The Happiness of Mankind in general, or of any valuable Part of it, is an *ultimate End* to that Series of Desires.

Men have
many ultimate
Ends.

[*219/222*] We may transiently observe one Mistake which many fall   20
into, who in their Philosophical Inquiries have learned to form very *abstract general Ideas:* They suppose, because they have formed some Conception of an *infinite Good*, or *greatest possible Aggregate*, or *Sum of Happiness*, under which all *particular Pleasures* may be included; that there is also some *one great ultimate End*, with a view to which every *particular Object* is desired; whereas, in truth, each *particular Pleasure* is desired without farther view, as an ultimate End in the *selfish Desires*. 'Tis true, the *Prospect* of a greater inconsistent Pleasure may surmount or stop this Desire; so may the *Fear* of a prepollent Evil. But this does not prove, that "all Men have formed Ideas of *infinite Good*, or *greatest possible Aggregate*, or that they have any *Instinct* or *Desire*, without an Idea   30
of its Object." Just so in the *benevolent* Affections, the Happiness of any one Person is an *ultimate End*, desired with no farther view: And yet the observing its *Inconsistency* with the Happiness of another more beloved, or with the Happiness of *many*, tho each one of them were but equally   35

beloved, may overcome the former Desire. Yet this will not prove, that in each *kind Action* Men do form the abstract Conception of *all Mankind,* or the *System of Rationals.* [*210*] The forming such large Conceptions is indeed useful, that so we may gratify either our [*223*] *Self-Love* or *kind Affections* in the fullest manner, as far as our Power extends; and may not content our selves with smaller Degrees either of *private* or *publick Good,* while greater are in our power: But when we have formed these *Conceptions,* we do not serve the *Individual* only from Love to the *Species,* no more than we desire *Grapes* with an Intention of the *greatest Aggregate* of Happiness, or from an Apprehension that they make a Part of the *General sum* of our Happiness. These Conceptions only serve to suggest *greater Ends* than would occur to us without Reflection; and by the *Prepollency* of one Desire toward the *greater Good,* either private or publick, to stop the Desire toward the *smaller Good,* when it appears inconsistent with the greater.

Let us examine the Truths assigned as *exciting* to the Pursuit of publick Good, even by those, who, tho they allow *disinterested Affections,* and a *moral Sense,* yet suppose something *reasonable* in it antecedently. They assign such as these "publick Good is the End proposed by the DE-ITY." Then what *Reason* excites Men to concur with the DEITY? Is it this, "Concurring with the DEITY will make the Agent *happy?*" This is an *exciting Reason* indeed, [*221*] but plainly supposes *Self-Love:* [*224*] And let any one assign the *exciting Reason* to the Desire of Happiness. Is the Reason exciting to concur with the DEITY this, "The DEITY is our *Benefactor?*" Then what *Reason excites* to concur with Benefactors? Here we must recur to an *Instinct.* Is it this Truth, "The divine Ends are *reasonable Ends?*" Then what means the Word [*reasonable?*] Does it mean, that "the Deity has *Reasons* exciting him to promote the publick Good?" What are these *Reasons?* Why, perhaps "we do not know them particularly, but in general are sure that the DEITY has Reasons for them." Then the Question recurs, What Reason excites us to *implicit Concurrence* with the Ends of the DEITY? The Reasons which excite *one Nature* may not excite another: The Tendency of an Action to the *Happiness of one Agent* may excite him, but will not excite another *Agent*

The common Reasons examined.

to concur, unless there appears a like Tendency to the Happiness of that *other.* They may say, "they are sure the *divine Ends* are good." What means *Goodness?* Is it *moral* or *natural?* If the divine Ends be *natural Good,* i.e. *pleasant,* or the *Cause of Pleasure,* to whom is this *Pleasure?* If to the DEITY, then why do we study the Happiness or the pleasing of the DEITY? What *Reason* excites us? All the possible Reasons must [*222*] either presuppose some *Affection,* if they are [*225*] exciting; or some *moral Sense,* if they are justifying.—Is the divine End naturally good to us? This is an exciting Reason, but supposes *Self-Love.* If we say the divine Ends are *morally Good,* we are just where we began. What is *moral Goodness? Conformity to Reason.* What are the *Reasons exciting* or *justifying?*

If any alledg as the Reason *exciting* us to pursue publick Good, this Truth, that "the Happiness of a *System,* a *Thousand,* or a *Million,* is a greater Quantity of Happiness than that of *one Person:* and consequently, if Men desire Happiness, they must have stronger Desires toward the *greater Sum,* than toward the *less.*" This Reason still supposes an *Instinct toward Happiness* as previous to it: And again, To *whom* is the Happiness of a System a greater Happiness? To one *Individual,* or to the *System?* If to the Individual, then his Reason exciting his Desire of a *happy System* supposes *Self-Love:* If to the *System,* then what *Reason* can excite to desire the greater *Happiness of a System,* or any *Happiness* to be in the Possession of *others?* None surely which does not suppose *publick Affections.* Without such *Affections* this Truth, "that an hundred Felicities is a greater Sum than one Felicity," will no [*223*] more excite to study the Happiness of the *Hundred,* than this Truth, "an hundred [*226*] Stones are greater than one," will excite a Man, who has no *desire of Heaps,* to cast them together.

The same may be observed concerning that *Proposition,* assigned by some as the *ultimate Reason* both *exciting* to, and *justifying* the Pursuit of publick Good, viz. *"It is best that all should be happy." Best* is most good: Good to whom? To the *Whole,* or to each *Individual?* If to the *former,* when this Truth excites to Action, it must presuppose *kind Affections;* if it is good to each *Individual,* it must suppose *Self-Love.*

Let us once suppose *Affections, Instincts* or *Desires* previously implanted in our Nature: and we shall easily understand the *exciting Reasons* for Actions, *viz.* "These Truths which shew them to be conducive toward some *ultimate End,* or toward the *greatest End* of that kind in our Power." He acts *reasonably,* who considers the various Actions in his Power, and forms *true Opinions* of their *Tendencies;* and then chuses to do that which will obtain the highest Degree of *that,* to which the *Instincts* of his Nature incline him, with the smallest Degree of those things to [224] which the *Affections* in his Nature make him averse.

[227] More particularly, the *exciting Reasons* to a Nature which had only *selfish Affections,* are those Truths which shewed "what Object or Event would occasion to it the greatest Quantity of *Pleasure:*" these would excite to the Prosecution of it. The *exciting Truths* about *Means,* would be only those which pointed out some Means as more certainly effectual than any other, or with less *Pain* or *Trouble* to the *Agent. Publick Usefulness* of *Ends* or *Means,* or *publick Hurtfulness* would neither excite nor dissuade, farther than the *publick State* might affect *that* of the Agent.

If there is any Nature with *publick Affections:* The Truths exciting to any *End* in this Order, are such as shew, "that any Event would promote the Happiness of others." That *End* is called most *reasonable,* which our Reason discovers to contain a greater Quantity of *publick Good,* than any other in our power.

When any Event may affect both the *Agent* and *others,* if the Agent have both *Self-Love* and *publick Affections,* he acts according to that Affection which is *strongest,* when there is any *Opposition* of Interests; [225] if there be no Opposition, he follows both. If he discovers this Truth, that "his constant [228] pursuit of *publick Good* is the most probable way of promoting his *own Happiness,*" then his Pursuit is truly reasonable and constant; thus both Affections are at once gratify'd, and he is consistent with himself. Without knowledge of that Truth he does not act *reasonably* for his own Happiness, but follows it by *Means* not tending effectually to this *End:* and must frequently, from the Power of *Self-Love,* neglect or counteract his other *End,* the *publick Good.* If there

The true Meaning of Reasons exciting to Actions, and reasonable Actions.

be also a *moral Sense* in such an Agent, while yet he is inadvertent to the *Connexion of private Happiness* with the *Study of the publick;* he must be perpetually yet more uneasy, either thro' the apprehended *Neglect of private Interest* when he serves the Publick; or when he pursues only *private Interest,* he will have perpetual *Remorse* and *Dissatisfaction* with his own   5
Temper, thro' his *moral Sense.* So that the Knowledge of this *Connexion* of private Interest, with the Study of publick Good, seems absolutely necessary to preserve a constant *Satisfaction* of Mind, and to prevent an *alternate Prevalence* of seemingly contrary Desires.

Should any one ask even concerning these two *ultimate Ends, private*   10
Good [226] and *publick,* is not the latter more *reasonable* than the former?—What means the Word *reasonable* in this Question? If we [229] are allowed to presuppose *Instincts* and *Affections,* then the Truth just now supposed to be discoverable concerning our State, is an *exciting Reason* to *serve the publick Interest,* since this Conduct is the most *effec-*   15
tual Means to obtain both ends. But I doubt if any Truth can be assigned which *excites* in us either the Desire of *private Happiness* or *publick.* For the *former* none ever alledged any *exciting Reason:* and a *benevolent Temper* finds as little *Reason exciting* him to the latter; which he desires without any view to *private Good.* If the meaning of the   20
Question be this, "does not every *Spectator approve* the Pursuit of publick Good more than private?" The Answer is obvious that he does: but not for any *Reason* or *Truth,* but from a *moral Sense.*

This leads to consider *Approbation* of Actions, whether it be for *Conformity to any Truth,* or *Reasonableness,* that Actions are ultimately approved, independently of any *moral Sense?* Or if all *justifying Reasons* do   25
not presuppose it?

Justifying Reasons suppose a moral Sense.

If *Conformity to Truth,* or *Reasonable,* denote nothing else but that "an Action is the *Object of a true Proposition,*" 'tis [227] plain, that all Ac-   30
tions should be approved [230] equally, since as many Truths may be made about the worst, as can be made about the best. See what was said above about exciting Reasons.

But let the *Truths* commonly assigned as *justifying* be examined.

Here 'tis plain, "*A Truth shewing an Action to be fit to attain an End,*" does not justify it; nor do we approve a *subordinate End* for any Truth, which only shews it to be fit to promote the *ultimate End;* for the worst Actions may be conducive to their *Ends,* and *reasonable* in that Sense. The *justifying Reasons* then must be about the *Ends* themselves, especially the *ultimate Ends.* The Question then is, "Does a *Conformity to any Truth* make us *approve* an *ultimate End,* previously to any *moral Sense?*" For example, we approve *pursuing the publick Good.* For what *Reason?* or what is the *Truth* for Conformity to which we call it a *reasonable End?* I fancy we can find none in these Cases, more than we could give for our liking any *pleasant Fruit.**

The Reasons assigned are such as these; "*'Tis the End proposed by the* Deity." But why do we *approve* concurring with [231] the divine Ends? This Reason is given, "*He is our Benefactor:*" But then, for [228] what *Reason* do we approve *Concurrence with a Benefactor?* Here we must recur to a *Sense.* Is this the Reason moving to *Approbation,* "*Study of publick Good tends to the Advantage of the Approver?*" Then the Quality moving us to *approve* an Action, is its being *advantageous to us,* and not *Conformity to a Truth.* This Scheme is intelligible, but not true in fact. Men *approve* without Perception of *private Advantage;* and often do not *condemn or disapprove* what is plainly pernicious; as in the Execution of a *just Sentence,* which even the Criminal may *approve.*

If any allege, that this is the *justifying Reason* of the *Pursuit of publick Good,* "*that it is best all be happy,*" then we approve Actions for their *Tendency to that State which is best,* and not for *Conformity to Reason.* But here again, what means *best? morally best,* or *naturally best?* If the *former,* they explain the same Word by itself in a Circle: If they mean the *latter,* that "it is the most happy State where all are happy;" then, *most happy,* for whom? the *System,* or the *Individual?* If for the *former,* what Reason makes us *approve the Happiness of a System?* Here we must

*This is what *Aristotle* so often asserts that the προαιρετὸν or βουλευτὸν is not the End, but the Means.

[[This note was added in the third edition. See *Nicomachean Ethics,* 1111b27.]]

recur to a *Sense* or *kind Affections.* Is [232] it most happy for the *Individual?* Then the Quality moving *Approbation* is [229] again *Tendency to private Happiness,* not *Reasonableness.*

Obligation supposes either Affections or a moral Sense.

There are some other *Reasons* assigned in Words differing from the former, but more confused, such as these: " *'Tis our Duty to study publick Good. We are obliged to do it. We owe Obedience to the Deity. The whole is to be preferred to a Part.*" But let these Words *Duty, Obligation, Owing,* and the meaning of that Gerund, *is to be preferred,* be explained; and we shall find our selves still at a Loss for *exciting Reasons* previously to *Affections,* or *justifying Reasons* without recourse to a *moral Sense.*

The meaning of Obligation.

When we say one is obliged to an Action, we either mean, 1. *That the Action is necessary to obtain Happiness to the Agent, or to avoid Misery:* Or, 2. *That every Spectator, or he himself upon Reflection, must approve his Action, and disapprove his omitting it, if he considers fully all its Circumstances.* The former Meaning of the Word *Obligation* presupposes *selfish Affections,* and the *Senses of private Happiness:* The latter Meaning includes the *moral* Sense. Mr. *Barbeyrac,* in his Annotations upon *Grotius,** [230/233] makes *Obligation* denote an *indispensable Necessity to act in a certain manner.* Whoever observes his Explication of this *Necessity,* (which is not *natural,* otherwise no Man could act against his Obligation) will find that it denotes only "such a Constitution of a powerful Superior, as will make it impossible for any Being to obtain *Happiness,* or avoid *Misery,* but by such a Course of Action." This agrees with the former Meaning, tho sometimes he also includes the latter.

Many other confused Definitions have been given of Obligation, by no obscure Names in the learned World. But let any one give a distinct Meaning, different from the two above-mentioned. To pursue them all would be endless; only let the *Definitions* be substituted in place of the Word OBLIGATION, in other parts of each Writer, and let it be observed whether it makes good Sense or not.†

---

* *Lib* J. *Chap.* 1. *Sect.* 10.
† The common Definition, *Vinculum Juris que necessitate aastringimur alicujus rei*

Before we quit this Character *Reasonableness,* let us consider the Arguments brought to prove that there must be some Standard of moral Good antecedent to any Sense. Say [234] they, "*Perceptions of Sense* are deceitful, we must have some Perception or Idea of *Virtue* more stable and certain; this must be *Conformity to Reason: Truth* discovered by our *Reason* [231] is certain and invariable: *That* then alone is the Original Idea of Virtue, *Agreement with Reason.*" But in like manner our *Sight* and *Sense of Beauty* is deceitful, and does not always represent the true *Forms* of Objects. We must not call that *beautiful* or *regular,* which pleases the *Sight,* or an *internal Sense;* but Beauty in external Forms too, consists in *Conformity* to *Reason.* So our *Taste* may be vitiated: we must not say that *Savour* is perceived by *Taste,* but must place the original Idea of *grateful Savours* in *Conformity to Reason,* and of *ungrateful* in *Contrariety to Reason.* We may mistake the real *Extent* of Bodies, or their *Proportions,* by making a Conclusion upon the first sensible Appearance: Therefore *Ideas of Extension* are not originally acquired by a *Sense,* but consist in *Conformity to Reason.*

If what is intended in this Conformity to Reason be this, "That we should call no Action *virtuous,* unless we have some *Reason* to conclude it to be virtuous, or some *Truth* shewing it to be so." This is very true; but then in like manner we should count no Action *vicious,* unless we [235] have some *Reason* for counting it so, or when 'tis *Truth* "that it is vicious." If this be intended by *Conformity to Truth,* then at the same rate we may make *Conformity to Truth* the original Idea of *Vice* [232] as well as *Virtue;* nay, of every Attribute whatsoever. That *Taste* alone is

---

praestandae, is wholly metaphorical, and can settle no Debate precisely.

[[This note was added in the third edition. This definition of obligation derives from Justinian, *Institutes,* III.1—"De Obligationibus." Cumberland renders it "*That bond of the Law, by which we are tied with the necessity of paying any thing*" (Richard Cumberland, *De Legibus Naturae,* V §11). It is commonly cited by the natural lawyers. For a discussion, see Pufendorf, *Of the Law of Nature and Nations,* I.vi.4, and Barbeyrac's n. 2. It seems likely that Hutcheson is deriving this from Cumberland's discussion, as Cumberland dismisses Justinian's definition in favor of Papinianus's definition (which rests not on the particular laws of a polity—Rome— but on "the bond of equity" and remarks "it breeds *obscurity,* that he uses *Metaphorical* words, which are generally of *doubtful* meaning," Ibid.]]

sweet, which there is *Reason* to count *sweet;* that Taste alone is *bitter,* concerning which 'tis *true* that it is *bitter;* that Form alone is *beautiful,* concerning which 'tis true that it is *beautiful;* and that alone *deformed,* which is truly *deformed.* Thus *Virtue, Vice, Sweet, Bitter, Beautiful, or Deformed,* originally denote *Conformity to Reason,* antecedently to Per- 5 ceptions of any *Sense.* The *Idea of Virtue* is particularly that concerning which 'tis *Truth,* that it is *Virtue;* or *Virtue* is *Virtue;* a wonderful Discovery!

So when some tell us, "that Truth is naturally pleasant, and more so than any *sensible Perception;* this must therefore engage Men more than 10 any other Motive, if they attend to it." Let them observe, that as much *Truth* is known about *Vice* as *Virtue.* We may *demonstrate* the publick *Miseries* which would ensue upon *Perjury, Murder,* and *Robbery.* These Demonstrations would be attended with that *Pleasure* which is peculiar to *Truth;* as well as the Demonstrations of the publick Happiness to 15 [236] ensue from *Faith, Humanity and Justice.* There is equal Truth on both sides.

Whence it is that Virtue is called reasonable and not Vice.

[233] We may transiently observe what has occasioned the Use of the Word *reasonable,* as an Epithet of only *virtuous Actions.* Tho we have 20 *Instincts* determining us to desire *Ends,* without supposing any previous *Reasoning;* yet 'tis by use of our *Reason* that we find out the Means of obtaining our *Ends.* When we do not use our Reason, we often are disappointed of our End. We therefore call those Actions which are *effectual* to their Ends, *reasonable* in one Sense of that Word. 25

Again, in all Men there is probably a *moral Sense,* making publickly useful Actions and kind Affections *grateful* to the Agent, and to every Observer: Most Men who have thought of human Actions, agree, that the *publickly useful* are in the whole also *privately useful* to the Agent, either in this Life or the next: We conclude, that all Men have the *same* 30 *Affections and Senses:* We are convinced by our Reason, that 'tis by publickly useful Actions alone that we can promote *all our Ends.* Whoever then acts in a contrary manner, we presume is *mistaken, ignorant of,* or *inadvertent* to, these Truths which he might know; and say he acts *unreasonably.* Hence some have [237] been led to imagine, some *Reasons* 35 either exciting or [234] justifying previously to all *Affections* or a *moral Sense.*

Two Arguments are brought in defense of this Epithet, as antecedent to any Sense, *viz.* "That we judge even of our *Affections* and *Senses* themselves, whether they are *morally Good* or *Evil.*"

The second Argument is, that "if all *moral Ideas* depend upon the *Constitution* of our *Sense,* then all *Constitutions* would have been alike reasonable and good to the DEITY, which is absurd."

As to the first Argument, 'tis plain we judge of our own *Affections,* or those of others by our *moral Sense,* by which we approve kind Affections, and disapprove the contrary. But none can apply *moral Attributes* to the very *Faculty* of perceiving *moral Qualities;* or call his *moral Sense morally Good* or *Evil,* any more than he calls the *Power of Tasting, sweet,* or *bitter;* or of *Seeing, strait* or *crooked, white* or *black.*

Every one judges the *Affections* of others by his own *Sense;* so that it seems not impossible that in these *Senses* Men might differ as they do in *Taste.* A *Sense approving Benevolence* would disapprove [235] *that Temper,* [238] which a *Sense approving Malice* would delight in. The *former* would judge of the *latter* by his *own Sense,* so would the *latter* of the *former.* Each one would at first view think the *Sense* of the other perverted. But then, is there no difference? Are both Senses equally *good?* No certainly, any *Man* who observed them would think the *Sense* of the *former* more desirable than of the *latter;* but this is, because the *moral Sense* of every Man is constituted in the former manner. But were there any Nature with no *moral Sense* at all observing these two Persons, would he not think the State of the *former* preferable to that of the *latter?* Yes, he might: but not from any Perception of *moral Goodness* in the one *Sense* more than in the other. Any rational Nature observing two Men thus constituted, with *opposite Senses,* might by reasoning see, not *moral Goodness* in one *Sense* more than in the contrary, but a *Tendency to the Happiness of the Person himself,* who had the former *Sense* in the one Constitution, and a *contrary Tendency* in the opposite *Consti-*

Objections from our judging even of our Affections and Senses themselves.

I. That we judge our Senses themselves.

Answer'd.

tution: nay, the Persons themselves might observe this; since the *former Sense* would make these Actions grateful to the Agent which were useful to others; who, if they had a like Sense, would *love* him, and return *good Offices;* whereas the *latter Sense* would make all such Actions as are *useful* [*236*] *to others,* and [239] apt to engage their *good Offices,* ungrateful to the Agent; and would lead him into *publickly hurtful Actions,* which would not only procure the Hatred of others, if they had a *contrary Sense,* but engage them out of their *Self-Love* to study his *Destruction,* tho their *Senses* agreed. Thus any *Observer,* or the *Agent* himself with this *latter Sense,* might perceive that the *Pains* to be feared, as the Consequence of *malicious Actions,* did over-ballance the *Pleasures* of this *Sense;* so that it would be to the Agent's *Interest* to counteract it. Thus one Constitution of the *moral Sense* might appear to be more *advantageous* to those who had it, than the contrary; as we may call that Sense of Tasting *healthful,* which made wholesom Meat pleasant; and we would call a contrary *Taste pernicious.* And yet we should no more call the moral Sense *morally good* or *evil,* than we call the *Sense of Tasting savoury* or *unsavoury, sweet* or *bitter.*

But must we not own, that we judge of all our *Senses* by our *Reason,* and often correct their *Reports* of the *Magnitude, Figure, Colour, Taste* of Objects, and pronounce them *right* or *wrong,* as they agree or disagree with *Reason?* This is true. But does it then follow, that *Extension, Figure, Colour, Taste,* are not [237] *sensible Ideas,* but only denote *Reasonableness,* or *Agreement with* [240] *Reason?* Or that these Qualities are perceivable antecedently to any *Sense,* by our *Power of finding out Truth?* Just so a *compassionate Temper* may rashly imagine the *Correction of a Child,* or the *Execution of a Criminal,* to be cruel and inhuman: but by *reasoning* may discover the *superior Good* arising from them in the whole; and then the same *moral Sense* may determine the Observer to approve them. But we must not hence conclude, that it is any *reasoning* antecedent to a *moral Sense,* which determines us to *approve* the Study of publick Good, any more than we can in the former Case conclude, that we perceive *Extension, Figure, Colour, Taste,* antecedently to a Sense. All these Sensations are often corrected by *Rea-*

soning, as well as our *Approbations* of Actions as Good or Evil:* and yet no body ever placed the *Original Idea* of *Extension, Figure, Colour, or Taste,* in *Conformity to Reason.*

Thus tho no Man can immediately either *approve* or *disapprove* as *morally good or evil* his own *moral Sense,* by which he approves only *Affections* and *Actions* consequent upon them; yet he [*238*] may see whether it be *advantageous* to him in other respects, to have it constituted *one way* rather than another. *One Constitution* may make these Actions grateful to this Sense which tend to procure *other Pleasures* also. A *contrary Constitution* may be known to the very Person himself to be *disadvantageous,* as making these Actions *immediately grateful,* which shall occasion all *other sorts* of Misery. His *Self-Love* may excite him, tho with *Dissatisfaction,* to counteract this Sense, in order to avoid a greater *Evil.* Mr. *Hobbes* seems to have had no better Notions of the *natural State* of Mankind. An Observer, who was *benevolent,* would desire that all had the former sort of *Sense; a malicious Observer,* if he feared no *Evil to himself,* [243] from the Actions of the Persons observed, would desire the *latter Constitution.* If this Observer had a *moral Sense,* he would think that *Constitution* which was contrary to *his own, strange* and *surprizing,* or *unnatural.* If the Observer had no *Affections* toward others, and were disjoined from Mankind, so as to have neither *Hopes* nor *Fears* from their Actions, he would be indifferent about their *Constitutions,* and have no *Desire* or *Preference* of one above another; tho he might see which were *advantageous* to them, and which pernicious.

[*239*] As to the second Argument, What means [*alike reasonable or good to the* DEITY?] Does it mean, "that the DEITY could have had no *Reasons exciting* him to make one Constitution rather than another?" 'Tis plain, if the DEITY had nothing *essential to his Nature,* corresponding to our *sweetest* and *most kind Affections,* we can scarce suppose he could have any *Reason exciting* him to any thing he has done: but grant such

The 2d Objection, that all Constitutions would have been alike reasonable, answered.

* See *Sect* 4. of this Treatise.

a *Disposition* in the DEITY, and then the manifest *Tendency of the pres-ent Constitution to the Happiness of his Creatures* was an exciting Reason for chusing it before the contrary.* Each sort of Constitution [244]

*A late Author on *the Foundation of Moral Goodness,* &c. *p. 9.* thus argues: "If such a Disposition is in the Deity, is it a Perfection, or is it not? is it better than the contrary, more worthy of his Nature, more agreeable to his other Perfections? If not, let us not ascribe it to him: If it be, then for what Reason, Account, or Ground is it better? That Reason, Account, or Ground, must be the Foundation of moral Good-ness. If there be no Reason why it is better, then God is acted by a blind unaccount-able Impulse." In Answer, one may first ask the precise Meaning of these vague Words, *Perfection, Betterness, Worthiness, Agreement.* If these Terms denote "whatever makes the Being possessed of them happier, than he would be without them;" then, 1. It is plain, kind Dispositions are Perfections to Men in our present Frame; are better for us than the contrary, and agree better with our other Powers; *i. e.* they tend to preserve them, and procure us many Enjoyments. 2. Our apprehending such Dis-positions in God, according to our Frame makes us esteem and love him. 3. Our Knowledge of God is so imperfect, that it is not easy to prove that such Dispositions tend to make or preserve him happy, or to procure him other Enjoyments. And yet, 4. We may have good Reason, Ground, or Evidence, from his Works and Administra-tion to believe him Benevolent. 5. If he has real Good-will to his Creatures, their Perfection or Happiness is to him an ultimate End, intended without farther View or Reason: And yet, 6. He is not *acted by a blind Impulse:* the ultimate End is known to him, and the best Means chosen; which never happen in what we call blind Im-pulses; unless one calls *willing any ultimate End* a blind Impulse. For thus each Man should desire his own Happiness by a blind Impulse: And God's willing to regard the *Fitness of Things,* must be a blind Impulse, unless he have a *prior Reason* why he wills what his Understanding represents as *fit,* rather than what is *unfit;* for his Un-derstanding represents both. And there must be a prior *Fitness* or *Reasonableness* that he should will what is *fit,* and a yet prior *Fitness* that he should regard the *Fitness* of willing what is fit, and so on.

If in these Questions is meant, not by what Argument do we prove that the Deity is benevolent? but, "what is the efficient Cause of that Disposition in God?" Those Gentlemen must answer for us, who tell us also of the *Reason or Ground of the Divine Existence;* and that not as a Proof that he does exist, or the *Causa Cognoscendi,* as the Schoolmen speak; but the *Causa Essendi* of that Being which they acknowledge un-caused and independent. See Dr. *Sam. Clarke's Boyle's Lectures.*

[[This footnote was added in the third edition. John Balguy (1686–1748) was, like Burnet, a follower of Samuel Clarke. His favored form was polemic, and over the course of his career his victims included Shaftesbury, Collins, Tindal, Henry Grove, and Hutcheson. *The Foundation of Moral Goodness, or a Further Inquiry into the Original of our Idea of Virtue* (1728–29) was a critique of Hutcheson's Treatises from a rationalist perspective. Balguy's criticisms of Hutcheson continued in the first part of *Divine Rectitude: or a Brief Inquiry Concerning the Moral Perfections of the Deity*

might have given Men an equal *immediate Pleasure* in present *Self-Approbation* for any sort of Action; but the Actions approved by the *present Sense,* procure all *Pleasures* of the *other Senses;* and the Actions which would have been approved by a *contrary* [245] *moral Sense,* would
5   have been productive of all *Torments of the other Senses.*

If it be meant, that "*upon this Supposition, that all our Approbation presupposes in us a moral Sense, the* DEITY *could not have approved one Constitution more than another:*" where is the Consequence? Why may not the Deity have [240] something of a superior Kind, analogous to
10 our *moral Sense,* essential to him? How does any Constitution of the *Senses of Men* hinder the DEITY to reflect and judge of his own Actions? How does it affect the divine Apprehension, which way soever *moral Ideas* arise with Men?

If it means "*that we cannot approve of one Constitution more than an-*
15 *other, or approve the* DEITY *for making the* present Constitution:" This Consequence is also false. The *present Constitution* of our *moral Sense* determines us to approve all *kind Affections:* [246] This Constitution the DEITY must have foreseen as *tending* to the *Happiness* of his *Crea-tures;* it does therefore evidence *kind Affection* or *Benevolence* in the DE-
20 ITY, this therefore we must *approve.*

We have got some strange Phrases, "*that some things are antecedently rea-sonable in the Nature of the thing,*" which some insist upon: "That oth-erwise, say they, if before Man was created, any Nature *without a moral*
25 *Sense* had existed, this Nature would not have approved as morally good in the Deity, his constituting our Sense as it is at present." Very true; and what next? If there had been no *moral Sense* in that Nature, there would have been no *Perception* [241] *of Morality.* But "could not such

The meaning
of antecedent
Reasonable-
ness.

(1730). For Samuel Clarke (1675–1729) see the Introduction to this volume.
30   The Boyle Lectures were instituted through a bequest from Robert Boyle's estate, to combat "atheism" (Spinoza, Hobbes, and Toland; "free thinkers" such as Anthony Collins; and fellow travelers such as Mandeville). Clarke's *A Discourse Concerning the Unchangeable Obligations of Natural Religion* (London, 1705) and *A Demonstration of the Being and Attributes of God* (London, 1704) were Boyle lectures.
35 Hutcheson is likely referring here to the proof of God in the latter work.]]

Natures have seen something *reasonable* in one Constitution more than in another?" They might no doubt have *reasoned* about the various *Constitutions,* and foreseen that the *present one* would tend to the *Happiness* of Mankind, and would evidence *Benevolence* in the DEITY: So also they might have *reasoned* about the *contrary Constitution,* that it would make Men miserable, and evidence *Malice* in the Deity. They would have *reasoned* about *both,* and found out *Truths:* are both Constitutions alike *reasonable* to these Observers? No, say they, "the *benevolent* one is *reasonable,* and [247] the *malicious unreasonable:*" And yet these Observers *reasoned* and *discovered Truths* about both: An Action then is called by us *reasonable* when 'tis *benevolent,* and *unreasonable* when *malicious.* This is plainly making the Word *reasonable* denote whatever is *approved* by our moral Sense, without Relation to *true Propositions.* We often use that Word in such a confused Manner: But these *antecedent Natures,* supposed without a *moral Sense,* would not have *approved* one Constitution of the DEITY as *morally* better than another.

Had it been left to the Choice of these *antecedent Minds,* what *manner of Sense* [242] they would have desired for Mankind; would they have seen no *difference?* Yes they would, according to their *Affections* which are presupposed in all *Election.* If they were *benevolent,* as we suppose the DEITY, the *Tendency of the present Sense to the Happiness of Men* would have excited their Choice. Had they been *malicious,* as we suppose the Devil, the *contrary Tendency* of the *contrary Sense* would have excited their *Election* of it. But is there nothing *preferable,* or *eligible* antecedently to all *Affections* too? No certainly, unless there can be *Desire* without *Affections,* or *superior Desire, i. e.* Election antecedently to all *Desire.*

Reasons for Election different from those for Approbation. [248] Some do farther perplex this Subject, by asserting, that "the same *Reasons* determining *Approbation,* ought also to excite to *Election.*" Here, 1. We often see *justifying Reasons* where we can have no *Election; viz.* when we observe the *Actions of others,* which were even prior to our *Existence.* 2. The Quality moving us to *Election* very often cannot excite *Approbation; viz. private usefulness,* not publickly pernicious. This both does and *ought* to move *Election,* and yet I believe few will say, "they *approve* as virtuous the *eating a Bunch of Grapes,* taking a *Glass of Wine,* or *sitting down* when [243] one is tired." *Approbation* is not what we can *voluntarily* bring upon our selves. When we are contemplating Actions, we do not *chuse* to approve, because *Approbation* is pleasant; otherwise we would always approve, and never condemn any Action; because this is some way uneasy. *Approbation* is plainly a *Perception* arising without previous *Volition*, or Choice of it, because of any *concomitant Pleasure.* The Occasion of it is the *Perception of benevolent Affections* in our selves, or the discovering the like in others, even when we are incapable of any *Action* or *Election.* The *Reasons* determining *Approbation* are such as shew that an Action evidenced *kind Affections*, and that in *others*, as often as in *our* [249] selves. Whereas, the *Reasons* moving to Election are such as shew the *Tendency of an Action to gratify some Affection* in the Agent.

The *Prospect* of the Pleasure of *Self-Approbation*, is indeed often a Motive to *chuse* one Action rather than another; but this supposes the *moral Sense*, or Determination to *approve*, prior to the *Election*. Were Approbation *voluntarily* chosen, from the Prospect of its concomitant Pleasure, then there could [244] be no *Condemnation* of our own Actions, for that is unpleasant.

As to that confused Word [ought] 'tis needless to apply to it again all that was said about *Obligation.*

SECTION II

Concerning that Character of Virtue and Vice,
The Fitness or Unfitness of Actions.

[245/250] We come next to examine some other Explications of Morality, which have been much insisted on of late * We are told, "that there are *eternal and immutable Differences* of Things, absolutely and antecedently: that there are also *eternal and unalterable Relations* in the Natures of the Things themselves, from which arise *Agreements* and *Dis-*

The Fitness and Unfitness in Morals.

---

* See Dr. *Samuel Clarke's Boyle's* Lectures; and many late Authors.
[[This is a synoptic description of Samuel Clarke, *A Discourse Concerning the*

agreements, Congruities and *Incongruities, Fitness* and *Unfitness* of the
Application of Circumstances, to the *Qualifications of Persons;* that Actions *agreeable to these Relations are morally Good,* and that the *contrary*
Actions are *morally Evil.*" These Expressions are sometimes made of the
same Import with those more common ones: "*acting agreeably to the*   5
eternal Reason and Truth [*246*] *of Things.*" 'Tis is asserted, that [251]
"God who knows all these *Relations,* &c. does guide his Actions by
them, since he has no wrong Affection" (the Word [wrong] should have
been first explained): "And that in like manner these *Relations,* &c.
ought" (another unlucky Word in Morals) "to determine the *Choice* of   10
all Rationals, abstractly from any *Views of Interest.* If they do not, these
Creatures are insolently *counteracting their Creator,* and as far as they
can, *making things to be what they are not,* which is the greatest Impiety."

  That Things are now *different* is certain. That *Ideas,* to which there
is no *Object* yet existing conformable, are also *different,* is certain. That   15
upon comparing two *Ideas* there arises a *relative Idea,* generally when
the two Ideas compared have in them any *Modes of the same simple Idea,*
is also obvious. Thus every *extended Being* may be compared to any
other of the same *Kinds of Dimensions;* and *relative Ideas* be formed of
greater, less, equal, double, triple, subduple, &c. with infinite variety. This   20
may let us see that Relations are not *real Qualities* inherent in external
Natures, but only *Ideas* necessarily accompanying our *Perception* of two
Objects at once, and comparing them. *Relative Ideas* do continue, when
the external [*247*] Objects do not exist, provided [252] we retain the *two*
Ideas. But what the *eternal Relations* in the Natures of Things do mean,   25
is not so easy perhaps to be conceived.

Unchangeable Obligations of Natural Religion, and the Truth and Certainty of the
Christian Revelation and particularly Proposition I. The "many late authors" include
Gilbert Burnet and William Wollaston.]]

To shew particularly how far *Morality* can be concerned in *Relations,* we may consider them under these Three Classes. 1. The *Relations of inanimate Objects,* as to their *Quantity,* or *active* and *passive Powers,* as explained by Mr. Locke."[43] 2. The *Relations of inanimate Objects to rational Agents, as to their active or passive Powers.* 3. The *Relations of rational Agents among themselves,* founded on their *Powers* or *Actions* past or continued.[44] Now let us examine what *Fitnesses* or *Unfitnesses* arise from any of these *sorts of Relations,* in which the *Morality* of Actions may consist; and whether we can place *Morality* in them, without presupposing a *moral Sense.* 'Tis plain, that ingenious Author says nothing against the Supposition of a *moral Sense:* But many do imagine, that his Account of moral Ideas is independent upon a moral Sense, and therefore are less willing to allow that we have such an immediate Perception, or Sense of Virtue and Vice.[45] What follows is not intended to oppose his Scheme, but rather to suggest what seems a necessary Explication of it; by shewing that it is no otherwise intelligible, [248/253] but upon Supposition of a *moral Sense.*

Three sorts of Relations considered.

43. As Locke does not emphasize the relation of quantity in *An Essay Concerning Human Understanding,* it is likely that Hutcheson means only to refer to the doctrine of active and passive powers, which Locke discusses at length in the chapter "Powers" (*Essay,* II.XXI). Although powers are simple modes and not relations, they are the basis for countless relations, such as the active power that fire has to melt gold is related to the passive power gold has to be melted by fire; this is the relation of cause and effect (*Essay,* II.XXI §1). For Locke, though, we only have very obscure notions of active powers of bodies; active powers are usually referred to the volitions of thinking beings (*Essay,* II.XXI §4).

44. This division is derived from Samuel Clarke, *A Discourse Concerning the Unchangeable Obligations of Natural Religion,* 46–47.

45. Burnet argues that although "Reason and *Pleasure* may both of them be properly enough . . . *Moral Senses*" (Burnet [ed.], *Letters,* 11), the sense of pleasure which we feel upon observing a moral action is a consequence of our rational judgment that an act is true or right. Thus for Burnet, Hutcheson's moral sense is mediated by reason which in turn is not immediate but is the "*Sense* of the *Agreement* or *Disagreement* of our *Simple Ideas,* or the *Combinations* of them" (ibid.). Wollaston would concur (cf. *Religion of Nature Delineated,* 23, 41–45).

None of them
explain Moral-
ity without a
Sense.
1. Relations *of inanimate Objects* being known, puts it in the Power of a rational Agent often to *diversify* them, to *change their Forms, Motions,* or *Qualities* of any kind, at his pleasure: but no body apprehends any *Virtue* or *Vice* in such Actions, where no *Relation* is apprehended to a *rational Agent's Happiness* or *Misery;* otherwise we should have got into   5 the Class of Virtues all the practical *Mathematicks*, and the Operations of *Chymistry.*

2. As to the *Relations of inanimate Objects to rational Agents;* the Knowledge of them equally puts it in one's Power to *destroy Mankind,* as to preserve them. Without presupposing *Affections,* this Knowledge   10 will not excite to one Action rather than another; nor without a *moral Sense* will it make us approve any Action more than its contrary. The Relation of *Corn* to human Bodies being known to a Person of *kind Affections,* was perhaps the *exciting Reason* of teaching Mankind *Husbandry:* But the Knowledge of the *Relations of Arsenick* would excite a   15 *malicious Nature,* just in the same manner, to the greatest Mischief. A *Sword,* an *Halter,* a *Musket,* bear the *same Relation* [249] to the Body of an *Hero,* which they [254] do to a *Robber.* The killing of either is equally agreeable to these *Relations,* but not equally *good* in a *moral Sense.* The Knowledge of *these Relations* neither excites to Actions, nor justifies   20 them, without presupposing either *Affections* or a *moral Sense. Kind Affections* with such Knowledge makes *Heroes; malicious Affections, Villains.*

3. The last *sort of Relations* is that among *rational Agents,* founded on their *Actions* or *Affections;* whence one is called *Creator,* another *Creature;*   25 one *Benefactor,* the other *Beneficiary* (if that Word may be used in this general Sense;) the one *Parent,* the other *Child;* the one *Governor,* the other *Subject,* &c. Now let us see what *Fitnesses* or *Unfitnesses* arise from these Relations.

There is certainly, independently of *Fancy* or *Custom,* a *natural Tendency*   30 in some Actions to give *Pleasure,* either to the Agent or to others; and a *contrary Tendency* in other Actions to give *Pain,* either to the Agent or others: This sort of *Relation* of Actions to the *Agents* or *Objects* is indisputable. If we call these Relations *Fitnesses,* then the most contrary Actions have *equal Fitnesses* for contrary Ends; and each one is *unfit*   35 for the End of [250] the *other.* Thus *Compassion* is *fit* to make *others happy,* and *unfit* to make others *miserable. Violation of* [255] *Property is fit* to make Men *miserable,* and *unfit* to make them happy. Each of these is both *fit* and *unfit,* with respect to different Ends. The bare *Fitness then to an End,* is not the Idea of moral Goodness.

Perhaps the *virtuous Fitness* is that of *Ends.* The Fitness of a *subordinate End* to the ultimate, cannot constitute the Action *good,* unless the *ultimate End* be good. To *keep a Conspiracy secret* is not a good *End,* tho it be fit for obtaining a farther *End,* the *Success of the Conspiracy.* The *moral Fitness* must be that of the *ultimate End* itself: The *publick Good* alone is a *fit End,* therefore the *Means* fit for this *End* alone are good.

What means the *Fitness of an ultimate End?* For what is it fit? Why, 'tis an *ultimate End,* not fit for any thing farther, but *absolutely fit.* What means that Word *fit?* If it notes a *simple Idea* it must be the *Perception of some Sense:* thus we must recur, upon this Scheme too, to a *moral Sense.**

[256] If Fitness be not a *simple Idea,* let it be defined. Some tell us, that it is "an *Agreement* of an *Affection, Desire,* [257] *Action, or End,* to the *Relations of Agents.*"⁴⁶ But what means *Agreement?* Which of these four Meanings has it? 1. We say one *Quantity* agrees with another of equal *Dimensions* every way. 2. A *Corollary* agrees with a *Theorem;* when our

Agreement with Relations presupposes also a moral Sense.

*A late Author who pleads that *Wisdom* is chiefly employed in choosing the ultimate Ends themselves, and that *Fitness* is a proper Attribute of *ultimate Ends,* in answer to this short Question, "What are they fit for?" "answers, they are fit to be approved by all rational Agents." Now his meaning of the word [*Approved*] is this, *discerned to be fit.* His Answer then is "they are fit to be perceived fit." When Words are used at this rate one must lose his Labour in Replies to such Remarkers. See a Paper called Wisdom the sole Spring of Action in the Deity.

[[This footnote was added in the third edition. Turco (*Saggio,* 260) identifies this as a reference to *Wisdom the first spring of action in the Deity* (London: J. J. and P. Knapton, 1734) by the Dissenter Henry Grove (1684–1738), tutor first in ethics and pneumatology, then mathematics and physics, and finally divinity at Taunton. Grove criticized T 3 in *Wisdom the first Spring* (n. 18): "Will any one say that there must be *natural inclinations* in God, because there can be no *exciting reasons* to action without them? . . . But to a Being of the most consummate wisdom, and unbounded power, what more *persuasive* reason can there be, than the eternal unchangeable reason, or *fitness,* of *things? 'Tis fit to be done, therefore God does it.*"]]

46. Hutcheson likely has the pre-1728 writings of Balguy in mind here.

knowing the latter to be Truth, leads us to know that the former is also a *true Proposition.* 3. *Meat* agrees with that *Body* which it tends to *preserve.* 4. Meat agrees with the *Taste* of that Being in whom it raises a *pleasant Perception.* If any one of these are the Meanings of *Agreement* in the Definition, then one of these is the Idea of *Fitness.* 1. That an Action or Affection is of the same *Bulk* and *Figure* with the *Relation.* Or, 2. When the *Relation* is a *true Proposition,* so is the *Action* or *Affection.* Or, 3. The *Action* or *Affection* tends to *preserve* the Relation; and *contrary Actions* would destroy it: So that, for instance, GOD would be no longer related to us as *Creator* and *Benefactor,* when we disobeyed him. Or, 4. The Action raises *pleasant Perceptions* in the *Relation.* All these Expressions seem absurd.*

[257] These Gentlemen probably have some other Meanings to these Words *Fitness* or *Agreement.* I hope what is said will shew the need for *Explication* of them, tho they be so common. There is one Meaning [252] perhaps intended, however it be obscurely expressed, That "certain *Affections* or *Actions* of an Agent, standing in a *certain Relation* to other Agents, is *approved* by every *Observer,* or raises in him a *grateful Perception,* or moves the Observer to *love* the Agent." This Meaning is the same with the Notion of pleasing a *moral Sense.*

Whoever explains *Virtue* or *Vice* by *Justice* or *Injustice, Right* or *Wrong,* uses only more ambiguous Words, which will equally lead to acknowledge a *moral Sense.*

---

* Several Gentlemen who have published Remarks or Answers to this Scheme, continue to use these words *Agreement, Conformity, Congruity,* without complying with this just Request of explaining or fixing precisely the meaning of these words, which are manifestly ambiguous.

[[This footnote was added in the third edition. Balguy did attempt to define "conformity" in response to Hutcheson's complaints about the vagueness of the moral rationalist's terminology (*The Foundation of Moral Goodness,* I:28), but Hutcheson found his attempt unsatisfactory. In Part II of the *The Foundation of Moral Goodness,* Balguy considers the possible criticism of his theory as providing too vague a discussion of "conformity," to which he responds with an even vaguer definition (II:4–5).]]

SECTION III

Mr. Woolaston's Significancy of Truth,
as the Idea of Virtue considered

[253/258] Mr. Woolaston* has introduced a new Explication of *moral Virtue,* viz. *Significancy of Truth in Actions,* supposing that in every Action there is some *Significancy,*[47] like to that which *Moralists* and *Civilians* speak of in their *Tacit Conventions,* and *Quasi Contractus!* [48]

The Word *Signification* is very common, but a little Reflection will shew it to be very ambiguous. In *Signification of Words* these things are included: 1. An *Association of an Idea with a Sound,* so that when any *Idea* is formed by the Speaker, the *Idea of a Sound* accompanies it. 2. The *Sound perceived* by the Hearer excites the *Idea* to which it is connected. 3. In like manner a *Judgment* in the Speaker's Mind is accompanied with the *Idea of a Combination of Sounds.* 4. This *Combination of* [254] *Sounds* heard raises the *Apprehension* of that *Judgment* [259] in the Mind of the Hearer. Nothing farther than these Circumstances seems to be denoted by *Signification.*

Hearing a Proposition does not of itself produce either *Assent* or *Dissent,* or *Opinion* in the Hearer, but only presents to his Apprehension the *Judgment,* or *Thema Complexum.*[49] But the Hearer himself often forms

> Signification wherein it consists.

> Conclusions drawn from Speech.

---

* *In his Religion of Nature delineated.*
[[see particularly I.ix.]]

47. "I lay down this as a fundamental maxim, *That whoever acts as if things were so, or not so, doth by his acts declare, that they are so, or not so;* as plainly as he could by words, and with more reality," Wollaston, *The Religion of Nature Delineated,* 13.

48. Tacit conventions and "quasi contractus" were standard natural law expressions, the latter derived from Justinian, *Institutes* I.iii.28. Hutcheson defines them as follows: "Some rights arise, not from any contract, but from some other action either of him who has the right, or of the person obliged. . . . the *Civilians* . . . call them * *obligationes quasi ex contractu ortae:* feigning a contract obliging men in these cases to whatever could reasonably have been demanded by the one party, and wisely promised by the other, had they been contracting about these matters" (*System,* II.2.14).

49. "A thema is whatever is able to be offered to the understanding to be known."

Judgments or *Opinions* upon this occasion, either *immediately* without Reasoning, or by some short *Argument*. These *Opinions* are some one or more of the following *Propositions*. 1. *That a* Sound *is perceived, and a Judgment apprehended*. 2. *Such a Person caused the Sound heard*. 3. *The Speaker intended to excite in the Hearer the Idea of the* Sound, *and the Apprehension of the Judgment, or* Thema Complexum. This Judgment is not always formed by the Hearer, nor is it always true, when Men are heard speaking. 4. *The Speaker intended to produce* Assent *in the Hearer:* This Judgment is not always true. 5. *The Speaker* assents *to the Proposition spoken:* This Judgment in the Hearer is often false, and is formed upon Opinion of the Speaker's *Veracity,* or speaking what expresses his *Opinion* usually. 6. *The Speaker does not assent to the Proposition spoken:* This Judgment of the Hearer is often false, when [255] what is spoken is every way [260] true. 7. *The Speaker intended that the Hearer should believe or judge, "that the Proposition spoken was assented to by the Speaker."* 8. *The Speaker had the contrary Intention, to that supposed in the last Judgment:* Both these latter Judgments may be *false,* when the Proposition spoken is every way *true.* 9. *The Proposition spoken represents the Object as it is, or is logically true.* 10. *The Proposition spoken does not represent the Object as it is, or it is logically false.*

Morality does not consist in Significancy. As to the first four *Circumstances* which make up the proper *Significancy* of Speech, 'tis scarce possible that any one should place *moral Good* or *Evil* in them. Whether the Proposition were *logically true* or *false,* the having a bare *Apprehension* of it as a *Thema Complexum,* or raising this in another, without intending to produce *Assent* or *Dissent,* can have no more *moral Good* or *Evil* in it, than the *Reception* of any other *Idea,* or raising it in another. This *Significancy of Falshood* is found in the very *Propositions* given in *Schools,* as *Instances* of *Falshood, Absurdity, Contradiction to Truth,* or *Blasphemy.* The *pronouncing* of which, are Actions *signifying* more properly than most of our other *Actions;* and yet no body condemns them as immoral.

A *thema complexum* is a "proposition or speech to be confirmed or explicated," (Hutcheson, *Logicae Compendium* (Glasgow: Foulis, 1756), "Appendix," III.ii, 100–101).

[256] As to the *Opinions* formed by the Hearer, they are all his own *Action* as much as [261] any other *Conclusion* or *Judgment* formed from *Appearances* of any sort whatsoever. They are *true* or *false,* according to the Sagacity of the Observer, or his *Caution.* The Hearer may form perfectly true *Opinions* or *Judgments,* when the *Speaker* is guilty of the basest *Fraud;* and may form *false Judgments,* when the Speaker is perfectly *innocent,* and spoke nothing *false* in any Sense.

Nor in Conclusions formed by Hearers.

The *Evils* which may follow from the false Judgments of the Hearer, are no otherwise chargeable on the *Speaker,* than as the evil Consequences of another's Action of any kind may be chargeable upon any Person who *co-operated;* or, by his *Action,* or *Omission,* the Consequence of which he might have *foreseen,* did either actually *intend* this Evil, or *wanted that Degree of kind Affection,* which would have inclined him to have prevented it.

The *Intention* of the Speaker is what all *Moralists* have hitherto imagined the *Virtue* or *Vice* of Words did depend upon, and not the bare *Significancy* of Truth or Falshood. This *Intention* is either, 1. *To lead the Hearer into a true or false Opinion about the Sentiments of the Speaker.* [257] 2. *To make the Hearer assent to the Proposition spoken.* Or, 3. *Both to make the Hearer assent to the Proposition, and judge that the* [262] *Speaker also assents to it.* Or, 4. *To accomplish some* End, *by means of the Hearer's assent to the Proposition spoken.* This End may be known by the Speaker to be either *publickly useful,* or *publickly hurtful.*

The Morality of Speech in the Intention.

Some Moralists* of late have placed all *Virtue in Speech* in the *Intention* of the last kind, *viz.* "Accomplishing some publickly useful End,

---

*Barberack's *Notes on* Puffendorf, *Lib.* iv. c. 1, 7.

[[Barbeyrac's extremely long note explains how speech is "to be governed by three great principles of Duty . . . *Religion, Self-love,* and *Sociability.*" In the note, Barbeyrac argued against theories that forbid all lies, on the grounds that sociability is intertwined with countless white lies and pragmatic lies are often necessitated by circumstances. Not all or even most lies are to be allowed, but at the very least, "As often as they, to whom we speak, have no right to require of us to speak freely what we think, we do them no injury, if we conceal the Truth from them." Thus, Barbeyrac, following Pufendorf, emphasized the sociable and functional character of language and separated it from absolute considerations on truth.]]

by speaking either *logical Truth* or *Falshood:* and that all *Vice* in speaking, consists in intending to effect something *publickly hurtful* by Speech, whether *logically true or false,* and known to be such; or by using Speech in a manner which we may foresee would be *publickly hurtful,* whether we actually *intend* this evil Consequence or not." Some stricter *Moralists* [50] assert, that "the *publick Evils* which would ensue from destroying mutual Confidence, by allowing to speak *Propositions known to be false* on any occasion, are so great, that no particular *Advantage* to be expected from speaking *known logical Falshoods,* can ever over-ballance [*258*] them; that all use of Speech supposes a *tacit Convention of Sincerity,* the *Violation* of which is always evil." Both sides in this Argument agree, that the *moral Evil* in Speech consists either in some *direct malicious Intention,* or a *Tendency to the publick Detriment* of [263] Society; which Tendency the Agent might have *foreseen,* as connected with his Action, had he not *wanted* that Degree of *good Affections* which makes Men *attentive* to the Effects of their Actions. Never was bare *Significancy of Falshood* made the Idea of *moral Evil.* Speaking *logical Falshood* was still looked upon as innocent in many cases. Speaking *contrary to Sentiment,* or *moral Falshood,* was always proved evil, from some *publickly hurtful Tendency,* and not supposed as evil *immediately,* or the same Idea with *Vice.* The *Intention to deceive* was the Foundation of the Guilt. This Intention the Speaker studies to *conceal,* and does not *signify* it: It is an *Act of the Will,* neither *signified* by his Words, nor itself *signifying* any thing else.

This Point deserved Consideration, because if any Action be *significant,* 'tis certainly the *Act of Speaking:* And yet even in this the *Virtue* is not the *signifying of Truth,* nor the *Vice* the *signifying Falshood.*

The Significancy of Actions.

[*259*] The *Signification of some Actions* depends upon a like *Association of Ideas* with them, made either by *Nature,* or *arbitrarily,* and by *Custom,* as with *Sounds. Letters* are by *Custom* the *Signs of Sounds.* A *Shriek* or *Groan* is a natural *Sign* of *Fear* or *Pain:* A *Motion of the Hand* or *Head* may signify [264] *Assent, Dissent,* or *Desire.* The *cutting down tall*

50. It is not clear to whom this refers. One possibility is Cumberland.

Poppies was an *answer:* The *sending Spurs, advice to Flight: Kindling many Fires* raises the Opinion of an *Encampment: Raising* a *Smoke* will raise Opinion of *Fire.*

The most important Distinction of *Signs* is this, that* 1. "Some *Appearances* are the Occasion upon which an Observer, by his *own reasoning,* forms a Judgment, without supposing, or having reason to believe, that the *Agent,* who caused these Appearances, did it with *design to communicate his Sentiments* to others; or when the Actions are such as are usually done by the Agents, without *designing to raise Opinions* in Observers. 2. Some Actions are never used but with *professed Design* to convey the *Opinions of the Agent* to the *Observer;* or such as the Observer [260] *infers* nothing from, but upon having *reason* to believe that the *Causer* of the Appearance *intended to convey some Sentiment to the Observer.*" 3. Other Signs are used, when "the *Signifier* gives no reason to conclude any other *Intention,* but only to raise an *Apprehension of the Judgment, or the Thema Complexum,* without *professing any design to communicate* [265] *his Sentiments,* or to produce any *Assent* in the Observer."

To do Actions from which the Observer will form *false Opinions,* without having reason to imagine an *Intention* in the Agent, is never of itself imagined *evil,* let the Signs be *natural* or *instituted;* provided there be no *malicious Intention,* or *neglect of publick Good.* 'Tis never called a Crime in a *Teacher,* to pronounce an *absurd Sentence* for an instance; in a *Nobleman,* to travel without *Coronets;* or a *Clergyman* in *Lay-Habit,* for private Conveniency, or to avoid troublesome Ceremony; to *leave Lights in a Lodge,* to make People conclude there is a *Watch kept.* This *Significancy* may be in any Action which is observed; but as *true Conclusions* argue no *Virtue* in the Agent, so *false ones* argue no *Vice.*

Raising *false Opinions* designedly by the *second Sort* of Signs, which reasonably [261] lead the Observer to conclude *Intention in the Agent to communicate his Sentiments,* whether the Signs be *customary, instituted,*

* *See* Grotius de Jure Bell. *Lib.* 3. *c.* 1.
[[See Grotius, *De Jure Belli et Pacis,* III.1.7.2, III.1.XI.3 and on the latter passages Barbeyrac's n. 3.]]

or *natural,* is generally *evil,* when the Agent knows the Falshood; since it tends to diminish *mutual Confidence.* To *send Spurs* to a Friend, whom the *Sender* imagines to be in no danger, to deceive by *Hierogly-phicks* or *Painting,* is as criminal [266] as a *false Letter.* This *Significancy* occurs in very few human Actions: Some of the most important *Virtues* profess no *design of communicating Sentiments,* or *raising Opinions* ei-ther true or false: Nor is there any more *Intention* in some of the most *vicious Actions.* Again, who can imagine any *Virtue,* in all Actions, where there is this *Significancy of Truth* with *Intention?* Is it Virtue to say at *Christmas,* that "the Mornings are sharp?" to *beckon with the Hand,* in sign of *Assent* to such an Assertion? And in *false Propositions* thus signified by *Actions* or *Words,* there is no *Evil* apprehended where the *Falshood* is only *logical.* When the Falshood is known by the Agent, the *Evil* is not imagined in the *Significancy,* but in doing what one may foresee tends to breed *Distrust in Society.* And did all *moral Evil* consist in *moral Falshood,* there could be no *Sins of Ignorance.* If Mr. *Woolaston* alledges, that "Ignorance of some things signifies this Falshood, *viz. We are not* [262] *obliged to know the Truth."* This Falshood is not signified with *Intention;* nor is it *moral Falshood,* but only *logical:* since no Man in an Error knows that "*he is obliged to know the contrary Truth,*" Mr. *Woolaston's* use of the Words [ought] or [obliged] without a distinct Meaning, is not peculiar to this Place.[51]

[267] The third sort of *Significancy of Falsehood* is never apprehended as *morally Evil:* if it were, then every *Dramatick Writer* drawing *evil Characters,* every *History Painter,* every *Writer of Allegories,* or *Epicks,* every *Philosopher* teaching the Nature of *contradictory Propositions,* would be thought criminal.

---

51. No passage in Wollaston matches these two quotes exactly, but Hutcheson seems to have in mind *Religion of Nature Delineated,* I §5, 16–18.

But since only the *first sort of Significancy* can be in all Actions, and that too supposing that every Action whatsoever is *observed* by some Being or other: Let us see if this will account for *Morality*. Perhaps either, 1st, "Every Action is *good* which leads the Observer into *true Opinions* concerning the *Sentiments of the Agent,* whether the *Agent's Opinions* be *true or false*." Or, 2dly. "That Action is good which leads the Observer into *true Opinions concerning the Object, the Tendency of the Action, and the Relation between the Agent and the Object*."

[263] Did *Virtue* consist in this *first sort of Significancy* of Truth, it would depend not upon the *Agent* but the *Sagacity of the Observer:* The acute Penetration of one would constitute an *Action virtuous,* and the Rashness or Stupidity of another would make it *vicious:* And the most *barbarous Actions* [268] would raise no *false Opinion of the Sentiments of the Agent,* in a judicious Observer.

The second *sort* of Significancy would also make *Virtue* consist in the *Power of Observers.* An exact Reasoner would receive no *false Opinion* from the worst Action concerning the *Object* or *Relation* of the Agent to it: And a *false Opinion* might be formed by a weak Observer of a *perfectly good Action.*—An Observer who knew an Agent to have the *basest Temper,* would not from his worst Action conclude any thing *false* concerning the *Object:* And all such *false Opinions* would arise only upon Supposition that *the Agent was virtuous.*

But may it not be said, that "whether Men reason well about Actions or not, there are some *Conclusions really deducible from every Action?* It is a *Datum* from which something may be inferred by *just Consequence,* whether any one [264] actually infers it or not. Then may not this *Quality* in Actions, whether we call it *Significancy* or not, *that only true Propositions can be inferred from them by just Reasoning,* be moral Goodness? And may it not be the *very Idea* of *moral Evil* in Actions, that *some false Conclusions* [269] *can by just Consequence, be deduced from them?*" Or if we will not allow these to be the *very Ideas* of moral Good and Evil, "are they not *universal just Characters* to distinguish the one from the other?"

One may here observe in general, that since the Existence of the Action is supposed to be a true *Premise* or *Datum,* no *false* Conclusion can

Significancy
different from
the Morality.

possibly be inferred from it by *just Reasoning*. We could perhaps often justly infer, that the Agent had *false Opinions;* but then this Conclusion of the Observer, *viz.* "that the Agent has false Opinions," is really true.

But again, it will not make an *universal Character* of good Actions, that a just Reasoner would infer from them, that *"the Opinions of the Agent are true."* For it is thus Men must reason from Actions; *viz. Given the Constitution of Nature, the Affections of Agents, and the Action, to conclude concerning the Opinions:* Or more generally *given any three* [265] *of these to conclude the* fourth. Thus suppose the *"Constitution of Nature such, that the private Interest of each Individual is connected with the publick Good."* Suppose an Agent's Affections *selfish* only, then from a *publickly useful* [270] *Action* we infer, that *"the Agent's Opinions are true:"* And from a *publickly hurtful Action* conclude his *Opinions* to be false.

The same *Constitution* supposed with *publick Affections* as well as *selfish*. The observing a *kind or publickly useful Action,* will not immediately infer, that the Agent's *Opinions* are either *true* or *false:* With false Opinions he might do *publickly useful Actions* out of his *publick Affections,* in those cases wherein they are not apparently opposite to his Interest. A *publick Action* opposite to some present *private Interest,* would generally evidence *true Opinions;* or if the *Opinions were false,* that his *publick Affections* were in this Case much stronger than his *Self-Love.* A cruel Action would indeed evidence *false Opinions.*

Suppose the *same Constitution* in all other respects, with *malicious Affections* in an Agent. *A cruel or ungrateful Action* would not always prove the *Opinions of the Agent to be false;* but only that his [266] *Malice* in this instance, was more violent than regard to his *Interest.* A *beneficent Action* would prove only one of these two, either that his *Opinions of the Constitution* were true; or, that if [271] he was mistaken about the *Constitution,* he had also a *false Opinion* of the natural Tendency of the Action. Thus *false Opinions* may be evidenced by contrary Actions.

Suppose *"a Constitution wherein a private Interest could be advanced in Opposition to the publick"* (this we may call an *evil Constitution:*) Suppose only *Self-Love* in the Agent, then a *publickly useful Action,* any way *toilsome* or *expensive* to the Agent, would evidence *false Opinions:* And the most *cruel selfish Actions* would evidence *true Opinions.*

In an *evil Constitution,* suppose *kind Affections* in the Agent; *a publickly useful Action* would not certainly argue either *true or false Opinions.* If his *Opinions* were true, but *kind Affections* stronger than *Self-Love,* he might act in the same manner, as if his *Opinions* were false, and *Self-Love* the *reigning Affection.*

In an *evil Constitution,* suppose *malicious Affections* in an Agent, all *publickly useful Actions* would argue *false Opinions;* [267] and *publickly hurtful Actions* would argue *true ones.*

[272] This may shew us that Mens Actions are generally *publickly useful,* when they have *true Opinions,* only on this account; that we neither have *malicious Affections* naturally, nor is there any probability, in our present *Constitution,* of promoting a *private Interest* separately from, or in Opposition to the *Publick.* Were there contrary *Affections* and a contrary *Constitution,* the most cruel Actions might flow from *true Opinions;* and consequently *publickly useful Actions* might flow from false ones.

In our *present Constitution,* 'tis probable no Person would ever do any-thing publickly hurtful, but upon some false Opinion. The *flowing from true Opinions* is indeed a tolerable Character or Property of *Virtue,* and *flowing from some false Opinion* a tolerable Character of *Vice;* tho neither be strictly universal. But, 1. This is not *proper Signification.* A judicious Observer never imagines any *Intention to communicate Opinions* in some of the most important Actions, either *good* or *evil.* 2. Did an Action *signify Falshood,* 'tis generally only *logical.* 3. The *false Opinion* in the Agent is not the *Quality* for which the evil Action is *condemned;* nor is the [268] *true Opinion* that for which the good Action is *approved.* True Opinions in Agents [273] often *aggravate* Crimes, as they shew higher Degrees of *evil Affection,* or total *Absence of good.* And *false Opinions* generally *extenuate* Crimes, unless when the very Ignorance or Error has flowed from *evil Affection,* or total *Absence of good.*

'Tis surprizing, for instance, how any should place the *Evil of Ingrat-*

How far it is a Character of Virtue, that it flows from true Opinions.

itude in *denying* the Person injured, to have been a *Benefactor*. The Observer of such an Action, if he supposed the Agent had really that *false Opinion*, would think the Crime the less for it: But if he were convinced that the Agent had a *true Opinion*, he would think his *Ingratitude* the *more odious*. Where we most abhor Actions, we suppose often *true Opinions*: And sometimes admire Actions flowing even from *false Opinions*, when they have evidenced no *want* of good Affection.

To write a Censure upon a Book so well designed as Mr. *Woolaston*'s, and so full of very good Reasoning upon the most useful Subjects, would not evidence much *good Nature*. But allowing him his *just Praise*, to remark any *Ambiguities* or *Inadvertencies* which may lead Men into Confusion in their Reasoning, I am confident would [*269*] have been acceptable to a Man of so much Goodness, when he was living.

[*274*] One may see that he has had some other Idea of *moral Good*, previous to this *Significancy of Truth*, by his introducing, in the very Explication of it, Words presupposing the *Ideas of Morality* previously known: Such as [*Right*,] [*Obligation*,] [*Lye*,] [*his*] denoting [Property.]

Mr. *Woolaston* acknowledges that there may be very little *evil* in some Actions signifying Falshood; such as *throwing away that which is of but little Use or Value*. It is objected to him, that there is equal *Contrariety to Truth* in such Actions, as in the greatest *Villany:* He, in answer to it, really unawares gives up his whole Cause. He must own, that there may be the *strictest Truth* and *Certainty* about Trifles; so there may be the most *obvious Falshood* signified by *trifling Actions*. If then *Significancy of Falshood* be the very same with *moral Evil*, all Crimes must be equal. He answers, that *Crimes* increase according to the *Importance* of the Truth denied; and so the *Virtue* increases, as the *Importance* of the Truths affirmed. Then

> [*270*] *Virtue* and *Vice* increase, as the *Importance* of Propositions affirmed or denied;
> [*275*] But *Signification of Truth and Falshood* does not so increase:
> Therefore *Virtue* and *Vice* are not the same with *Signification of Truth or Falshood*.

Margin note: Signifying of Truth equal in unequal Virtue.

But what is this *Importance of Truth?* Nothing else but the *Moment* or *Quantity* of good or evil, either *private* or *publick,* which should be produced by Actions, concerning which these *true Judgments* are made. But it is plain, the *Signification* of Truth or Falshood is not varied by this *Importance;* therefore *Virtue* or *Vice* denote something different from this *Signification.*

But farther, The *Importance* of Actions toward publick Good or Evil, is not the *Idea of Virtue* or *Vice:* Nor does the one prove *Virtue* in an Action, any farther than it evidences *kind Affections;* or the other *Vice,* farther than it evidences either *Malice* or *Want* of kind Affections: Otherwise a *casual Invention,* an Action wholly from *views of private Interest,* might be as virtuous as the most *kind* and *generous Offices:* And *Chance-Medley,* or *kindly-intended,* but *unsuccessful Attempts* [271] would be as *vicious* as *Murder* or *Treason.*

One of Mr. *Woolaston's* Illustrations that *Significancy of Falshood* is the Idea of moral [276] Evil, ends in this, " *'Tis acting a Lye.*"[52] What then? Should he not first have shewn what was *moral Evil,* and that every Lye was such?

Another Illustration or Proof is that, " *it is acting contrary to that Reason which* GOD *has given us as the Guide of our Actions.*"[53] Does not this place the original Idea of *moral Evil* in *counteracting the* DEITY, and not in *signifying Falshood?* But, he may say, "Counteracting the DEITY denies him to be our *Benefactor,* and signifies Falshood." Then why is *signifying Falshood* evil? Why, 'tis *counteracting the* DEITY, who gave us Reason for our Guide. Why is this evil again? It denies the Truth, that " *he is our Benefactor.*"

Some Ambiguities in Mr. Woolaston.

---

52. Wollaston argues that someone who violates another's property rights "acts a lie," (*Religion of Nature Delineated,* VI §§15, 138). The exact formulation is found in John Clarke's attack on Wollaston: "I suppose this Sort of Language of denying Truth by Action, or acting a Lie, as the Author somewhere expresses himself, will be a little surprising to the Reader" (John Clarke, *An Examination of the Notion of Moral Good and Evil* [London: A. Bettesworth, 1725], 6).

53. See *Religion of Nature Delineated,* I.4, 14–15.

Another Illustration is this, "That *signifying Falshood is altering the Natures of Things, and making them be what they are not,* or *desiring at least to make them be what they are not.*"[54] If by *altering the Natures* be meant *destroying Beings,* then moral Evil consists in *desiring the Destruction of other Natures,* [272] or in *Evil Affections.* If what is meant be *altering the Laws of Nature,* or *desiring that they were stopped;* this is seldom desired by any but *Madmen,* nor is this *Desire* evidenced by some of the [277] worst Actions, nor is *such Desire* always criminal; otherwise it were as great a Crime as any, to wish, when a *Dam* was broken down, that the Water would not overflow the Country.

If *making Things be what they are not,* means "attempting or desiring that any Subject should have two *opposite Qualities at once,* or a *Quality* and its *Privation;*" 'tis certain then, that according to the *Stoicks,* all *vicious Men are thorowly mad.* But 'tis to be doubted, that such Madness never happened to even the *worst of Mankind.* When a Man *murders,* he does not desire his *Fellow-Creature* to be both *dead* and *living.* When he *robs,* he does not desire that both *he* and the *Proprietor* should at the *same time* possess. If any says, that he desires to have a *Right* to that, to which another has a *Right;* 'tis probably false. Robbers neither think of *Rights* at all, nor are solicitous about acquiring them: Or, if they retain some *wild Notions of Rights,* they think their *Indigence, Conquest* or *Courage* gives them a *Right,* and makes the other's Right to *cease.* If *attempting to make* [273] *old Qualities or Rights give place to new,* be the Idea of *moral Evil,* then every *Artificer, Purchaser,* or *Magistrate invested with an Office* is criminal.

[278] Many of Mr. *Woolaston's* Propositions contradicted by Actions, are about *Rights, Duties, Obligation, Justice, Reasonableness.* These are *long Words, principal Names,* or *Attributes* in Sentences. The little Word [his,] or the Particles [*as, according*] are much better: they may escape Observation, and yet may include all the Ambiguities of *Right, Property, Agreement, Reasonableness:* "*Treating Things as they are, and not as they are not.*" Or, "*According to what they are, or are not,*" are Expressions he

54. See *Religion of Nature Delineated,* I.4, 13.

probably had learned from another truly great Name, who has not explained them sufficiently.

It may perhaps not seem improper on this occasion to observe, that in the *Quasi Contractus,* the *Civilians* do not imagine any Act of the Mind of the *Person obliged* to be really signified, but by a sort of *Fictio juris* supposing it, order him to act as if he had contracted, even when they know that he had *contrary Intentions.*

In the *Tacit Conventions,* 'tis not a *Judgment* which is signified, but an *Act of the Will transferring Right,* in which [274] there is no Relation to *Truth* or *Falshood* of itself. The *Non-performance of Covenants* is made [279] *penal,* not because of their *signifying Falshoods,* as if this were the Crime in them: But it is necessary, in order to preserve *Commerce* in any Society, to *make effectual* all *Declarations of Consent to transfer Rights* by any usual *Signs,* otherwise there could be no *Certainty* in Mens Transactions.

> In Quasi Contracts, or Tacit, no Signification of Truth.

SECTION IV

*Shewing the Use of Reason concerning Virtue
and Vice, upon Supposition that we receive
these Ideas by a Moral Sense.*

[275/280] Had those who insist so much upon the *antecedent Reasonableness of Virtue,* told us distinctly what is *reasonable* or *provable* concerning it, many of our Debates had been prevented. Let us consider what *Truths* concerning Actions Men could desire to know, or prove by *Reason.* I fancy they may be reduced to these Heads. 1. "To know whether there are not *some Actions* or *Affections* which obtain the *Approbation* of any Spectator or Observer, and others move his *Dislike* and *Condemnation?*" This Question, as every Man can answer for himself, so *universal Experience* and *History* shew, that in all Nations it is so; and consequently the *moral Sense is universal.* 2. "Whether there be any par-

> Truths about Morals, four sorts.

ticular *Quality,* which, wherever it is apprehended, gains *Approbation,* and the contrary raises *Disapprobation?*" We shall [*276*] find this *Quality* to be *kind Affection,* [281] or Study of the Good of others; and thus the *moral Senses* of Men are generally *uniform.* About these two Questions there is little reasoning; we know how to answer them from reflecting on our own *Sentiments,* or by consulting others. 3. "What Actions do really *evidence kind Affections,* or do really *tend to the greatest publick Good?*" About this Question is all the special *Reasoning* of those who treat of the particular *Laws of Nature,* or even of *Civil Laws:* This is the largest Field, and the most useful Subject of *Reasoning,* which remains upon every *Scheme of Morals.* 4. "What are the Motives which, even from Self-Love, would excite each Individual to do those Actions which are publickly useful?" 'Tis probable indeed, no Man would *approve* as virtuous an Action *publickly useful,* to which the Agent was excited only by *Self-Love,* without any *kind Affection:* 'Tis also probable that no view of *Interest* can raise that *kind Affection,* which we *approve* as virtuous; nor can any *Reasoning* do it, except that which shews some *moral Goodness,* or *kind Affections* in the Object; for this never fails, where it is observed or supposed in any Person to raise the *Love* of the Observer; so that *Virtue* is not properly *taught.*

[*277/282*] Yet since all Men have naturally *Self-Love* as well as *kind Affections,* the former may often counteract the latter, or the latter the former; in each case the Agent is *uneasy,* and in some degree *unhappy.* The first *rash Views* of human Affairs often represent *private Interest* as opposite to the *Publick:* When this is apprehended, *Self-Love* may often engage Men in *publickly hurtful Actions,* which their *moral Sense* will condemn; and this is the ordinary Cause of Vice. To represent these Motives of *Self-Interest,* to engage Men to publickly useful Actions, is certainly the most necessary Point in Morals. This has been so well done by the *antient Moralists,* by Dr. *Cumberland, Puffendorf, Grotius, Shaftesbury;* 'tis made so certain from the *divine Government* of the World, the *State of Mankind,* who cannot subsist without Society, from universal *Experience* and *Consent,* from *inward Consciousness* of the Pleasure of kind Affections, and *Self-Approbation,* and of the *Torments* of *Malice,* or *Hatred,* or *Envy,* or *Anger;* that no Man who considers these things, can ever imagine he can have any possible *Interest* in opposing the publick Good; or in checking or restraining his kind Affections; nay, if he had no *kind Affections,* his very *Self-Love* and Regard to his private Good might excite [*278*] him to publickly [*283*] useful Actions, and dissuade from the contrary.

What farther should be provable concerning Virtue, whence it should be called *reasonable antecedently to all Affection, or Interest, or Sense,* or what it should be *fit* for, one cannot easily imagine.

Perhaps what has brought the Epithet *Reasonable,* or *flowing from Reason,* in opposition to what flows from *Instinct, Affection,* or *Passion,* so much into use, is this, "That it is often observed, that the very best of our particular *Affections* or *Desires,* when they are grown violent and *passionate,* thro' the *confused Sensations* and *Propensities* which attend them, do make us incapable of considering calmly the whole *Tendency* of our Actions, and lead us often into what is *absolutely pernicious,* under some Appearance of *relative* or *particular Good.*" This indeed may give some ground for distinguishing between *passionate Actions,* and *those* from *calm Desire* or *Affection* which employs our *Reason* freely: But can never set *rational Actions* in Opposition to those from *Instinct, Desire* or *Affection.* And it must be owned, that the most perfect Virtue consists in the *calm, unpassionate Benevolence,* [*279*] rather than in particular Affections.

[*284*] If one asks "how do we know that *our Affections are right when they are kind?*" What does the Word [right] mean? Does it mean *what we approve?* This we know by *Consciousness* of our *Sense.* Again, how do we know that our *Sense* is right, or that we *approve our Approbation?* This can only be answered by another Question, *viz.* "How do we know we are pleased when we are pleased?"—Or does it mean, "how do we know that we shall *always* approve what we *now* approve?" To answer this, we must first know that the *same Constitution* of our *Sense* shall always remain: And again, that we have applyed our selves carefully to consider the *natural Tendency* of our Actions. Of the *Continuance* of the same Constitution of our *Sense,* we are as sure as of the Continuance of *Gravitation,* or any other *Law of Nature:* The *Tendency* of

How we judge of our Moral Sense.

our own Actions we cannot always know; but we may know certainly that we *heartily* and *sincerely* studied to act according to what, by all the Evidence now in our Power to obtain, appeared as most *probably tending to publick Good.* When we are conscious of this *sincere Endeavour,* the *evil Consequences* which we could not have foreseen, [*280*] never will make us *condemn* our Conduct. But without this *sincere Endeavour,* [*285*] we may often approve at *present* what we shall *afterwards* condemn.

How our
Moral Sense is
corrected by
Reason.

If the Question means, "How are we sure that what *we* approve, *all others* shall also approve?" Of this we can be sure upon *no Scheme;* but 'tis highly probable that the *Senses* of all Men are pretty *uniform:* That the DEITY also approves *kind Affections,* otherwise he would not have implanted them in us, nor determined us by a *moral Sense* to approve them. Now since the *Probability that Men shall judge truly,* abstracting from any presupposed *Prejudice,* is greater than that *they shall judge falsly;* 'tis more probable, when our Actions are really *kind* and *publickly useful,* that *all Observers* shall judge *truly* of our *Intentions,* and of the *Tendency* of our Actions, and consequently approve what *we* approve our selves, than that they shall judge *falsly* and condemn them.

If the Meaning of the Question be, "Will the doing what our *moral Sense* approves tend to *our Happiness,* and to the avoiding Misery?" 'Tis thus we call a *Taste wrong,* when it makes that *Food* at present *grateful,* which shall occasion *future Pains,* or *Death.* This Question [*281*] concerning our *Self-Interest* must be answered by such *Reasoning* as was mentioned above, [*286*] to be well managed by our *Moralists* both antient and modern.

Thus there seems no part of that *Reasoning* which was ever used by *Moralists,* to be superseded by supposing a *moral Sense.* And yet without a *moral Sense* there is no Explication can be given of our *Ideas of Morality;* nor of that *Reasonableness* supposed *antecedent* to all *Instincts, Affections,* or *Sense.*

"But may there not be a *right* or *wrong State* of our *moral Sense,* as there is in our other *Senses,* according as they represent their Objects to be *as they really are,* or represent them otherwise?" So may not our *moral*

Sense approve that which is *vicious,* and *disapprove Virtue,* as a *sickly Palate* may dislike *grateful Food,* or a *vitiated Sight* misrepresent *Colours* or *Dimensions?* Must we not know therefore *antecedently* what is *morally Good* or *Evil* by our *Reason,* before we can know that our *moral Sense* is *right?*

To answer this, we must remember that of the *sensible Ideas,* some are allowed to be only *Perceptions* in our Minds, and not Images of any like *external Quality,* as [282] *Colours, Sounds, Tastes, Smells, Pleasure, Pain.* Other Ideas are *Images* of something *external,* [287] as *Duration, Number, Extension, Motion, Rest:* These *latter,* for distinction, we may call *concomitant Ideas of Sensation,* and the former *purely sensible.* As to the *purely sensible Ideas,* we know they are *alter'd* by any Disorder in our *Organs,* and made *different* from what arise in us from the same Objects at other times. We do not denominate Objects from our *Perceptions during the Disorder,* but according to our *ordinary Perceptions,* or those of others in *good Health:* Yet no body imagines that therefore *Colours, Sounds, Tastes,* are not *sensible Ideas.* In like manner many *Circumstances* diversify the *concomitant Ideas:* But we denominate Objects from the Appearances they make to us in an *uniform Medium, when our Organs are in no disorder, and the Object not very distant from them.* But none therefore imagines that it is *Reason* and not *Sense* which discovers these *concomitant Ideas,* or *primary Qualities.*

Just so in our *Ideas of Actions.* These three Things are to be distinguished, 1. The Idea of the *external Motion,* known first by *Sense,* and its *Tendency to the Happiness or Misery* of some *sensitive Nature,* often inferr'd by *Argument* or *Reason.* 2. *Apprehension* or *Opinion of the Affections* [283] in [288] the Agent, concluded by our *Reason:* So far the Idea of an *Action* represents something *external* to the Observer. 3. The *Perception of Approbation or Disapprobation* arising in the Observer, according as the *Affections of the Agent* are apprehended *kind* in their *just Degree,* or *deficient,* or *malicious.* This *Approbation* cannot be supposed an *Image of any thing external,* more than the *Pleasure of Harmony, of Taste, of Smell.* But let none imagine, that calling the *Ideas of Virtue* and *Vice* Perceptions of a *Sense,* upon apprehending the *Actions* and *Affections* of another does diminish their *Reality,* more than the like *Assertions* concerning all *Pleasure* and *Pain, Happiness* or *Misery.* Our *Reason* does often correct the *Report of our Senses,* about the *natural Tendency* of the external Action, and corrects *rash Conclusions* about the *Affections* of the Agent. But whether our *moral Sense* be subject to such a Disorder, as to have *different Perceptions,* from the same apprehended *Affections* in an 5 Agent, at *different times,* as the *Eye* may have of the Colours of an un-altered Object, 'tis not easy to determine: Perhaps it will be hard to find any Instances of such a *Change.* What *Reason* could correct, if it fell into such a *Disorder,* I know not; except suggesting to its *Remembrance* its *former* [289] *Approbations,* and representing the *general Sense* of Man- 10 kind. [*284*] But this does not prove Ideas of *Virtue* and *Vice* to be pre-vious to a *Sense,* more than a like *Correction* of the Ideas of *Colour* in a Person under the *Jaundice,* proves that *Colours* are perceived by *Reason,* previously to *Sense.*

If any say, "this *moral Sense* is not a *Rule:"* What means that Word? 15 It is not a *strait rigid Body:* It is not a *general Proposition, shewing what Means are fit to obtain an end:* It is not a *Proposition, asserting, that a Superior will make those happy who act one way, and miserable who act the contrary way.* If these be the Meanings of *Rule,* it is no *Rule;* yet by reflecting upon it our Understanding may find out a *Rule.* But what 20 *Rule* of Actions can be formed, without Relation to some *End* pro-posed? Or what *End* can be proposed, without presupposing *Instincts, Desires, Affections,* or a *moral Sense,* it will not be easy to explain.

25

SECTION V

Shewing that Virtue may have whatever is meant by Merit; and be rewardable upon the Supposition, that it is perceived by a Sense, and elected from Affection or Instinct. 30

[*285/290*] Some will not allow any *Merit* in *Actions* flowing from *kind Instincts:* "*Merit,* say they, attends Actions to which we are excited by *Reason* alone, or to which we *freely* determine ourselves. The Operation 35 of *Instincts* or *Affections* is *necessary,* and not *voluntary;* nor is there more *Merit* in them than in the *Shining of the Sun,* the *Fruitfulness of a Tree,* or the *Overflowing of a Stream,* which are all *publickly useful."*

5   But what does *Merit* mean? or *Praiseworthiness?* Do these Words denote   Merit, what.
the "Quality in Actions, which gains *Approbation* from the Observer?"
Or, *2dly,* Are these Actions called [291] meritorious, "which, when any
Observer does *approve* all other [286] *Observers* approve him for his *Approbation* of it; and would condemn any *Observer* who did not *approve*
10   these Actions?" These are the only Meanings of *meritorious,* which I can
conceive as distinct from *rewardable,* which is considered hereafter separately.

Now we endeavoured already to shew, that "no *Reason* can excite to Action previously to some *End,* and that no *End* can be proposed with-
15   out some *Instinct* or Affection." What then can be meant by being *excited by Reason,* as distinct from all Motion of *Instincts* or *Affections?*

Then *determining our selves freely,* does it mean *acting without any Motive or exciting Reason?* If it did not mean this, it cannot be opposed to *acting from Instinct or Affections,* since all *Motives* or *Reasons* presup-
20   pose them. If it do mean this, that "Merit is found only in Actions done without *Motive* or *Affection,* by *mere Election,* without prepollent *Desire* of one *Action* or *End* rather than its opposite, or without *Desire of that Pleasure* which* some do suppose follows [287] upon any *Election,* by a *natural Connexion:"* Then let any Man [293] consider whether he ever
25   acts in this manner by *mere Election,* without any previous *Desire?* And again, let him consult his own Breast, whether such kind of Action gains his *Approbation?* Upon seeing a Person not more disposed by *Af-*

---

¹ This is the Notion of *Liberty* given by the Archbishop of *Dublin,* in his most ingenious Book, *De Origine Mali.* This Opinion does not represent *Freedom* of
30   Election, as opposite to all *Instinct* or *Desire;* but rather as arising from the *Desire* of that *Pleasure supposed to be connected with every Election.* Upon his Scheme there is a *Motive* and *End* proposed in every Election, and a natural Instinct toward Happiness presupposed: Though it is such a *Motive* and *End* as leaves us in perfect *Liberty.* Since it is a Pleasure or Happiness, not connected with one thing more
35   than another, but following upon the *Determination* itself.

fection, Compassion, or Love or Desire, to make his Country happy than miserable, yet choosing the one rather than the other, from no *Desire of publick Happiness,* nor *Aversion to the Torments of others,* but by such an *unaffectionate Determination,* as that by which one moves his *first Finger* rather than the *second,* in giving an Instance of a *trifling Action;* let any one ask if this Action should be *meritorious:* and yet that there should be no *Merit* in a *tender compassionate Heart,* which shrinks at every *Pain* of its *Fellow-Creatures,* and triumphs in their *Happiness;* with *kind Affections* and *strong Desire* labouring for the publick Good. If this be the Nature of *meritorious Actions;* I fancy every honest [*288*] Heart would disclaim all *Merit in Morals,* as violently as the old *Protestants* rejected it in *Justification.*

But let us see which of the two Senses of *Merit* or *Praise-worthiness* is founded on this (I won't call it *unreasonable* or *casual*) but *unaffectionate Choice.* If Merit denotes the *Quality moving the Spectator to approve,* then there may be *unaffectionate Election* of the greatest Villany, as well as of the most [294] useful Actions; but who will say that they are *equally approved?*—But perhaps 'tis not the *mere Freedom of Choice* which is approved, but the *free Choice of publick Good,* without any *Affection.* Then *Actions* are approved for *publick Usefulness,* and not for *Freedom.* Upon this Supposition the *Heat of the Sun,* the *Fruitfulness of a Tree,* would be *meritorious:* or if one says, "these are not Actions;" they are at least *meritorious Qualities, Motions, Attractions,* &c. And a *casual Invention* may be *meritorious.*—Perhaps *Free Election* is a *Conditio sine qua non,* and *publick Usefulness* the immediate *Cause* of Approbation; neither separately, but both jointly are *meritorious: Free Election alone* is not *Merit; Publick Usefulness alone* is not *Merit;* but both concurring. Then should any Person by *mere Election,* without any *Desire* to serve the publick, set about *Mines,* [*289*] or any *useful Manufacture;* or should a Person by *mere Election* stab a Man, without knowing him to be a *publick Robber;* here both *free Election* and *publick Usefulness* may concur: Yet will any one say there is *Merit* or *Virtue* in such Actions? Where then shall we find Merit, unless in *kind Affections,* or *Desire* and *Intention* of the publick Good? This moves our *Approbation* wherever we observe it: and the want of this is the true *Reason* why a *Searcher for Mines,* a *free Killer* of an unknown [295] Robber, the *warming Sun,* or the *fruitful Tree,* are not counted *meritorious.*

But it may be said, that to make an Action *meritorious,* it is necessary not only that the Action be *publickly useful,* but that it be *known* or *imagined* to be *such,* before the Agent freely chuses it. But what does this add to the former Scheme? Only a *Judgment* or *Opinion* in the *Understanding,* concerning the *natural Tendency* of an Action to the publick Good: Few, it may be presumed, will place *Virtue* in *Assent* or *Dissent,* or *Perceptions.* And yet this is all that is superadded to the former Case. The Agent must not *desire* the publick Good, or have any *kind Affections.* This would spoil the *Freedom of Choice,* according to their Scheme, who insist on a *Freedom opposite to Affections* [290] *or Instincts:* But he must *barely know* the Tendency to publick Good, and without any *Propensity* to, or *Desire* of, the Happiness of others, by an *arbitrary Election,* acquire his Merit. Let every Man judge for himself, whether these are the Qualities which he *approves.*

What has probably engaged many into this way of speaking, "that Virtue is the Effect of *rational Choice,* and not of *Instincts or Affections,*" is this; they [296] find, that "some Actions flowing from particular kind Affections, are sometimes condemned as *evil,*" because of their *bad Influence* upon the State of larger Societies; and that the *Hurry* and *confused Sensations* of any of our Passions, may divert the Mind from considering the *whole Effect* of its Actions: They require therefore to *Virtue a calm and undisturbed Temper.*

There is indeed some ground to recommend this *Temper* as very necessary in many Cases; and yet some of the most *passionate Actions* may be perfectly *good.* But in the *calmest Temper* there must remain *Affection* or *Desire,* some implanted *Instinct* for which we can give no *reason;* otherwise there could be no Action of any kind. As it was shewn above in the first Section.

[291] If *meritorious Actions* are these which whosoever does not *approve,* is himself *condemned* by others; the Quality by which they are constituted *meritorious* in this Sense, is the same which moves our *Approbation.* We *condemn* any Person who does not *approve* that which we our selves *approve:* We presume the *Sense* of others to be constituted like

our own; and that any other Person, would he attend to the [297] Actions which we *approve,* would also *approve* them, and love the Agent; when we find that another does not *approve* what we approve, we are apt to conclude, that he has not had *kind Affections* toward the Agent, or that some *evil Affection* makes him overlook his Virtues, and on this   5
account condemn him.

Perhaps by meritorious is meant the same thing with another Word used in like manner, *viz. rewardable.* Then indeed the *Quality* in which *Merit* or Rewardableness is founded, is different from that which is denoted by Merit in the former Meanings.   10

Rewardable, or *deserving Reward,* denotes either that *Quality which would incline a superior Nature to make an Agent happy:* Or, 2dly, That *Quality of Actions which would make a Spectator approve* [292] *a superior Nature, when he conferred Happiness on the Agent, and disapprove that*   15
Superior, who inflicted Misery on the Agent, or punished him. Let any one try to give a Meaning to the Word *rewardable* distinct from these, and not satisfy himself with the Words *worthy of,* or *deserving,* which are of very complex and ambiguous Signification.

[298] Now the *Qualities* of an Action determining a powerful Nature   20
to reward it, must be various, according to the *Constitution* and *Affections* of that Superior. If he has a *moral Sense,* or *something analogous* of a more excellent sort, by which he is determined to *love* those who evidence *kind Affections,* and to desire their Happiness, then *kind Affection* is a Quality moving to Reward.   25

But farther, if this Superior be *benevolent,* and observes that inferior Natures can by their mutual Actions promote their mutual Happiness; then he must incline to excite them to *publickly useful Actions,* by Prospects of *private Interest* to the Agent, if it be needful: Therefore he will engage them to publickly useful Actions by *Prospects of Rewards,* what-   30
ever be the internal Principle of their Actions, or whatever their *Affections* be. These *two Qualities* in Actions, *viz. flowing from kind* [293] *Affections,* and *publick Usefulness* concurring, undoubtedly incline the *benevolent Superior* to confer Happiness: The *former alone,* where, thro' want of *Power,* the Agent is disappointed of his kind Intentions, will   35

incline a benevolent Superior to reward; and the *want of Power* in the Agent will never incline him to punish. But the *want of kind Affections,* altho [299] there be *publickly useful Actions,* may be so offensive to the *moral Sense* of the *superior Nature,* as to prevent *Reward,* or excite to punish; unless this Conduct would occasion *greater publick Evil,* by withdrawing from many Agents a *necessary Motive* to publick Usefulness, *viz.* the *Hope of Reward.*

But if the Superior were *malicious* with a *moral Sense contrary to ours,* the contrary *Affections* and *Tendency of Actions* would excite to reward, if any such thing could be expected from such a *Temper.*

If Actions be called *rewardable,* when "a *Spectator* would approve the *superior Mind* for conferring Rewards on such Actions:" Then various Actions must be rewardable, according to the *moral Sense* of the Spectator. *Men* approve rewarding all *kind Affections:* And if it will promote publick Good to promise [294] Rewards to *publickly useful Actions* from whatsoever *Affections* they proceed, it will evidence Benevolence in the Superior to do so. And this is the Case with *human Governors,* who cannot dive into the Affections of Men.

Some strongly assert (which is often the only Proof) that "to make an Action *rewardable,* the Agent should have had Inclinations to evil as well as to good." What does this mean, That a good governing MIND is only inclined to make an Agent happy, or to confer a *Reward* on him when he has some *evil Affections,* which yet are surmounted by the *benevolent Affections?* But would not a *benevolent Superior* incline to make any *benevolent Agent* happy, whether he had any weaker evil Inclinations or not? Evil Inclinations in an Agent would certainly rather have some Tendency to *diminish* the Love of the superior Mind. Cannot a good Mind *love* an Agent, and *desire* his Happiness, unless he observes some Qualities, which, were they alone, would excite *Hatred* or *Aversion?* Must there be a Mixture of *Hatred* to make *Love* strong and effectual, as there must be a Mixture of Shade to set off the Lights in a Picture, where there are no *Shades?* Is there any Love, where there is no *Inclination to* [295] *make happy?* Or is strong Love made up of *Love* and *Hatred?*

Whether Motives or Inclinations to Evil be necessary to make an Agent rewardable?

'Tis true indeed, that *Men* judge of the *Strength* of kind Affections generally by the contrary Motives of *Self-Love,* which they surmount: But must the DEITY do so too? Is any Nature the less lovely, for its having no Motive to make itself *odious?* If a Being which has no Motive to evil can be *beloved* by a Superior, shall he not *desire the Happiness* of that Agent whom he loves? 'Tis true, such a Nature will do good Actions [301] without Prospect of any *Self-Interest;* but would any benevolent Superior study the less to make it happy on that account?—But if they apply the Word *rewardable* to those Actions alone, *which an Agent would not do without Prospect of Reward:* then indeed to make an Action in this Sense *rewardable,* 'tis necessary that the Agent should either have *no kind Affections,* or that he should live in such Circumstances, wherein Self-Love should lead to Actions *contrary* to the publick Good, and over-power any kind Affections; or that he should have *evil Affections,* which even in a good Constitution of the World, his *Self-Love* could not over-ballance without *Reward.*

[*296*] This poor Idea of *Rewardableness* is taken from the *Poverty* and *Impotence of human Governors:* Their Funds are soon exhausted; they cannot make happy all those whose Happiness they desire: Their *little Stores* must be frugally managed; none must be rewarded for what good they will do without Reward, or for abstaining from Evils to which they are not inclined. Rewards must be kept for the *insolent Minister,* who without reward would fly in the Face of his Prince; for the *turbulent Demagogue,* who will raise Factions if he is not bribed; for the *covetous, mean-spirited,* but *artful Citizen,* who will serve his Country no farther [302] than it is for his private Interest. But let any kind honest Heart declare what *sort of Characters* it *loves? Whose* Happiness it most desires? *Whom* it would reward if it could? Or what these *Dispositions* are, which if it saw rewarded by a superior Nature, it would be most pleased, and most *approve* the Conduct of the Superior? When these Questions are answer'd, we shall know what makes Actions *rewardable.*

If we call all Actions *rewardable,* the rewarding of which we *approve;* then indeed we shall approve the rewarding of all *Actions which we approve,* whether the [*297*] Agent has had any *Inclinations* or *Motives* to Evil or not: We shall also approve the *promising of Rewards* to all *pub-*

lickly useful Actions, whatever were the Affections of the Agents. If by this *Prospect of Reward* either *malicious* Natures are restrained from Mischief, or *selfish* Natures induced to serve the Publick, or *benevolent* Natures not able without reward to surmount real or apparent *selfish Motives:* In all these Cases, the *proposing Rewards* does really advance the Happiness of the *Whole,* or diminish its *Misery;* and evidences *Benevolence* in the superior Mind, and is consequently *approved* by our *moral Sense.*

[303] In this last Meaning of the Word *rewardable,* these Dispositions are rewardable. 1. *Pure unmixed Benevolence.* 2. *Prepollent good Affections.* 3. *Such weak Benevolence, as will not without Reward overcome apparently contrary Motives of Self-Love.* 4. *Unmixed Self-Love, which by Prospect of Reward may serve the publick.* 5. *Self-Love, which by Assistance of Rewards, may overballance some malicious Affections.* If in these Cases *proposing Rewards* will increase the Happiness of the System, or diminish its Misery, it evidences *Goodness* in the Governor, when he cannot so well otherwise accomplish so much good for the whole.

[298] If we suppose a Necessity of making all virtuous Agents *equally happy,* then indeed a *Mixture of evil Dispositions,* tho surmounted by the good, or of *strong contrary Motives* overballanced by *Motives to Good,* would be a Circumstance of some Importance in the Distribution of Rewards: Since such a Nature, during the *Struggle of contrary Affections* or Motives, must have had less *Pleasure* than that virtuous Nature which met with no Opposition: But as this very Opposition did give this Nature *full Evidence* of the Strength of its Virtue, this *Consciousness* may be a peculiar *Recompence* to which the unmixed Tempers are Strangers: [304] And there seems no such necessity of an *equal Happiness of all Natures.* It is no way inconsistent with perfect Goodness, to make different *Orders of Beings;* and, provided all the Virtuous be at last *fully content,* and as happy as they desire, there is nothing absurd in supposing *different Capacities* and *different Degrees;* and during the Time of *Probation,* there is no necessity, not the least shew of it, that all be equal.

Those who think "*no Person punishable for any Quality or Action, if he had it not in his Power to have had the opposite Quality, or to have abstained* [299] *from the Action if he had willed it;*" perhaps are not mis-

taken: but then let them not assert on the *other Hand,* that it is unjust
to reward or make happy those, who neither had any *Dispositions to
Evil,* nor could possibly *desire* any such Dispositions. Now if Mens Affections are naturally good, and if there be in their Fellows no *Quality*
which would necessarily raise *Malice* in the Observer; but, on the con-   5
trary, *all Qualities* requisite to excite at least *Benevolence* or *Compassion:*
It may be justly said to be in the *Power* of every one, by due Attention,
to prevent any *malicious Affections,* and to excite in himself *kind Affections* toward all. So that the intricate Debates about human *Liberty* do
not affect what is here alledged, concerning our [305] *moral Sense* of Af-   10
fections and Actions, any more than any other Schemes.

Some alledge, that MERIT supposes, beside *kind Affection,* that the
Agent has a *moral Sense, reflects* upon his own Virtue, *delights* in it, and
chuses to adhere to it for the *Pleasure* which attends it.* We need not
debate the Use of this Word *Merit:* 'tis plain, we *approve* a generous   15
kind Action, tho the Agent had not made this *Reflection.* [*300*] This Reflection shews to him a Motive of Self-Love, the joint View to which
does not increase our *Approbation:* But then it must again be owned,
that we cannot form a just Conclusion of a *Character* from one or two
kind, generous Actions, especially where there has been no very strong   20
Motives to the contrary. Some apparent Motives of *Interest* may afterwards overballance the *kind Affections,* and lead the Agent into vicious
Actions. But the *Reflection* on Virtue, the being once *charmed* with the
lovely Form, will discover an *Interest* on its side, which, if well attended
to, no other Motive will overballance. This Reflection is a great *Security*   25
to the *Character;* this must be supposed in such Creatures as *Men* are,
before we can well depend upon a *Constancy in Virtue.* The same may
be said of many other Motives [306] to Virtue from *Interest;* which, tho
they do not *immediately* influence the *kind Affections* of the Agent, yet
do remove these *Obstacles* to them, from *false Appearances of Interest.*   30
Such are these from the Sanctions of *divine Laws* by future Rewards and
Punishments, and even the manifest *Advantages of Virtue in this Life:*

---

*See Lord *Shaftesbury's* Inquiry concerning Virtue. *Part* 1.

without *Reflection* on which, a steddy *Course of Virtue* is scarce to be expected amidst the present Confusion of human Affairs.

SECTION VI

How far a Regard to the Deity is necessary to make an Action virtuous

[*301*/307] I. Some do imagine, that "to make an Action virtuous, it is necessary that the Agent should have previously known his Action to be *acceptable to the* DEITY, and have undertaken it chiefly with design to please or obey him. We have not, say they, reason to imagine a *malicious Intention* in many of the worst Actions: the very *want of good Affections in their just Degree,* must constitute *moral Evil.* If so, then the *moral Evil* in the *want of Love or Gratitude,* must increase in proportion to the *Causes of Love or Gratitude* in the Object: by the Causes of Love, they mean *those Qualities in the Object* upon Observation of which Love or Gratitude do arise in every good Temper. Now the *Causes of Love* toward the DEITY are infinite; therefore the want of the highest possible Degree of Love to him, must be infinitely evil.—To be excited more by *smaller* [302] *Motives* or *Causes* [308] than by greater; to love those who are less *lovely,* while we neglect him in whom are *infinite Causes of Love,* must argue great *Perverseness* of Affections. But the *Causes of Love* in the DEITY, his infinite *Goodness* toward all, and even toward our selves, from whence springs all the Happiness of our Lives, are infinitely above any *Causes of Love* to be found in *Creatures:* Therefore to act from Love to them without *Intention* to please GOD, must be infinitely evil."

If this Reasoning be just, the best of Men are infinitely evil. The Distinction between *habitual* and *actual Intention* will not remove the Difficulty, since these Arguments require *actual Intention.* An *habitual Intention* is not a present act of Love to the DEITY, influencing our Actions more than actual Love to *Creatures,* which this Argument requires; but a prior general *Resolution* not at present repeated.

To find what is just on this Subject, we may premise some Propositions of which Men must convince themselves by *Reflection*.

How we compute the Goodness of Temper. II. There is in Mankind such a *Disposition* naturally, that they desire the Happiness of any known *Sensitive Nature*, [303] when it is not inconsistent with something more [309] strongly desired; so that were there no *Oppositions of Interest* either private or publick, and *sufficient Power*, we would confer upon every Being the highest Happiness which it could receive.

But our *Understanding* and *Power* are limited, so that we cannot know many other Natures, nor is our utmost *Power* capable of promoting the Happiness of many: our Actions are therefore influenced by some *stronger Affections* than this general *Benevolence*. There are certain *Qualities* found in some Beings more than in others, which excite stronger *Degrees* of *Good-will*, and determine our *Attention* to their Interests, while that of others is neglected. The Ties of *Blood, Benefits conferred* upon us, and the Observation of *Virtue* in others, raise much more vigorus *Affections*, than that general *Benevolence* which we may have toward all. These *Qualities* or *Relations* we may call the *Causes of Love.*

However these *Affections* are very different from the *general Benevolence* toward all, yet it is very probable, that there is a *Regularity* or *Proportion* observed in the Constitution of our Nature; so that, abstracting from some acquired *Habits*, or [304] *Associations of Ideas*, and from the more sudden *Emotions* of some particular Passions, *that* Temper [310] which has the most lively *Gratitude*, or is the most susceptive of *Friendship* with virtuous Characters, would also have the strongest *general Benevolence* toward indifferent Persons: And on the contrary, where there is the weakest *general Benevolence*, there we could expect the least *Gratitude*, and the *least Friendship*, or *Love toward the Virtuous*. If this *Proportion* be observed, then, if we express all these Desires of the good of others by the Name of *Benevolence*, we may denote the several *Degrees* in which Men possess these several kind Dispositions by the *Goodness of the Temper:* And the Degrees of Desire toward the Happiness of any Person, we may call the *Quantity of Love* toward him. Then,

The *Quantity of Love* toward any Person is in a compound Proportion of the apprehended *Causes of Love* in him, and of the *Goodness of Temper* in the Observer. Or $L = C \times G$.[55]

When the *Causes of Love* in two Objects are apprehended equal, the *Love* toward either in different Persons is as the *Goodness of Temper;* or $L = G \times I$.

[*305*] When the *Goodness of Temper* is the same or equal, the *Love* toward any Objects will be as the *Causes;* or $L = C \times I$.

The *Goodness of any Temper* is therefore as the *Quantity of Love*, divided by the apprehended *Causes,* or $G = \dfrac{L}{C}$. And since we [311] cannot apprehend any Goodness in having the *Degree of Love* above the *Proportion* of its Causes, the most virtuous Temper is that in which the *Love* equals its *Causes*, which may therefore be expressed by Unity.*

Hence it follows, that if there were any Nature incomparably more excellent than any of our *Fellow-Creatures,* from whom also we our selves, and all others had received the greatest *Benefits;* there would be less Virtue in any small Degree of *Desire of his Happiness,* than in a like *Degree of Love* toward our Fellow-Creatures. But *not loving* such a Being, or having a *smaller Degree of Love,* must evidence a much greater *Defect* in Virtue, than a like *want of Love* toward our Fellow-Creature. For the *Causes of Love* being [*306*] very great, unless the *Love* be also

55. Hutcheson toned down or removed the mathematical language in the third edition of the *Essay with Illustrations* as well as in later editions of the *Inquiry.* This included not only the mathematical notation (also purged from T2), but also the word "axioms" which is replaced by "maxims" in the text, although it persists in the marginal titles. The desire to render morals into mathematically quantifiable ratios likely derives from Cumberland, cf. *De Legibus Naturae,* I §§5–9.

*See *Treat.* 2. *Sect.* 3. *Art.* II. last Paragraph.

In many Questions of this Nature we must have recourse with *Aristotle* to a *Sense,* which is the last Judge in particular Cases.[318]

[[This footnote was added in the third edition and is not indicated in the text. Hutcheson likely had in mind Aristotle's discussion of our ability to judge good and bad as natural, like the sense of vision, *Nicomachean Ethics,* III. 5, 1114a30–b12.]

very great, the *Quotient* which expresses the *Goodness of Temper* will be very much below Unity.

III. To apply this to the DEITY is very obvious. Our *Affections* toward him arise in the same manner as toward our Fellows, in [312] proportion to our *Attention* to the *Causes of Love* in him, and the *Goodness of our Temper.* The Reflection on his Goodness raises *Approbation* and *Complacence,* his *Benefits* raise *Gratitude,* and both occasion *Good-will* or *Benevolence.* Some imagine, that "his *Happiness* is wholly detached from all Events in this World, absolute, and unvaried in himself." And yet the same *Inclination* of Mind might remain in us, tho we had this Opinion. When the *Happiness of a Friend* is in *Suspense,* we desire it; when he has obtained all that which we desired, the same *Inclination of Mind* seems to remain toward him, only without that *Uneasiness* accompanying Desire of an *uncertain* Object: Thus *Gravity* may be said to be the same when a Body is resting on a fixed Base, as when it caused descent.

Upon this Scheme of the divine Happiness, it is not easy to account how our Love to him could excite us to promote the *Happiness of our Fellows.* Our frequent *Contemplation* of such an amiable excellent [307] Nature, might indeed tend to *reform* or *improve* our Temper.

If we imagine that the DEITY has such *Perceptions* of *Approbation* or *Dislike* toward [313] Actions as we have our selves, then indeed our *Love* to him would directly excite us to do whatever he approves, and shun what he condemns. We can scarce avoid imagining, that the frequent recurring of Events *disapproved,* must be uneasy to any Nature, and that the observing *approved Actions* must be delightful.

If we imagine that the *divine Happiness,* or any part of it is connected with the Happiness of his Creatures, so that their Happiness is constituted the Occasion of his; then indeed our *Love to the* DEITY will directly excite us to all manner of *beneficent Actions.* 'Tis true, many good Men deny these two last Opinions, yet it is probable, when their Minds are diverted from *Speculations,* by Opportunities of Action, there recurs some Imagination of *Offence, Uneasiness,* and *Resentment* in the DEITY, upon observing *evil Actions;* of *Delight* and *Joy* in beholding good

Actions; of *Sorrow* upon observing the *Misery* of his Creatures, and *Joy* upon seeing them happy: So that by their *Love to the* DEITY they are influenced to beneficent Actions, notwithstanding their [*308*] *speculative Opinions*. In our Conceptions of the DEITY, we are continually led to imagine a Resemblance to what we feel in our selves.

[314] Whoever maintains these Opinions of the DEITY to be true, must also suppose "a particular *Determination* of all Events in the Universe;" otherwise this *part* of the divine Happiness is made *precarious* and *uncertain,* depending upon the *undetermined Will* of Creatures.

The Diversity of Opinions concerning the *divine Happiness,* may lead Men into different ways of accounting for the *Influence* which the *Love of* GOD may have upon our Actions toward our Fellows: But the Affections toward the DEITY would be much the same upon both Schemes. Where there were the same just *Apprehensions* of the *divine Goodness* in two Persons, the *Love* to the DEITY in both would be proportioned to the *Goodness of Temper.* Tho the highest possible *Degree* of Love to a perfectly good DEITY, would evidence no more *Virtue of Temper,* than a proportioned *Love to Creatures;* yet the having only *smaller Degrees* of Love to the DEITY, would evidence a greater *Defect* of Goodness in the Temper, than any want of *Affection* toward Creatures.

[*309*] Here it must be remembred, that in arguing concerning the *Goodness of Temper* [315] from the *Degree* of Love directly, and the *Causes* of Love inversly, *actual Attention* to the *Causes of Love* is supposed in the Person. For 'tis plain, that in the best Temper no one *Affection or Idea* can always continue present, and there can be no *Affection* present to the Mind, toward any Object, while the *Idea* of it is not present. The bare *Absence* therefore of Affection, while the Mind is employed upon a different Object, can argue no *evil* in the Temper, farther than want of *Attention* may argue want of *Affection.* In like manner, in the *best Temper,* there can be no Love toward an Object *unknown:* The want therefore of Love to an *Object unknown,* can argue no evil in the Temper, farther than *Ignorance* may argue want of *Affection.* It is certain indeed, that he who knows that there is a good DEITY, and actually thinks of him, and of all his Benefits, yet has not the *strongest Love and*

Gratitude toward him, must have a Temper void of all Goodness; but it will not follow, that that Mind is void of Goodness which is not *always thinking* of the DEITY, or actually *loving* him, or even does not know him. How far the want of *Attention* to the DEITY, and *Ignorance* of him, may argue an *evil Temper,* [*310*] must be shown from different *To-* 5 *picks,* to be considered hereafter.

What Degrees
of Affection
necessary to
Innocence.

[316] IV. But previously to these Inquiries we must consider "what *Degrees* or Kinds of Affection are necessary to obtain the simple *Approbation* of *Innocence.*" 'Tis plain, the *bare Absence* of all *Malice* is not 10 enough. We may have the general *Benevolence* toward a mere *sensitive Nature,* which had no other desire but *Self-Love;* but we can apprehend no *moral Goodness* in such a Being: Nay, 'tis not every *small Degree* of kind Affections which we *approve.* There must be some *proportion* of kind Affections to the *other Faculties* in any Nature, particularly to its 15 *Understanding* and *active Powers* to obtain *Approbation.* Some Brutes evidence small Degrees of *Good-will,* which make them be *approved* in *their Kind;* but the same Degrees would not be approved in a *Man.* There is an higher Degree expected in Mankind, to which, if they do not come up, we do not account them *innocent.* It is not easy to fix 20 precisely that *Degree* which we approve as *innocent* by our moral Sense. Every kind Affection, if it be considered only with relation to its own Object, is indeed approved; such as *natural Affection, Gratitude, Pity, Friendship:* And yet when we take a more *extensive* View of the Tendency of [*311*] some Actions proceeding even from these *Affections,* [317] 25 we may often condemn these Actions when they are apprehended as pernicious to *larger Systems* of Mankind. In the same manner we often condemn Actions done from Love to a particular Country, when they appear to be *pernicious to Mankind* in general. In like manner, *Self-Preservation* and pursuing *private Advantage* abstractly considered, is *in-* 30 *nocent:* But when it is apprehended as very pernicious in any case to the Safety of *others,* it is condemned.

Mankind are capable of large extensive Ideas of *great Societies.* And it is expected of them, that their *general Benevolence* should continually direct and limit, not only their *selfish Affections,* but even their *nearer* 35

Attachments to others: that their Desire of *publick* Good, and Aversion to *publick* Misery, should overcome at least their Desire of *positive private Advantages,* either to themselves or their particular Favourites; so as to make them abstain from any Action which would be positively pernicious or hurtful to *Mankind,* however *beneficial* it might be to *themselves,* or their *Favourites.* To undergo *positive Evil* for the sake of *positive Good* to others, seems some degree of Virtue above *Innocence,* which we do not universally expect: But to reject *positive* attainable [*312/*318] good, either for our selves or our particular Favourites, rather than occasion any considerable *Misery* to others, is requisite to obtain the Approbation of *Innocence.* The *want* of this Degree we positively condemn as evil; and an Agent must rise above it by *positive Services* to Mankind, with some *Trouble* and *Expence* to himself, before we approve him as virtuous. We seem indeed universally to expect from all Men those good Offices which give the Agent no trouble or expence: Whoever refuses them is below Innocence. But we do not *positively condemn* those as evil, who will not sacrifice their private Interest to the Advancement of the *positive Good* of others, unless the private Interest be *very small,* and the publick Good *very great.*

But as the Desire of *positive private Good* is weaker than Aversion to *private Evil,* or Pain; so our *Desire* of the positive Good of others, is weaker than our *Aversion* to their Misery: It seems at least requisite to [*313*] *Innocence,* that the stronger *publick Affection, viz.* our Aversion to the Misery of others, should surmount the *weaker private Affection,* the Desire of positive private Good; so that no prospect of [319] Good to our selves, should engage us to that which would occasion *Misery* to others. It is in like manner requisite to *Innocence,* that our Aversion to the Misery of *greater* or *equal Systems,* should surmount our Desire of the *positive Good* of these to which we are more particularly attached.

How far it may be necessary to Innocence to submit to smaller *private Pains* to prevent the *greater Sufferings* of others, or to promote some great *positive Advantages;* or how far the Happiness of *private Systems* should be neglected for the Happiness of the *greater,* in order to obtain the *Approbation of Innocence,* it is perhaps impossible precisely to determine, or to fix any *general Rules;* nor indeed is it necessary. Our business is not to find out "at how *cheap* a Rate we can purchase *Innocence,* but to know what is *most noble, generous* and *virtuous* in Life." This we know consists in sacrificing all *positive Interests,* and bearing all *private Evils* for the publick Good: And in submitting also the Interests of all *smaller Systems* to the Interests of the whole: Without any other *Exception* or *Reserve* than this, that every Man may look upon himself as a *Part* of this System, and consequently not sacrifice an *important private Interest* to a [320] *less important Interest* of others. We may find the same sort of Difficulty about all our other Senses, in determining precisely what Objects are *indifferent,* [314] or where Pleasure ends, and Disgust begins, tho the positive Degrees of the *grateful* and *ungrateful* are easily distinguished.

It is also very difficult to fix any precise *Degree* of Affection toward the DEITY, which should be barely requisite to Innocence. Only in general we must disapprove that Temper, which, upon Apprehension of the perfect Goodness of the DEITY, and of his innumerable Benefits to Mankind, has not *stronger Affections* of *Love* and *Gratitude* toward him, than those toward any other Being. Such Affections would necessarily raise frequent *Attention* and Consideration of our Actions; and would engage us, if we apprehended any of them to be offensive to him, or contrary to that *Scheme of Events* in which we apprehended the DEITY to *delight,* to avoid them with a more firm Resolution than what we had in any other Affairs. *Positive Virtue* toward the DEITY must go farther than a *resolute abstaining from Offence,* by engaging us with the greatest Vigor, to do whatever we apprehend as *positively pleasing,* or conducive to those Ends in which we apprehend the DEITY delights. It is [321] scarce conceivable that any *good Temper* can want such Affections toward the DEITY, when once he is known, as were above supposed necessary to *Innocence.* Nor [315] can we imagine *positive Degrees* of Goodness of Temper above Innocence, where Affections toward the DEITY do not arise proportionably.

What is here said relates only to the *Apprehensions of our moral Sense,* and not to those Degrees of Virtue which the DEITY may require by *Revelation:* And every one's Heart may inform him, whether or no he does not *approve,* at least as *innocent,* those who omit many good Offices which they might *possibly* have done, provided they do a great deal of good; those who carefully abstain from every *apprehended Offence* toward the DEITY, tho they might possibly be more frequent in Acts of *Devotion.* 'Tis true indeed, the *Omission of what we know to be required* is positively evil: so that by a *Revelation* we may be obliged to farther Services than were requisite previously to it, which we could not innocently omit, after this *Revelation* is known: But we are here only considering our *moral Sense.*

V. Now let us inquire how far *simple Ignorance* of a DEITY, or *unaffected Atheism* does evidence an *evil Disposition,* or *Defect* of good Affections below *Innocence.*

How far Ignorance of DEITY is Evil.

1. Affections arising upon *apparent Causes,* or present *Opinions,* tho false, if [*316*] they be such as would arise in the *best Temper,* were these Opinions *true,* cannot argue any present *want of Goodness* in any Temper, of themselves: the *Opinions* indeed may often argue a *want of Goodness* at the *time* they were formed: But to a benevolent Temper there is no *Cause of Malice,* or Desire of the *Misery* or *Non-existence* of any Being for itself. There may be Causes of Dislike, and Desire of Misery or Non-existence, as the Means of greater Good, or of lessening Evil.

2. No Object which is entirely *unknown,* or of which we have no *Idea,* can raise *Affection* in the best Temper; consequently *want of Affection* to an unknown Object evidences no evil. This would be the Case of those who never heard even the *Report of a* DEITY, if ever there were any such: Or who never heard of any *Fellow-Creatures,* if one may make a Supposition like to that made by *Cicero.** And this is perhaps the Case, as to the DEITY, of any unfortunate Children, who may have some [*323*] little *Use of Reason,* before they are instructed in any *Religion.*

---

*De Nat. Deor. *Lib.* 2. *cap.* 37. Ex Aristotele.
[[Hutcheson is citing Cicero's dicussion of a passage from Aristotle's lost dialogue *De Philosophia.* Aristotle imagines beings who always lived under the earth but finally surfaced. Seeing the extraordinary beauty and purposiveness (*efficientiam*) of the world they must conclude that the gods exist and the world is their work. This is a *locus classicus* for the argument from design and occurs within Cicero's argument that the world exhibits design and providence.]]

If there really were an *Innate Idea* of a DEITY so imprinted, that no Person could [*317*] be without it; or if we are so disposed, as *necessarily* to receive this *Idea*, as soon as we can be called moral Agents: then no *Ignorance* of a DEITY can be innocent; all *Atheism* must be affected, or an Opinion formed, either thro' *evil Affection*, or *want* of *good Affection* below Innocence. But if the *Idea of a* DEITY be neither imprinted, nor offer itself even previously to any *Reflection*, nor be universally excited by *Tradition*, the bare *Want* of it, where there has been no *Tradition* or *Reflection*, cannot be called criminal upon any Scheme. Those who make *Virtue* and *Vice* relative to a *Law*, may say, "Men are required to reflect, and thence to know a DEITY. "But they must allow *Promulgation* necessary, before Disobedience to a Law can be criminal. Now previously to *Reflection* it is supposed impossible for the Agent to know the *Legislator*, or to know the *Law requiring him to reflect*, therefore this *Law requiring him to reflect*, was not antecedently to his *Reflection* published to him.

The Case of *human Laws*, the Ignorance of which does not excuse, is not parallel [324] to this. No Person under any Civil Government can be supposed ignorant that there are *Laws* made for the whole State. But in the present Supposition, Men antecedently to *Reflection* may be ignorant of the DEITY, or that there are *Laws of Nature*. [*318*] If any Subject could thus be *unapprized*, that he lived under Civil Government, he should not be accounted *Compos Mentis*. The Supposition indeed in both Cases is perhaps wholly *imaginary;* at least as to Persons above Childhood. One can scarce imagine that ever any Person was wholly unapprized of a *governing Mind*, and of a *Right* and *Wrong* in Morals. Whether this is to be ascribed to *innate Ideas*, to *universal Tradition*, or to some *necessary Determination* in our Nature, to imagine a designing *Cause* of the beautiful Objects which occur to us, with a *moral Sense*, let the curious inquire.

3. Suppose an Idea formed in a *benevolent Mind*, of other *sensitive Natures*, *Desire* of their Existence and Happiness would arise.

4. A good *Temper* would incline any one to wish, that other Natures were *benevolent*, or morally Good, since this is the chief *Happiness*.

[325] 5. A good *Temper* would desire that the Administration of Nature were by a *benevolent* or *good Mind*.

6. All Desire of any Event or Circumstance inclines any Mind to search into the *Truth* of that Event or Circumstance, [*319*] by all the *Evidence* within its power to obtain.

7. Where there is such *Desire,* and sufficiently obvious *Evidence* given in proportion to the *Sagacity* of the desiring Mind, it will come to the Knowledge of the Truth, if its Desire be strong.

Now from these Propositions we may deduce the following Corollaries.

1. Supposing the Idea of a good DEITY once apprehended, or excited either by *Report,* or the slightest *Reflection;* if there be *objective Evidence* in Nature proportioned to the *Capacity* of the Inquirer, for the Existence of a good DEITY, *Atheism* directly argues want of good Affection below *Innocence.*

2. If there be only the simple *Tradition* or *Presumption* of a governing Mind once raised; and if there be *Evidence* as [326] before for his *Goodness,* to conclude the DEITY *evil or malicious,* must argue want of *good Affection* as before.

3. Suppose the Idea of an *evil* DEITY once excited, and some Presumptions for his *Malice* from *Tradition,* or slight *Reflection* upon particular *Evils* in Nature; to rest in this Opinion without Inquiry, [*320*] would argue *want of good Affection;* to desire to *reject* this Opinion, or *confute* it by contrary Evidence, would argue *good Affection:* Suppose such contrary *Evidences* obvious enough in Nature to one who inquired as diligently about it as about his own *Interest;* to continue in the *false Opinion* cannot be innocent.

VI, In like manner concerning our Fellow-Creatures, who are actually known to us.

4. To imagine Fellow-Creatures *morally Good,* either according to *Evidence* upon Inquiry, or even by a rash *Opinion,* evidences *good Affection.*

5. Imagining them Evil contrary to obvious *Evidence,* argues *want of good Affection* below Innocence.

6. Retaining and *inculcating* an Opinion either of the *Causes of Love* in [327] others, or of the *Causes of Aversion,* induces an *Habit;* and makes the Temper prone to the *Affection* often raised. Opinion of *Good-*

How Ignorance in human Affairs evidences a bad Temper.

ness in the DEITY and our Fellows, increases *good Affection,* and improves the *Temper: Contrary Opinion* of either, by raising frequent *Aversions,* weakens *good Affection,* and impairs the *Temper.*

[*321*] This may shew how cautious Men ought to be in passing Sentence upon the *Impiety* of their Fellows, or representing them as *wicked* and *profane,* or *hateful* to the DEITY, and justly given over to eternal Misery: We may see also what a wise *Mark* it is to know the *true Church* by, that "it pronounces Damnation on all others." Which is one of the Characters of the *Romish* Church, by which it is often recommended as the safest for Christians to live in.

The same *Propositions* may be applied to our Opinions concerning the *natural Tendencies* of Actions. Where the Evidence is obvious as before, good Affection will produce *true Opinions,* and *false Opinions* often argue *want of good Affection* below Innocence. Thus, tho in *Assent* or *Dissent* of themselves, there can neither be *Virtue* nor *Vice,* yet they may be *Evidences*[328] of either in the Agent, as well as his *external Motions.* 'Tis not possible indeed for Men to determine precisely in many cases the *Quantity of Evidence,* and its *proportion* to the Sagacity of the Observer, which will argue *Guilt* in him, who contrary to it, forms a *false Opinion.* But Men are no better judges of the *Degrees of Virtue* [*322*] *and Vice* in external Actions. This therefore will not prove that all *false Opinions* or *Errors* are innocent, more than *external Actions:* The Searcher of Hearts can judge exactly of both. Human *Punishments* are only *Methods of Self-Defence;* in which the *Degrees of Guilt* are not the proper Measure, but the *Necessity of restraining Actions for the Safety of the Publick.*

How want of Attention evidences a bad Temper. VII. It is next to be considered, how far *want of Attention* to the DEITY can argue *want of good Affections,* in any Agent, to whom he is known.

Every *good Temper* will have strong Affections to a good DEITY, and where there is *strong Affection* there will be *frequent Reflection* upon the Object beloved, *Desire* of pleasing, and *Caution* of offence. In like manner every Person of good Temper, who has had the Knowledge of a [*329*] *Country,* a *System,* a *Species,* will consider how far these great Societies may be affected by his Actions, with such Attention as he uses in his own Affairs; and will abstain from what is injurious to them.

Attention to a DEITY apprehended as good, and governing the Universe, will increase the *Moment of Beneficence* in any [*323*] good Agent, various ways, such as by Prospects of *Reward,* either present or future, by improving his Temper thro' Observation of so amiable a *Pattern,* or
5 by raising Sentiments of *Gratitude* toward the DEITY, a part of whose Happiness the Agent may imagine depends upon the Happiness of the Universe. In like manner, the considering a *Species* or *System* may increase our *good Offices,* since *their* Interests are advanced by good Offices to *Individuals.*
10   But then from a like Reasoning to that in *Art.* II. 'tis plain, that in *equal Moments* of good produced by two Agents, the *Goodness of the Temper* is inversly as the several *additional Helps,* or *Motives* to it. So that *more Virtue* is evidenced by any given *Moment* of Beneficence from good Affections only toward our *Fellows,* or particular Persons, than by
15 the *same Moment* produced from the joint Considerations of the DEITY, or of a general *System* or *Species.**
    But an injurious Action which appeared to the Agent not only *pernicious to his Fellows,* or to particular Persons, but *offensive to the* DEITY, and pernicious to a *System,* is much more vicious than when the
20 Agent did not reflect upon the DEITY, or a *Community.*

[*324*] VIII. We must not hence imagine, that in order to produce greater Virtue in our selves, we should regard the DEITY no farther, then merely to *abstain from Offences.* Were it our sole Intention in beneficent
25 Actions, only to obtain the *private Pleasure* of *Self-Approbation* for the Degree of our Virtue, this might seem the proper Means of having *great Virtue* with the least *Expence.* But if the real Intention, which constitutes an Action virtuous, be the *promoting publick Good;* then *voluntarily* to reject the Consideration of any Motive which would increase the

Nothing in this Scheme supersedes the Duty of Love to the DEITY, *and general Benevolence.*

30 * See Luke x. 12, 13, 14.
    [[This note, added in the third edition, refers to the following passage from Luke: "I tell you, on that day it will be more tolerable for Sodom than for that town. Woe to you, Chorazin! Woe to you, Bethsaida! For if the deeds of power done in you had been done in Tyre and Sidon, they would have repented long ago,
35 sitting in sackcloth and ashes," (*Holy Bible,* II. 72–73). For the exact passage it is attached to, see the Textual Note reference for 199/13–16.]]

Moment of publick Good, or would make us more vigorous and stedfast in Virtue, must argue *want of good Affection.* In any *given Moment* of Beneficence, the unaffected *Want* of Regard to the DEITY, or to *private Interest,* does really argue greater Virtue. But the *retaining these Motives* with a View to increase the *Moment* of publick Good in our Actions, if they really do so, argues Virtue equal to, or greater than that in the former Case: And the *affected Neglect* of these Motives, that so we may acquit our selves virtuously with the *least Expence* to our selves, or with the least Moment of publick Good, must evidence *want of good Affections,* and base *Trick* and *Artifice* to impose upon [325] Observers, or our own Hearts. Therefore

Since Gratitude to the DEITY, and even Consideration of *private Interest,* tend to increase the Moment of our Beneficence, and to strengthen good Affections, the voluntary *Retaining* them with this View evidences Virtue, and *affecting* to neglect them evidences Vice.* And yet,

[332] If the Moment produced by the Conjunction of these Motives, be not greater than that produced with unaffected Neglect of these Motives, from particular good [326] Affection, there is less Virtue in the former than in the latter.

Men may use Names as they please, and may chuse to call nothing

---

*This may sufficiently justify the *Writers of Morality* in their proving, that "Virtue is the surest Means of Happiness to the Agent." 'Tis also plain from universal *Experience,* that a *Regard to the Deity,* frequent *Reflection* on his Goodness, and consequent *Acts of Love,* are the strongest and most universally prevailing *Means* of obtaining a good Temper. Whatever Institution therefore does most effectually tend to raise Mens *Attention,* to *recall* their Minds from the Hurry of their common Affairs, to *instruct* them in the Ways of promoting publick Good farther than the busy Part of the World without assistance would probably apprehend, must be so *wise* and *good,* that every honest Mind should rejoice in it, even though it had no other *Authority* than *human* to recommend it. Every one will understand that by this is meant a *publick Worship* on set Days, in which a stop is put to Commerce, and the busy part of Mankind instructed in the Duties of *Piety* and *Humanity.*

[[Hutcheson likely has Shaftesbury in mind: "*Every thing which is an Improvement of Virtue, or an Establishment of right Affection and Integrity, is an Advancement of Interest, and leads to the greatest and most solid Happiness and Enjoyment*" "An Inquiry Concerning Virtue," "Conclusion."]]

Virtue but "what is intended chiefly to evidence *Affection* of one kind or other toward the DEITY." Writers on this Scheme are not well agreed about what this *virtuous Intention* is; whether only to evidence *Submission,* or *Submission* and *Love,* or to *obtain the divine Benevolence,* and *private Happiness* to the Agent, or to *give Pleasure to the Deity.* But let them not assert, against universal *Experience,* that we *approve* no Actions which are not thus intended toward the DEITY. 'Tis plain, a *generous compassionate Heart,* which, at first view of the Distress of another, flies impatiently to his Relief, or spares no Expence to accomplish it, meets with strong *Approbation* from every Observer who has not perverted his *Sense of Life* by *School-Divinity,* or *Philosophy.* 'Tis to be suspected, that some *Vanity* must be at the Bottom of these Notions, which place Virtue in some *Nicety,* which *active Tempers,* have not leisure to apprehend, and only the *Recluse Student* can attain to.

[327] To be led by a *weaker Motive,* where a *stronger* is alike present to the Mind, to love a Creature *more* than GOD, or to have *stronger Desires* of doing what is grateful to Creatures than to GOD, when we equally attend to both, would certainly argue some *Perversion of our Affections;* or to study the *particular Good* of one, more than that of a *System,* when we reflected on both: But as no *finite Mind* can retain at once a [334] *Multiplicity of Objects,* so it cannot *always* retain any one Object. When a Person therefore not thinking at present of the DEITY, or of a *Community* or *System,* does a beneficent Action from *particular Love,* he evidences *Goodness of Temper.* The bare *Absence* of the Idea of a DEITY, or of *Affections* to him, can evidence no evil; otherways it would be a Crime to *fall asleep,* or to think of any thing else: If the *bare Absence* of this Idea be no evil, the Presence of *kind Affections* to Fellow-Creatures cannot be evil. If indeed our Love to the DEITY excited to any Action, and at the *same time* Love to a *Creature* excited to the Omission of it, or to a contrary Action, we must be very criminal if the *former* do not prevail; yet this will not argue all Actions to be evil in which *pleasing the* DEITY, [328] is not directly and chiefly intended. Nay, that Temper must really be very *deficient* in Goodness, which needs to excite it to any good Office, to recal the Thoughts of a DEITY, or a *Community,* or a *System.* [335] The frequent recalling these Thoughts, indeed, does strengthen all good Affections, and increases

the *Moment* of Beneficence to be expected from any Temper; and with
this *View* frequently to recal such Thoughts, must be one of the best
Helps to Virtue, and evidence high Degrees of it. Nay, one cannot call
that Temper *entire* and *complete,* which has not the *strongest Affection*
toward the greatest Benefactor, and the most worthy Object.   5

Beings of such Degrees of *Knowledge,* and such *Extent* of Thought,
as Mankind are not only capable of, but generally obtain, when nothing
interrupts their Inquiries, must naturally arise to the Knowledge of the
DEITY, if their Temper be good. They must form *general Conceptions*
of the whole, and see the *Order, Wisdom,* and *Goodness* in the *Admin-*   10
istration of Nature in some Degree. The Knowledge and Love of the
DEITY, the *universal* MIND, is as *natural* a Perfection to such a Being
as Man, as any Accomplishment to which we arrive by [*329*] cultivating
our natural Dispositions; nor is that Mind come to the *proper State* and
Vigor of its kind, where *Religion* is not the main *Exercise* and *Delight.*   15

Whether the
DEITY is the
sole proper
Object of
Love.

IX. There is one very subtle Argument on this Subject. Some alledge,
"That [*336*] since the DEITY is really the *Cause* of all the Good in the
Universe, even of all the *Virtue,* or *good Affection* in Creatures, which
are the seeming *Causes of Love* toward them, it must argue strange *Per-*   20
version of Temper to love those in whom there is no *Cause of Love,* or
who are (as they affect to speak) *nothing,* or *Emptiness of all Goodness.*
The DEITY alone is amiable, in whom there is infinite *Fulness of every*
amiable Quality. The DEITY, say they, not without some Reason, is the
Cause of every *pleasant Sensation,* which he immediately excites accord-   25
ing to a *general Law,* upon the Occasion of *Motions* arising in our Bodies; that likewise he gave us that general *Inclination,* which we modify
into all our different *Affections;* GOD therefore, say they, is alone *lovely.*
Other Things are not to be beloved, but only the *Goodness of God ap-*
pearing in them; nay some do make the *loving* of them, without consid-   30
ering GOD as displaying [*330*] his Goodness in them, to be infinitely
evil."

In answer to this it must be owned, that "God's being the Cause of
all the Good in the Universe, will no doubt raise the highest Love to
him in a good Temper, when it reflects upon it."

[337] But 1st, had all Men this Apprehension that "there was no good in any Creature," they really would not love them at all. But Men generally imagine with very good ground, that there are *good Beings* distinct from God, tho produced by him: And whether this Opinion be true or false, it evidences no evil.

2. As upon this Scheme GOD is the Cause of all *pleasant Sensation,* so is he the Cause of all Pain: He is, according to them, the Cause of that *Inclination* which we modify into *evil Affection,* as well as into *good.* If then we are to love GOD only, for what we call *good Affection* in Creatures, and not the Creatures themselves, we must also only love GOD upon observing *evil Affections* in Creatures, and have no *Aversion* to the *basest Temper,* since God gave the general INCLINATION alike in both Cases.

[331] 3. If we may suppose *real Beings* distinct from GOD, that *their Affections* are not GOD's Affections, if GOD is not the only *Lover* and *Hater,* if our *moral Sense* is determined to approve *kind Affections,* and our *Love* or *Benevolence* must arise toward what we *approve;* or if we find an *Instinct* to desire the Happiness of every sensitive [338] Nature, we cannot avoid loving Creatures, and we must *approve* any *kind Affections* observed in others toward their Fellows. 'Tis true, we must approve the *highest Affections* toward the DEITY, and *condemn,* as a *Deficiency* of just Affections toward GOD any Degree which is not superior to our other Affections. But still, *Affections* towards Creatures, if they be *distinct Natures* from GOD, must be approved.

4. If to make a Mind virtuous, or even innocent, it be necessary that it should have such sublime Speculations of GOD, as the $\tau\grave{o}\ \pi\hat{a}\nu$ in the *Intellectual active System* (if we call *one Agent* in many *Passive Organs* an *active System*) then God has placed the Bulk of Mankind in an absolute *Incapacity* of Virtue, and inclined them perpetually to infinite Evil, by their very *Instincts* and *natural Affections.* Does the *parental Affection* direct [332] a Man to love the DEITY, or his *Children?* Is it the DIVINITY, to which our *Pity* or *Compassion* is directed? Is God the Object of *Humanity?* Is it a *Design* to support the DIVINITY, which we call *Generosity* or *Liberality?* Upon *Receipt of a Benefit,* does our Nature suggest only *Gratitude toward* GOD? Affections toward the DEITY may indeed

often accompany Affections toward Creatures, and do so in a virtuous Temper: but [339] these are distinct Affections. This Notion of making all virtuous Affections to be only directed toward GOD, is not suggested to Men by any thing in their *Nature,* but arises from the long subtle *Reasonings* of Men at leisure, and unemployed in the natural Affairs of Life.

5. If there be no Virtue or Cause of Love in Creatures, it is vain for them to debate wherein their Virtue consists, whether in regard toward the DEITY, or in any thing else, since they are supposed to have none at all.

To conclude this Subject. It seems probable, that however we must look upon that Temper as exceedingly *imperfect, inconstant,* and *partial,* in which *Gratitude toward the universal Benefactor, Admiration* and *Love* of the *supreme* [333] *original Beauty, Perfection and Goodness,* are not the *strongest* and most *prevalent* Affections; yet *particular Actions* may be innocent, nay virtuous, where there is no actual *Intention* of pleasing the DEITY, influencing the Agent.

FINIS.

TEXTUAL NOTES

TREATISE I: *An Essay on the Nature and Conduct of the Passions*

4/17 remembred] remembred,

4/18 will] may

5/15–16 Illustrations of . . . are so,] Illustrations of this Point, that we have a *moral Sense,* and a Sense of Honour, by which we discern an immediate Good in Virtue and Honour, not referred to any further Enjoyment, are not much insisted on since they are already laid down

5/24 tho *Seven* or *Ten* might] though a larger Number might perhaps

5/26 *Perceptions,*] *Perceptions immediately*

5/26–27 *Bodies;*] *Bodies,*

5/34 I . . . do,] Mr. *Locke* declares expressly, calling it *internal Sensation,* that [See John Locke, *Essay,* II. 1 §4. Locke is interested in giving an account of how and from where experience furnishes us with ideas, not with using the idea of reflection as a basis for multiplying senses which

is more a characteristic of Shaftesbury.]

6/2 *natural . . . as*] *natural* and *necessary* and *ultimate,* without reference to any other, as

6/14– The principal Objec-
7/4 tions . . . complete the Scheme] THE Author takes nothing in bad part from any of his Adversaries, except that Outcry which one or two of them made against these Principles as opposite to *Christianity,* though it be so well known that they have been and are espoused by many of the most zealous Christians. There are Answers interspersed in the later Editions to these Objections, to avoid the disagreeable Work of *Replying* or *Remarking,* in which one is not generally upon his Guard [xiii] sufficiently to avoid Cavils and offensive Expressions.

7/10   to establish.] to establish
        in *Treat.* IV.
7/22   some other natural]
        some of the natural
8/6–8   every one . . . to ap-
        prove] *om.*
8/9   tend] are intended
8/9–10 in the . . . Agent] *om.*
8/10–14 it can . . . *Affections.*"]
        our Power can reach, is
        approved as the highest
        Virtue; and that the *uni-
        versal calm Good-will or
        Benevolence,* where it is
        the leading Affection of
        the Soul, so as to limit
        or restrain all other Af-
        fections, Appetites, or
        Passions, is the Temper
        which we esteem in the
        highest Degree, accord-
        ing to the natural Con-
        stitution of our Soul:
        And withal, that we in a
        lower Degree approve
        every particular kind *Af-
        fection* or *Passion,* which
        is not inconsistent with
        these higher and nobler
        Dispositions."
8/15   this to be] this calm ex-
        tensive Affection to be
9/3   Actions, are,] Actions,
9/3   *Natural,*] *Natural,* yet are
9/4   yet if] but if
9/5–6   tend to the greater] tend
        to the
9/7   whereas a . . . find his]
        while yet one may better
        find his *private*
9/12–15 I hope . . . Gentlemen,]
        GENTLEMEN,

9/20   Δύναμις αγαθοειδὴς]
        Φιλάνθρωπον καὶ
        αγαθοειδὲς
10/1   Journals,] *Journals* in
        1728,
10/2   them bore] them in
        those weekly Papers bore
10/6–12 I have . . . I have] He
        was soon after informed,
        that his Death disap-
        pointed the Author's
        great Expectations from
        so ingenious a Corre-
        spondent. The *Objec-
        tions* proposed in the
        first *Section* of *Treatise*
        IV, are not always those
        of *Philaretus,* though the
        Author endeavoured to
        leave no Objections of
        his unanswered; but he
        also interspersed what-
        ever Objections occurred
        in Conversation on these
        Subjects; and has not
        used any Expressions in-
        consistent with the high
        Regard he has
15/12   several *Senses*] several
        Powers of Perception or
        Senses
15/13   There seems . . . or *Pain.*]
–16   It is by some Power of
        Perception, or *Sense,* that
        we first receive the Ideas
        of these Objects we are
        conversant with, or by
        some *Reasoning* upon
        these perceived Objects
        of Sense. By Sensation
        we not only receive the
        Image or *Representation,*

but some Feelings of
Pleasure or *Pain;* nay
sometimes the sole Per-
ception is that of Plea-
sure or Pain, as in *Smells,*
and the Feelings of *Hun-
ger* and *Thirst.*

15/18 *Extension . . . one of*]
–16/1 *Duration* or *Time,*

16/3 *Idea,* or *Assemblage*] *Idea,*
or *Image,* or *Assemblage*

16/4 Pleasures,] Pleasures

16/13 is ridiculously] seems
very

16/25 Ideas, as] Ideas, and yet
may also accompany any
other Ideas, as

16/25 Sensations.] Sensations.
Brutes, when several
Objects are before them,
have probably all the
proper Ideas of Sight
which we have, without
the Idea of Number.

16/32 Senses.] Senses; since
they can be received
sometimes without the
Ideas of Colour, and
sometimes without those
of Touching, though
never without the one or
the other.

16/33 *Smells, . . . &c.*] *Smells,
colours, Sound, Cold,
Heat,* &c.

16/38 "the] "those

17/6 *every*]" *every*

17/8 SENSE,] SENSE,"

17/14 *Perceptions*] *Perceptions,*

17/15 as also] as also,

17/16 ADDISON,] ADDISON

17/17 them,] them

17/22 Antients. 4. The] Antients. This inward Pain
of Compassion cannot
be called a Sensation of
Sight. It solely arises
from an Opinion of *Mis-
ery felt by another,* and
not immediately from a
visible Form. The same
Form presented to the
Eye by the exactest
Painting, or the Action
of a Player, gives no Pain
to those who remember
that there is no Misery
felt. When Men by
Imagination conceive
real Pain felt by an Ac-
tor, without recollecting
that it is merely feigned,
or when they think of
the real Story repre-
sented, then, as there is a
confused Opinion of real
Misery, there is also Pain
in Compassion. 4.

17/23 *Virtue,* or *Vice*] *Virtue* or
–24 *Vice,*

17/26 *Virtue,* or *Vice*] *Virtue* or
Vice,

18/3 "which] which

18/5 Pleasure;] pleasure;

18/7 them."] them.

18/15 *Plato** accounts] *Plato*
makes one of his Dialo-
gists* account

18/24 our *selves*] ourselves

18/28 Senses);] Senses, of Taste
and Touch chiefly);

19/6–12 The third . . . of Love.]
om.

19/14 Now] AND

19/18   Desires, with] Desires,
          and that with
19/20   Hence it is that] Thus
19/23   Power,] Power
20/2   Character:] Character:"
20/4   Actions?"] Actions?
20/14   "Further,] FURTHER,
20/16   Sense, by] Sense, yet by
20/18   Aversion."] Aversion.
20/22   *Posture*] *Posture,*
20/26   this] all this,
20/34   *Sect. 6.*] *Sect. 2.*
21/7   **Uses**] **Use**
21/11   consider] consider,
21/26   such as] such as those of
21/30   a Desire of *Distinction,*]
  –22/1   an *Emulation* or desire of
          Eminence,
23/33   II.] II. in his *Foundation
          of Morality in Theory and
          Practice.*
24/4–10   *Desire is* . . . is plain,]
          there is a certain *Pain* or
          Uneasiness accompany-
          ing most of our violent
          Desires. Though the
          Object pursued be
          Good, or the Means of
          Pleasure, yet the Desire
          of it generally is at-
          tended with an uneasy
          Sensation. When an Ob-
          ject or Event appears
          Evil, we desire to shun
          or prevent it. This De-
          sire is also attended with
          uneasy Sensation of *Im-
          patience:* Now this Sen-
          sation [16] immediately
          connected with the De-
          sire, is a distinct Sensa-

          tion from those which
          we dread, and endeavour
          to shun. It is plain then,
24/12   *itself.* ". . . be uneasy:] it-
  –15   self." Uneasy Sensations
          previously felt, will raise
          a Desire of whatever will
          remove them; and this
          Desire may have its con-
          comitant Uneasiness.
          Pleasant Sensations ex-
          pected from any Object
          may raise our Desire of
          it; this Desire too may
          have its concomitant un-
          easy Sensations:
24/22   *pleasant*] peculiar pleas-
          ant
24/31   the *Pleasure of gratified*]
          that *Pleasure which
          merely arises from gratify-
          ing of*
24/32   since the] since this
24/34   that,] that
25/12   *Desire or Affection*] De-
          sire, or the mere Affection,
25/24   our Happiness,] our fu-
          ture Happiness
26/9   these are either . . .
  –10   shewing,] the two for-
          mer are Motives only to
          external Actions; and the
          other two only shew
26/11   of the Happiness of oth-
          ers,] *of the Happiness of
          others,*
26/12   *Event* . . . desired] *Event*
          desired
26/19   Deity,] DEITY,
26/22   but as conceiving it] ex-
          cept we imagined their
          Happiness to be

27/16   *Pleasures] Pleasure*

27/17   unaccountable] unac-
        countable,

27/23   might,] *might*

27/30   but to continue him in
        Misery,] or to harden
        our Hearts against all
        feelings of Compassion,
        on the one hand, while
        yet the Object continued
        in Misery;

28/6   Drink] Drink and his
        Sensations of Hunger
        and Thirst

28/14   Life.] Life, which must
        be the Case with those
        who voluntarily hazard
        their Lives, or resolve on
        Death for their Country
        or Friends,

28/30   attempting] from the at-
        tempting

29/5   toward] towards

29/13   "befooled] "outwitted by
        nature

30/7   no] less

30/17   or certainly future] or
        future

30/18   are sure] expect or judge

30/24   in some sense also be
-25   called a Sensation.] be
        called a Sort of *Sensa-
        tion:* as the Physicians
        call many of our Pas-
        sions *internal Senses.*

30/28   includes, beside . . . im-
-31   pending Evil,] includes a
        strong Brutal Impulse of
        the Will, sometimes
        without any distinct no-
        tions of Good, publick
        or private, attended with

31/14   it appears] they appear

31/20   manner,] Manner

32/6   Temper. We] Temper.
        Sometimes the calm
        Motion of the *Will* con-
        quers the *Passion,* and
        sometimes is conquered
        by it. Thus *Lust* or *Re-
        venge* may conquer the
        calm Affection toward
        private Good, and some-
        times are conquered by
        it. *Compassion* will pre-
        vent the necessary Cor-
        rection of a Child, or the
        use of a severe Cure,
        while the calm *parental*
        Affection is exciting to
        it. Sometimes the latter
        prevails over the former.
        All this is beautifully
        represented in the 9th
        book of *Plato's Repub-
        lick.* We

32/9   *Passions.] Passions.**

33/32   *In the third edition* The
        same . . . finite Evils. *is
        connected to, and con-
        cludes, the previous para-
        graph.*

33/33   about . . . that tho] even
-34   in the acts of the *Under-
        standing,* or in *Judging,*
        that though

34/19   by the *Moment*] by the
        Importance or *Moment*

34/25   the *Axioms* subjoined]
        the *Maxims* subjoined

34/30   apt,] apt

34/34   *Treat. 4] Treat.* II. [As
        noted by Turco, Hutche-
        son incorrectly emended

the third edition. The
reference should be to
the final paragraph of T4
6.6.]

35/11   *Cor.* RELATIVE] [36]
         HENCE relative
35/15   *Particular*] *Particular,*
35/17   *Good,*] *Good*
35/29   Instances;] Instances:
35/31   *Cor.* 2.] 2.
36/1–2   the Powers . . . Goods]
         Goods of several sorts
36/7–8   at once . . . Evil:] at once
         Good and Evil:
36/18   Action is . . . *Sense,*] Ac-
         tion is morally good,
36/25   (*which is . . . Pas-
–26   sions;)] (*universal Evil
         is scarce ever intended,
         and particular Evil only
         in violent Passion)
37/8   AXIOMS,] MAXIMS,
37/16   beloved.] for whose sake
         it is desired.
37/25   *Intenseness:*] *Intenseness,*
         or Dignity of the Enjoy-
         ment:
38/8   *Cor.* HENCE] HENCE
38/10   Ratio] Proportion
40/17   selves . . . Systems,]
         Hearts,
41/7   And we] We
41/23   We do] We
41/25   do not seem] seem not
42/30   of Good,] *of Good,*
43/8   good] Good
43/25   ours. There] ours. There
         are [51] perhaps Orders
         of rational Beings also
         without these particular
         limited Attachments, to
         which our Natures are

subjected; who may per-
haps have no *Parental*
Affection, Friendships,
or Love to a Country, or
to any special smaller
Systems; but have *Uni-
versal Good-will* to all,
and this solely propor-
tioned to the moral Ex-
cellencies of the several
Objects, without any
other Bonds of Affec-
tion. There

44/2   upon] on
46/24   Virtue,] Virtue
47/16   possible] possible,
47/33   do accompany] accom-
         pany
49/31   from a like] from a cer-
         tain Prospect of future
         pleasant Sensations on
         the one hand, or from a
         like
50/2   others."] others."*
50/13   *Desire*] *Desire,*
50/14   Joy of Love . . . *Sorrow
–19   of Aversion:*] raises *joyful
         Love:* Good in suspense,
         the *Love of Desire,* or *de-
         sirous Love:* Good lost,
         sorrowful Love. Evil pres-
         ent, raises *sorrowful Aver-
         sion:* Evil expected, *desir-
         ous Aversion;* and Evil
         removed, *joyful Aversion.*
         The joyful Love, and
         joyful Hatred, will possi-
         bly be found nearly the
         same sort of Sensations,
         though upon different
         Occasions; the same may
         be said of the sorrowful

Love, and the sorrowful
Aversion:
51/3   itself.] itself.*
52/10   tho . . . often [tho' other
Degrees may often
54/29   shewing] shewing, [*In
the third edition the five
numbered paragraphs fol-
lowing* "shewing" *are
connected to form one
paragraph. The small caps
used to offset* "How" *at
the beginning of each paragraph are rendered in regular print as* "How"]
55/4   *State,*] *State*
56/23   absent . . . others;] Hap-
−24   piness of others while it
is in suspense;
57/23   *Diffidence* of] *Diffidence*
in
58/3   do raise] raise
58/20   this Passion,] it,
58/21   *malicious,* and designing]
malicious, designing
58/22   we . . . pursue] we naturally pursue
59/25   Let . . . especially] Let
one reflect on this Class
of Passions,
60/11   Disappointment] Disappointment,
60/30   *Racine;*] *Racine,*
64/24   Advantage:] Advantage?
64/26   them;] them?
64/28   others.] others?
65/22   would give us;] gives us;
65/32   external] other sorts of
66/2   *under*] *in*
(in title)
66/15   others:] others, or Consciousness of moral Evil:

67/16   fellow Creatures.]
Fellow-creatures.
67/24   it self;] itself:
68/13   proportioned] generally
proportioned
69/4   satisfied:] satisfied;
74/27   have any] secure constant
75/22   enjoy] obtain
76/2−3 all . . . Cruelty,] all Cruelty,
76/30   "It] It
77/8   *Self-Condemnation.*"]
Self-Condemnation.
78/27   Praise . . .Style,] Praise,
−28
78/32   Approbation] Approbation,
79/7   pursued,] pursued
79/26   them,] them
79/30   Fortunes,] Fortunes
−31
80/7   Wise:] wise:
81/14   Life:] Life;
82/23   but] and that
83/1   Whole,] Whole;
83/4−5 of the lower . . . boast-
ing] Expressions of the
Stoicks, boasting, one
would imagine, who did
not remember other
parts of their Scheme,
84/25   *quoddam*] *quádam*
84/32   obtained;] obtained:
87/1 2 find , , . Misfortunes;]
when under Misfortunes
find in being pitied by
others;
87/25   their] the
87/26   their] the
88/28   *Fly* or *Maggot*] Brute or
−29   Insect

89/24   Luxurious *Debauchee*]
         DEBAUCHEE
90/27   An Hobby-Horse . . . a
−29   *Son.*] Our former Toys
         we more easily procured,
         kept in good order, and
         managed, than the pres-
         ent Objects of our
         Cares, an Employment,
         a Son, a Friend, a Coun-
         try, a Party.
91/15   luxurious Debauchees,]
         Debauchees
91/24   "that] that
91/28   Enjoyments."] Enjoy-
         ments.
92/12   *Compassion*] *Compassion,*
92/23   "fantastick] fantastick
92/27   Pain."] Pain.
93/14   Ideas,] Ideas,*
95/8   given to *Castle-building,*]
         amusing himself with
         imaginary Scenes of
         Life,
95/24   When we] When indeed
         we
95/26   begin indeed from] be-
         gin from
95/29   "That had we] That we
         had
96/1–2   Time"—No Mortal,]
         Time—No mortal,
96/25   *Absence . . . revenged?*]
−26   Safety from Injury, to
         the having revenged an
         Injury?
99/14   *Life: The*] *Life,* the
99/20   *Necessity,* do] *Necessity,*
100/11   World, . . . themselves,]
         World,
100/12   incapable . . . without]
−13   without,

100/14   "Set] Set
100/16   them,"] them,
100/28   any one] one
101/9   Men should neglect]
         Men neglect
102/6   *Praise . . .* represent]
−7   World imagines
102/20   *Self-Defence*] *Self-*
         Defence,
102/28   Purpose,] Purpose
102/29   *Duels,*] our *Duels,*
105/14   no] little
105/14   *Reflection;* nor] *Reflec-*
         tion; and that almost
         solely arises from the re-
         turn of *Appetite;* and
         some Prospect of re-
         peated Enjoyment, or
         some moral Notions of
         Love or *Friendship* or
         Communication of Plea-
         sure: without these the
         Remembrance of past
         sensual Enjoyments is
         more generally nauseous.
         Nor
106/25   "it] it
106/27   nor ever] never
106/29   in every] in almost
         every
107/12   our *selves,*] ourselves,
107/15   Being."] Being.
107/18   our *selves;*] ourselves;
108/22   perpetual.] perpetual;
108/22   no . . . these.] least *Relief*
−23   from them.
109/31   violent.] violent."
109/34   Pains."] Pains.
110/3   *habet,*] *habeat,*
110/12   We see therefore,]
         THUS,
110/13   that] we see that

110/14 *Honour . . . to*] *Honour:*
–15   To
110/25 affect] effect
111/1–2 us . . . by] us, by
111/7   necessary.] necessary:
111/31 "the] the
111/31 itself,] itself
111/35 Temptation."] Temptation.
113/7   Passions do often] Passions often
113/24 Authors . . . to] Authors to
113/29 publickly useful.] useful to the Publick.
114/19 others,] others;
114/20 Enjoyment] Enjoyment,
115/10 Merit do] Merit
117/10 The] WHEN we have the
117/11 is indeed . . . We] we
–13
117/17 The Conceptions] Conceptions
–18
118/16 Nature] nature
118/28 Author.] Author. *See Treat. I. Sect. ult.*
118/32 external *Pains*] the most severe external *Pain*

118/35 Ruin?] Ruin.
118/35 the *Pains*] Pain
119/1   kinds.] kinds,
120/10 Presumptions] ground
120/33 who,] who
120/35 their natural . . . *Neces-*
–121/1 *saries.*] the common Necessaries, or even of the natural Conveniences of Life,
122/4   Beauty] Beauty,
122/17 *Par. lost,*] Par. Lost,
123/7   *Whole*] whole
124/6   *Frauds . . . what*] *Frauds* in other points, yet probably
124/20 "no] no
124/30 Violence."] Violence
127/8   *carisque*] carisq;
127/12 a generous] generous
129/22 Good."] Good.
129/24 End:] End;
129/33 "This] This
130/3   it."] it.
130/4   do,] do
130/31 Nature] Species
132/8   *Attention*] *Attention,*

TREATISE II: *Illustrations upon the Moral Sense*

133/10 called *privately*] *called* for
11   shortness, [208] *privately*
133/22 into:] into;
134/5   with] with,
134/7–8 is pleasant . . . Agent.] has some little Pleasure attending it in the Observer, and raises Love toward the *Agent,* in whom the Quality ap

proved is deemed to reside, and not in the *Ob-server,* who has a Satisfaction in the Act of approving.*
134/22 Mr. *Hobbes,*] Hobbes, *Rochefocault,* and others of the last Century,
134/26 *Moralists*] *Moralists* of this Scheme

134/27 "'tis the *Prospect*] it is the
        "*Prospect*
135/22 in] about
136/7   manner] manner,
136/8   be] have been
136/23 imagined do] imagine
138/1   *Object;*] *Object:*
138/2   Object,] Objects,
138/22 Action] Action,
138/30 *exciting*] *exciting,*
138/33 *Suasoriae.*] *Suasoriæ,* or
        these, *sub ratione utilis.*
139/5   these;] these:
139/8–9 *Affection,* . . . *Affection*):]
        Affection or *Passion:*
        This paragraph follows in
        the third edition: WRIT-
        ERS on these Subjects
        should remember the
        common Divisions of
        the Faculties of the Soul.
        That there is 1. *Reason*
        presenting the natures
        and relations of things,
        antecedently to any Act
        of *Will* or *Desire:* 2. The
        Will, or *Appetitus Ra-*
        tionalis, or the disposi-
        tion of Soul to pursue
        what is presented as
        good, and to shun Evil.
        Were there no other
        Power in the Soul, than
        that of mere contempla-
        tion, there would be no
        Affection, Volition, De-
        sire, Action. Nay without
        some motion of *Will* no
        Man would voluntarily
        persevere in Contempla-
        tion. There must be a
        Desire of Knowledge,

        and of the Pleasure
        which attends it: this too
        is an Act of *Willing.*
        Both these Powers are by
        the Antients included
        under the λόγος or
        λογικὸν μήρος. Below
        these they place two
        other powers dependent
        on the Body, the *Sensus,*
        and the *Appetitus Sensiti-*
        vus, in which they place
        the particular Passions:
        the former answers to
        the *Understanding,*
        [220] and the latter to
        the *Will.* But the Will is
        forgot of late, and some
        ascribe to the *Intellect,*
        not only *Contemplation*
        or Knowledge, but
        Choice, Desire, Prosecut-
        ing, Loving. Nay some
        are grown so ingenious
        in uniting the Powers of
        the Soul, that *contem-*
        plating with Pleasure,
        Symmetry and Propor-
        tion, an Act of the *Intel-*
        lect as they plead, is the
        same thing with *Good-*
        will or the virtuous *De-*
        sire of publick Happi-
        ness.
140/20 one . . . *Ideas:*] a Mistake
 –22   some fall into;
140/30 prove, that "all] prove
        "that all
140/31 *Desire,*] *Desire,* actually
        operating
140/32 Object."] Object.
141/2   do form] form

141/3–4 The . . . is] Such Conceptions are
141/13 either] to either
141/20 these] these,
141/21 Is it] It is
142/12 *justifying?*] *justifying.*
143/9 to] from
143/33 frequently,] frequently
144/4 serves the] serves in
144/22 obvious] obvious,
144/23 *Sense*] *Sense* in the Constitution of the Soul.
145/11 *Fruit.*] *Fruit.**
145/22 Criminal] Sufferer
146/9 Gerund,] Gerund or Participle,
146/18 Words] Words,
146/32 not] not.†
149/11 I. **That**] *That*
149/15 *sweet,*] *sweet*
This paragraph follows in the third edition: 'Tis manifest we have in our *Understanding moral Ideas,* or they are Perceptions of the Soul: we reason about them, we compare, we judge; but then we do all the same Acts about *Extension, Figure, Colour, Taste, Sound,* which Perceptions all Men call *Sensations.* All our Ideas, or the materials [241] of our reasoning or judging, are received by some immediate Powers of Perception internal or external, which we may call *Senses;* by these too we have Pleasure and Pain. All Perception is by the Soul, not by the Body, tho' some Impressions on the bodily Organs are the Occasions of some of them; and in others the Soul is determined to other sorts of *Feelings* or *Sensations,* where no bodily Impression is the immediate Occasion. A certain *incorporeal Form,* if one may use that Name, a *Temper* observed, *a Character, an Affection, a State* of a sensitive Being, known or understood, may raise *Liking, Approbation, Sympathy,* as naturally from the very Constitution of the Soul, as any bodily Impression raises external Sensations. Reasoning or *Intellect* seems to raise no new Species of Ideas, but to discover or discern the *Relations* of those received. Reason shews what Acts are conformable to a *Law,* a *Will* of a Superior; or what Acts tend to Private Good, or to Publick Good: In like manner, Reason discovers contrary Tendencies of contrary Actions. Both Contraries are alike the Object of the Understanding, and may give that sort of Pleasure

which arises upon Dis-
covery of Truth. A Dem-
onstration that certain
Actions are detrimental
to Society is attended
with the peculiar *Plea-
sure of new Knowledge,* as
much as a like Demon-
stration of [242] the
Benefit of Virtue. But
when we *approve* a kind
beneficent Action, let us
consider whether this
Feeling, or *Action,* or
Modification of the Soul
more resembles an Act
of *Contemplation,* such
as this [when strait Lines
intersect each other, the
vertical Angles are
equal;] or that *Liking* we
have to a beautiful
Form, an harmonious
Composition, a grateful
Sound.

151/17   observed,] observed
151/29   corresponding] resem-
          bling or analogous
152/3   contrary.] contrary.*
153/14   *of one*] one
154/4   Deity:] Deity;
154/14   Manner:] Manner;
154/18   Mankind;] Mankind,
154/29   Some do] Some
156/8   (the Word] the (Word
156/23   do continue,] continue
156/25   *Relations*] *Relations,*
157/6   *themselves,*] *themselves*
157/11   many do] many
158/2   *Motions,*] *Motions*
158/5   *Agent's*] or *sensitive
          Being's*

158/6   *Mathematicks,*] *Mathe-
          maticks*
158/19   *good* in a *moral Sense.*]
          good.
158/31   or to] or
159/33   others:] others.
159/15   *Sense.*] *Sense.**
159/17   [*This marginal title was
  −19   omitted from the third
          edition*]
160/9   instance,] Instance,
160/12   absurd.] absurd.†
160/16   That "certain] "That
  −17   certain
161/3   like to] like
161/6   **Signification**] *Significa-
          tion,*
163/1   **Nor**] *Not*
163/11   *Action*] *Action,*
163/16   imagined] imagined,
  −17
163/24   *useful,*] *useful*
163/26   "Accomplishing] accom-
          plishing
164/5   not."] not.
164/6   assert, that "the] assert
          that the
164/11   evil."] evil.
164/19   evil,] Evil,
164/29   **of**] *of some*
  −30
165/4–7   *In the third edition there
          is the following marginal
          title next to this para-
          graph:*] **Three Sorts of
          Signifying**.
165/9   *designing*] *professing a
          Design*
165/20   without . . . Agent,]
          while yet the Agent is
          not understood to *profess
          any Intention of commu-*

nicating to him his Opin-
ions or Designs,

165/30   *Intention . . . his]* a Pro-
−31   *fession of communicating*
166/8   imagine any] imagine
166/20   *Truth."] Truth,"*
167/30   *Consequence]* Conse-
         quence,
168/3   Opinions,"] Opinions"
168/7   *Given]* When
168/8   *Action,] Action,* are given,
168/23   *Opinions.] Opinions,* or a
         very violent unkind Pas-
         sion.
170/33   Therefore *Virtue . . . or*
−34   *Falshood.]* Therefore *Sig-*
         nification of Truth or
         Falshood, are not the
         same with *Virtue* and
         Vice.
171/20   is that,] is, that
174/11   *Morals.] Morals,* and
         here we may discover as
         certain, invariable, or
         eternal Truths, as any in
         Geometry.
174/19   Observer; . . . *taught.]*
−20   Observer; so that *Vir-*
         tue is not properly
         taught.
174/35   *Hatred,] Hatred;*
175/14   do make] make
176/2   studied] study
176/3   appeared] appears
177/26   *Reason.] Reason,* which
         on these Subjects, sug-
         gests as invariable eternal
         or necessary Truths as
         any whatsoever.
177/27   concluded] inferred
177/28   Observer.] Observer, re-
         ally existing whether he

had perceived it or not,
and having a real Ten-
dency to certain Ends.
177/32   *Pleasure]* Pleasures
178/1–2 does often correct] often
         corrects
179/6   Observer?"] Observer,
         according to the present
         Constitution of the hu-
         man Mind?"
179/8   *approve]* approve,
179/11   separately.] separately.
−12   Let those who are not
         satisfied with either of
         these Explications of
         Merit, endeavour to give
         a Definition of it reduc-
         ing it to its simple Ideas:
         and not, as a late Author
         has done, quarrelling
         these Descriptions, tell
         us only that it is *Deserv-*
         ing or being worthy of
         Approbation, which is
         defining by giving a syn-
         onimous Term.[[In his
         polemic against Hutche-
         son, Balguy uses Cicero's
         De Officiis 1.14 to define
         "*Merit* or *Praiseworthi-*
         ness" as "*the Quality in*
         Actions which not only
         gains the Approbation of
         the Observer, but which
         also *deserves* or is *worthy*
         of it," (Balguy, *The*
         Foundation of Moral
         Goodness, I:20).]]
179/16   *Affections?] Affections?*
         Some perhaps take the
         Word [Instinct] solely
         for such Motions of

Will, or bodily Powers, as determine us without Knowledge or Intention of any End. Such Instincts cannot be the Spring of Virtue. But the Soul may be as naturally determined to Approbation of certain Tempers and Affections, and to the Desire of certain Events when it has an Idea [292] of them, as Brutes are, by their lower Instincts, to their Actions. If any quarrel the Application of the Word *Instinct* to any thing higher than what we find in Brutes, let them use another Word. Though there is no Harm in the Sound of this Word, more than in a *Determination to pursue Fitness,* which they must allow in the Divine *Will,* if they ascribe any Will to him at all.

179/20   do mean] means
179/23   do suppose] suppose
180/10   I fancy every] every
180/14   *casual*) but] *casual,* but)
180/21   Supposition] Supposition,
180/30   Man,] Man
181/14   of,] of
181/22   *Sensations*] *Sensation*
181/32   others;] others:
182/12   In the third edition
−14   Hutcheson added the marginal head "**What Actions rewardable.**"

next to this paragraph.
182/21   various,] various
182/29   *Interest . . .* Agent,] *Interest,*
182/30   publickly useful] such
183/4   *superior*] *Superior*
183/12   *superior*] *Superior*
183/22   What . . . mean,] [300] What means this?
183/32   Picture, . . . *Shades?*] Pic-
−33   ture?
185/24   did give] gave
186/26   this] and
186/29   yet do] do
−30
187/11   Some do] SOME
187/20   Gratitude do] Gratitude
188/31   then, if . . . *C* × *G.*]
−189/3   then we may denote the Propensity of mind, or the disposition to receive or to be moved with any tender or kind Affections by the *Goodness of Temper.* Then,

THE *degree of kind Affection* toward any Person is in a compound Proportion of the apprehended *Causes of Love* in him, and of the *Goodness of Temper* in the Observer.

189/5−6   *Temper . . . I.*] *Temper.*
189/8   as the . . . *I.*] proportioned to the *Causes.*
189/10   *Causes,* . . . $\frac{L}{C}$.] *Causes.*

190/1−2   the *Quotient . . .* Unity.] there must be some depravation of the Temper, some want of the natural

Proportion, or of that calm Deliberation and calm Affections, toward Objects of the Understanding.

190/8–9 Benevolence . . . Happiness is] Benevolence. "His Happiness is perhaps imagined

190/21 Temper.] Temper, by presenting an Example engaging our Imitation.

192/2 that] the

193/11 positively . . . as] con-
–12 demn as positive

193/26 occasion] occasion praepollent

193/30 to Innocence] to the Character of Innocence

194/11 positive] higher

194/26 apprehend] apprehended

194/34 him,] him

195/11 does evidence] evidences

195/18 or Desire] or of the ultimate Desire

196/7 itself even] itself

197/7–8 Corollaries] Conclusions.

198/3 Affection,] Affections,

199/2–3 Moment . . . such as] Disposition to Beneficence in any good Agent various ways;

199/3 future,] future;

199/4 Pattern,] Pattern

199/5–7 a part . . . the Universe.] to whom we may imagine the publick Happiness to be acceptable.

199/12 inversly] rather inversly

199/13 more Virtue . . . Species.]
–16 where no more good is

done, in equal Abilities, by one Agent who had presented to him the joint Motives of Piety toward God and Humanity toward Men, than is done by another from mere Humanity, the latter gives a better Evidence of a [330] good Temper. And where higher Motives of Gratitude to God are presented to one than to another, unless the Good done from these stronger Motives is greater, the Temper must be so much the worse.*

200/2 In any . . . these] [331]
–4 Good Offices done from mere Humanity, while the Motives of Piety were not present to the Mind, provided they were not excluded by direct Design, or blameable Inadvertence, may in this particular Case be a better Indication of a good Temper, than Offices only of equal Importance done by another of equal Abilities, from the joint Motives of Piety and Humanity; yet the retaining designedly and frequently recalling all these

200/22 that "Virtue] "that Virtue
–23

201/4–5 obtain . . . Deity.] express

Gratitude by compliance with the Divine Will, or to express a disinterested *Esteem,* or to obtain our own Happiness by means of the Divine Favour. This last [333] Intention may influence a very corrupt Mind in some things. And the former more generous Intentions must really increase the Goodness of every Action, and are the highest Virtues of themselves.

201/10 Observer] Observer,
201/11 'Tis to be . . . attain to.]
—14 Joining frequently and habitually the Acts of Piety with those of Humanity is, no doubt, the *Perfection* of Goodness and Virtue. But we must not deny the *Reality* of Virtue in these Actions, which are not of the most perfect Sort.

201/18 some] great
201/23 *Community*] *Community,*
201/34 needs to excite . . . *System.*] ever needs to recall
—35 the Thoughts of a Divine *Command* and its *Sanctions,* or even the Thoughts of the Interests of greater Societies or *Systems,* before it can be engaged into any particular Acts of Kindness. Accordingly we find in Nature that the particular kind *Passions* generally move the Mind first. And upon Reflection, more *extensive Motives* begin to occur, and Regards to the great Head of the rational *System.*
202/30 do make] make
203/24 *Natures* from GOD,] *Natures.*
204/16 nay] nay,

INDEX

Note: Page numbers followed by (*n*) indicate material in footnotes.

This book is set in Adobe Garamond, a modern adaptation by Robert Slimbach of the typeface originally cut around 1540 by the French typographer and printer Claude Garamond. The Garamond face, with its small lowercase height and restrained contrast between thick and thin strokes, is a classic "old-style" face and has long been one of the most influential and widely used typefaces.

Printed on paper that is acid free and meets the requirements of the American National Standard for Permanence of Paper for Printed Library Materials, z39. 48-1992. ⊗

Book design by Louise OFarrell, Gainesville, Florida
Typography by Impressions Book and Journal Services, Inc., Madison, Wisconsin
Printed and bound by Worzalla Publishing Company, Stevens Point, Wisconsin